THE FABER REPORT

The **FABER** REPORT

How Wall Street *Really* Works — And
How You Can Make It Work for You

David Faber

with KEN KURSON

Little, Brown and Company

BOSTON | NEW YORK | LONDON

Originally published by Little, Brown and Company, May 2002
First paperback edition, October 2003

ISBN 0-316-08742-4 (hc) / 0-316-16492-5 (pb)
LCCN 2002102890

10 9 8 7 6 5 4 3 2 1

Q-MART

Designed by Victoria Hartman

Printed in the United States of America

To Jenny

CONTENTS

THE FABER REPORT

INTRODUCTION

In January 1987 I accepted a position to cover corporate banking for a newsletter owned by *Institutional Investor* magazine. I had graduated from college eighteen months earlier with a B.A. in English. I had worked in politics since graduating. I had never taken an economics course during college or high school. I had never read the *Wall Street Journal.* I had never owned a stock, never owned a bond, and had never met an investment banker, a risk arbitrageur, a CEO, or an analyst. Upon being led to my dingy cubicle on the fourteenth floor of 488 Madison Avenue, I nervously eyed the telephone, the typewriter, and the condiment-stained walls. I was certain I would be fired before the month was out.

Fifteen-plus years, thousands of business meals, and close to a million phone calls later, I'm still covering Wall Street. The world has changed since my early days in financial journalism — and not just because I no longer use a typewriter. Wall Street and the stock market have taken over a rather large piece of real estate in our national consciousness. Kids in high school can rattle off the words behind the initials IPO, and CEOs have become celebrities. Still, I think back to the winter of 1987 and how much I had yet to learn.

My first three months as a reporter were terrifying. I would have trouble breathing some mornings, as though the stress of it all were crushing my lungs. It wasn't just the pressure of having to call complete strangers, trying to find out things they might not want to tell me. That can be tense, but I've always found it an exciting challenge. The real tension derived from the fact that I knew nothing about the field I was being asked to cover — even more so, because I couldn't really fake it. There is a language of finance, a language that belongs only to Wall Street. Though not difficult to understand once explained, it is an idiom designed to intimidate. I was intimidated. But I was also determined not to fail. I had no money. I was living at home in Queens after having moved from Washington, D.C., and was not about to give up without a fight the luxurious annual salary of $21,000 and the promise of an apartment of my own.

Slowly, but with certainty, I learned about Wall Street. First came the ability to speak the language, then the ability to understand it. I'll never forget the first time I was able to ask a follow-up question after receiving a particularly stupid but jargon-heavy answer. It took quite a few years, but in time I gained some perspective on how Wall Street really works. I also managed not to get fired.

I spent almost seven years at *Institutional Investor*. I started on the banking beat, moved over to cover the stock market a year later, and became an executive editor of the newsletter division a year after that. It was a wonderful time in which to learn. I covered the heady deal days of the mid to late 1980s, complete with corporate raiders and insider trading. I covered the demise of the commercial banking industry, swollen with losses from failed buyouts and real estate loans. I covered the emergence of capital markets in developing countries in the early 1990s and at one point embarked on a round-the-world business trip that still provides me valuable perspective to this day. And then I made my move to television, joining a fledgling cable network in September 1993.

When I joined CNBC, the economy was just getting roused from a deep slumber and few of us had any idea how successful and influential our network would soon become. My ambitions were fairly modest: I wanted to find out things before anyone else and tell the world. And I wanted to make Wall Street accessible and comprehensible to people who might have been much the same as I had been in the winter of 1987.

This book is simply a continuation of that ambition.

The same traits that make a good journalist make a good investor. It really is that simple. Skepticism. Curiosity. A penchant for research. Quick analysis. The ability to sniff out a story. A nose for rumor and an ear for BS. The courage to go with your gut when you're right and the prudence not to leap too soon.

Combing through balance sheets, cutting through the well-rehearsed corporate-speak of company executives, discerning relevant fact from rumor (and true rumors from false ones!) — these strategies and techniques are available to any investor with a little gumption. And they're the same strategies and techniques I used to break stories such as the takeover of MCI in 1996, United Technologies' and GE's offers for Honeywell, the fall of Long-Term Capital, Amgen's purchase of Immunex, and the massive fraud at WorldCom, among others.

The people I've spent my career getting information from share one overriding ambition: to make as much money as possible. No doubt, they enjoy the challenge of their jobs and the gratification that comes from a job well done. But of the many thousands of bankers, traders, money managers, and brokers I've spoken to, not one came to Wall Street in order to do good for his or her fellow man. In fact, many of these same people do devote themselves to improving humanity after their Wall Street careers have ended. But while they're working, their interests are not always aligned with those of investors. So although I have certainly not been curing world hunger during my time at CNBC, I have been trying to level the playing field. I have tried to give anyone who cares to watch and learn an opportunity to use the same information that is available to those who make their consider-able living working on Wall Street. There have been plenty of wealthy people whom I have helped make even wealthier. That's the price of doing business. But I like to think that there have also been people of more modest means who have come to un-derstand how Wall Street works and have used that knowledge to help them make sound investment decisions.

In the fall of 2001, before the collapse of Enron became front-page news, there was a maudlin but typically funny e-mail making its way around Wall Street:

> If you bought $1,000 worth of Nortel stock one year ago, it would now be worth $49.
> $1,000 worth of BroadVision is now worth $22.
> $1,000 worth of JDSU is now worth $52.
> Now consider this . . .
> If you bought $1,000 worth of Budweiser (the beer, not the stock) one year ago, drank all the beer, and traded in the cans for the nickel deposit, you would have $79.
> My advice . . . start drinking heavily.

Wall Street loves to proclaim "a new paradigm" where the old rules don't apply. But that's never true. In the end, the old rules simply adapt, and always apply. Because if we've learned anything over the past three years, it's that stocks do go down. And when they do, the pain is ample.

Much of the information imparted in this book may help you make money. But I can't guarantee that following my advice un-failingly leads to fortune. Still, if information is power, and the ability to understand that information more power still, this book should stand you in good stead. If you want to know how Wall Street really works, if you want to know what your broker or fund manager is really doing, if you want to know why analysts are sometimes dirty and short sellers often are not, if you want to know how Wall Street frauds function or the stories behind some of my best stories, then read on. It may not be pretty, but I guar-antee it will be worth your time.

1

FRAUD: IT CAN HAPPEN TO YOU

Somewhere deep in the recesses of my mind, I suppose I had always expected it. But when I confirmed late one June day that WorldCom had made up at least $3.6 billion in profits over the past five quarters, I was still shocked.

I stumbled on the story, as is often the case with the big ones. I had called one of my better sources to inquire about the goings-on at Vivendi — the French media company that was in turmoil at the time. Before letting me ask a question, my source offered one of his own: "Can you believe it?" he asked with a chuckle.

"What?" I asked.

"WorldCom."

WorldCom, one of the nation's biggest companies, had been in some very rough financial straits at the time, but its survival seemed likely. Its banks had been working with the company to restructure its balance sheet, and my read was that the restructuring was going to occur.

I could tell from my source's tone that this was not about any bank negotiations. Something was very wrong. It took me the entire day to figure out what that something was. Only a handful of people had been told the truth, and a few others knew bits and pieces of the story. I was able to put it all together by about 6 P.M. and went on to break the biggest story of my career.

WorldCom, the greatest success story in telecom the markets have ever produced, was a sham. Its profits had been made up. And the information I was getting on that day only dealt with the previous fifteen months. A few weeks later I would report that WorldCom's investigators had identified another $4 billion or so in fictional profits.

WorldCom's fraud was far different from the other titanic crime in corporate America allegedly committed by Andrew Fastow and friends at Enron. Enron used names from the *Star Wars* movies for the complicated partnerships that hid much of its fraud — they truly were out of this world. By contrast, World-Com's CFO Scott Sullivan is alleged to have done some pretty simple stuff in creating what is now believed to be at least $9 billion in false profits.

One of Sullivan's favorite techniques was to simply treat costs that should have been expensed immediately as those allowed by accounting standards to be expensed over many years. Such capitalization of costs is permitted, as the name would imply, for capital expenditures, but Sullivan used it for the expenses that WorldCom incurred in the ordinary course of its business. That low-tech fraud was good enough to net WorldCom $4 billion in profits it never really made.

Sullivan employed other crude techniques to hide World-Com's true financial condition. When WorldCom made an acquisition, he set up reserves that were much larger than needed and then quietly emptied those reserves when he needed to pad the company's earnings. Despite the lack of artistry, WorldCom's board of directors and its shareholders were not able to uncover the massive fraud taking place at the company. And that fraud had ramifications far beyond WorldCom itself.

Competitors, chief among them AT&T, always wondered how WorldCom could price its services, particularly to the most important corporate customer, at a discount to what AT&T could offer that same customer. Execs at AT&T scratched their heads for years, and the company's former CEO, C. Michael Armstrong, sent some of those heads flying when his company was unable to compete. No wonder it couldn't compete. WorldCom had single-handedly brought the price of telecom services to such a low level that while corporate America was saving big, the telecom companies were engaged in a price war that was ruining them.

And it never should have happened. The reason WorldCom was able to offer the best rates to its customers and still make more money than its competitors had nothing to do with its oft-lauded management. The only reason that WorldCom was able to offer those low prices was that it was the biggest cheat in corporate history. Any losses the company was suffering from pricing its services below their actual cost would be made up by fraud.

Fraud finds its way into corporate America in many different ways. Some companies are frauds from inception. Others are well-established brand names that suffer from a breakdown in governance that allows for a slow progression into criminal behavior.

Either way, frauds are awfully fun for me to cover. They typically feature colorful characters and a complicated web of facts to weave together. But, good stories aside, they're also quite useful for investors to understand, for several reasons:

- By learning to identify the signs of fraud *before* you invest, you can avoid the costly — and infuriating — result of owning the stock of a company that turns out to be a fiction.

- Frauds make excellent shorting candidates. A fraudulent company's stock doesn't just lose a couple of points and then recover. The frauds I'm talking about here go to zero. And stay there.

- Most important, frauds remind investors of a lesson that cannot be repeated enough: there ain't no such thing as a free lunch. When an investment comes along that sounds as if it can't miss, and seems cheap to boot, you have only yourself to blame when you wind up losing your shirt.

Who Protects Investors?

You really can't count on anyone but yourself to keep from being defrauded. The Securities and Exchange Commission (SEC) is a well-meaning public agency, but it has nowhere near the resources to uncover enough fraud to either deter other wrongdoers or obtain realistic restitution for burned investors. Perpetrators of fraud have been prosecuted, but it's a rare remedy — and it won't get you your money back. Even when the perps have not yet plundered every last cent, there's seldom enough left over to make equity investors whole.

Class actions? Most companies carry insurance to cover securities-fraud suits, so the threat of a securities-fraud class action has no deterrent effect. Congress is actually trying to limit such suits, but even multimillion-dollar settlements still equal only pennies on the dollar. Outside auditors can help, but don't rely on them too much. They will tell you — and this line comes up every time they get sued in connection with a fraudulent company they were allegedly auditing — "Auditors aren't supposed to look for fraud. We're supposed to look for whether the financial presentation was consistent with generally accepted accounting principles." Even when they're doing just that, the auditors can fail to protect investors. Arthur Andersen let Enron get away with financial reporting that its own accountants either did not fully understand or chose to ignore. Enron was, after all, a huge generator of fees for Arthur Andersen. Rather than force Enron to explain itself or change its accounting, Arthur Andersen was happy to play the obsequious adviser. And when the feds started to move in, the company proved only too happy to shred documents to cover its ass. Arthur Andersen's CEO admitted to Congress that in the wake of Enron, it's clear his profession will have to reform itself and improve its system of regulation and discipline. One can always hope. Arthur Andersen, which was also WorldCom's auditor, no longer has any hope. It was shuttered by the government.

The good news is that fraud rarely goes undetected forever. Everybody with some interest in a company's financial results — the SEC, auditors, short sellers, good guys in management, stock exchanges, money managers, even analysts — eventually gets clued in. The problem is that by the time these people wake up, you may have already lost a fortune.

Take the most common means of securities fraud: manipulating sales to enhance quarterly numbers. If you start stealing sales from the next quarter to make this quarter look good or simply ship unordered products to customers at the end of the quarter, you face an even bigger shortfall in the future. It has to catch up with you sometime. In addition, the number of people who see this funny business going on keeps growing: officers of the company, salespeople who are pushed to exhaustion at the end of every quarter, inside and outside auditors, customers, and potential merger partners may all become aware that something is amiss.

How a Rig Works

Some of the most sophisticated frauds resemble espionage thrillers more than investment vehicles. They are known as "rigs," and investors who spot any of the telltale signs should flee. Most rigs are variations on a theme. The tune follows similar notes: a quiet beginning, a loud period of promotion, followed by a mad scramble for the exits by insiders before the crescendo.

Here's how one type of rig plays.

The principals behind the rig choose locations such as Bermuda and the Cayman Islands — places without effective scrutiny that don't require a lot of legal documents. The owners then set up a number of offshore funds there, typically naming the funds vaguely, as in "Minnow 1, a Bermuda-based investment partnership." Each of, say, four participants contributes perhaps half a million to three funds, so there's $2 million in each fund, and each partner has invested $1.5 million. They control these funds but their control is not noted, and they often have a front man.

The funds then invest in some kind of company in the United States or Canada. Ideally, it's a shell company that's got a dormant publicly traded penny stock. Because these shell companies are already public, there isn't the need for detailed filings with the SEC. Once a shell has been secured, it does a private placement in which warrants — which give the holder the right to purchase shares at a set price — are sold to the same offshore funds. Once the funds have secured the right to purchase millions of shares in the company for a small sum, they can begin what's aptly termed the promote.

The promote works by trying to interest shareholders in the prospects of the company. Rigs work best when the company's business involves stuff that's also hard to track down or understand, such as mineral or oil deposits of vast potential value — businesses whose revenue sources are in remote locations, capital intensive, and hard to investigate. With technology becoming more complex, there's also been a spate of software- and hardware-related rigs. Noncommittal, difficult-to-disprove stories about "potential mineral reserves" or "revolutionary software applications" are leaked to inexperienced and faraway reporters. If anyone bites and writes an item, that item is reproduced en masse, posted everywhere possible, and then used to generate further stories, in hopes of these unwitting dupes helping to spread the word. Early-stage, nearly free shares are distributed to those close to the principals of the company. Options are also given to so-called experts whose opinions may sway future investors.

As investor interest grows, the promoters can stimulate trading by selling shares back and forth between their own funds. With volume intensifying, investors can easily be convinced to take a flier on a stock that might be trading at 50 cents. That 50 cents already represents a giant return for the rig's principals, who paid pennies for their warrants to buy those same shares. Meanwhile, the promote is in full swing. Trading volume is multiplying and is clearly no longer only the product of offshore sham trading between the participants. Optimistic rumors about the richness of the distant find or the huge software contract in a foreign land are floated in chat rooms and elsewhere. Occasionally, the rig can even catch the eye of an institutional investor whose subsequent purchase can be used to validate the merit of the investment.

I don't think much of tracking sales of stock by insiders. But in the case of a rig, such insider selling is a key. No matter how well constructed a rig is in its early stages, if it can't be extended long enough for its engineers to sell out, it's a failure. So when it comes to fraud, insider selling is something to watch for. In the case of our model rig, that time would be when Minnow 1, 2, and 3 exercise their warrants and start selling the shares received. The height of that selling normally comes right before the SEC, short sellers, or general investors close in on the fraud. The trouble is that given the steps insiders have taken to shield their holdings from scrutiny, you have to be a detective simply to recognize when they are selling.

If the rig works to perfection, nothing stops the promoters from collecting their money and watching the stock price deflate, only to start the promotion all over again a few years later. The memories of those who work on Wall Street are often short, one reason that rigs from years past can and do reappear with similar claims, the same company name, and the same cast of characters.

Naturally, given the allure of get-rich-quick schemes, the rig is fairly common.

THE SOLV-EX STORY

Solv-Ex crept up on me slowly; no one incident made me spring up and shout, "This is a fraud!" It was more that things didn't add up. And the more I looked, the more dubious the company's claims and prospects seemed.

Here's what happened.

If you read the *Wall Street Journal* on September 18, 1996, you saw a boastful ad that promised "Our Technology Will Reduce American Dependence on Middle East Oil." Solv-Ex, a New Mexico–based company, claimed its patented process could wring crude oil from tar sands. The idea behind SOLVent EXtraction was that bitumen, a distillate residue of oily sand, could be filtered into crude oil at prices similar to conventional drilling. Even more appealing, the process supposedly produced by-products such as aluminum and titanium that were three times more valuable than the oil. The process could even extract gold and silver from the tar sands.

By the time of the ad, the stock had already ridden up and down plenty, from 8 to 38 to 6 to 28 to 9 to 20 in under a year. But for me, the story really started to heat up well before most of that ride.

On April 1, 1996, Solv-Ex chairman John S. Rendall issued a press release saying that the company had "discovered" that there are "at least two federal inquiries into what appears to be stock manipulation that resulted in a precipitous drop." That drop had occurred near the end of March. Rendall went on to blame the manipulation on a report by Weir-Jones Engineering that had been quoted in the media, which he said was erroneous, adding that Weir-Jones "acknowledged that its information regarding Solv-Ex was . . . incomplete."

In fact, my reporting revealed that the FBI had served the company a subpoena that "commanded all documents, letters, papers, notes, trading records, SEC filings, company prospectuses, press releases" on March 15 — *before* the late-March "precipitous drop" and two weeks before Rendall said that "neither Solv-Ex nor its officers have received any formal notification of the inquiries; nor have they been requested to supply any information."

The next day, April 2, I got my hands on a personal letter to John Rendall from Iain Weir-Jones, founder of the engineering company Solv-Ex blamed for the incomplete information that was hurting the stock. Weir-Jones says, "I should be greatly obliged if you would cease issuing misleading statements to the media about our work. I reiterate that the report I have prepared for my client has not been withdrawn, modified, or qualified. Furthermore, I have never 'acknowledged that (our) information regarding Solv-Ex and the Solv-Ex process was incomplete in [a] number of material respects.' I made it very clear to you at the beginning of our discussion last Tuesday that our primary sources of information on Solv-Ex are the documents issued by the company and interviews with your Directors, employees and consultants."

The following day, April 3, 1996, I got hold of the actual confidential report by Weir-Jones — a lengthy and detailed piece of forensic engineering that had been commissioned by an investor who was short Solv-Ex stock. The report took as a given the veracity of the information Solv-Ex provided and did not seek to analyze the marketability of the products or validate the capital and operating costs of the company. Even given that head start, Solv-Ex fell woefully short of impressing the firm, which concluded, "We do not consider the bitumen extraction procedure . . . particularly unique, nor does it appear to be capable of being protected by defensible comprehensive patents." As for the bonus minerals, "anticipated cash flow . . . is as yet unsubstantiated, at best, and probably highly speculative." And what about the idea that gold and silver could be by-products of the extraction process? Weir-Jones said of this, "We see no evidence."

This wasn't the first time Solv-Ex had contorted an engineer's opinion to seem more favorable. After hearing Solv-Ex refer to "validation" by Pace Consultants of its business plan and its estimate on per barrel production costs, I tried to find the Pace report that would confirm such support. I couldn't. Proving a negative is hard for an investor or an investigative reporter, and since Solv-Ex had hired Pace, Pace wasn't going to release a report that I suspected was negative to its client. Finally, I reached Dan Foley at Pace, who said that Pace had not "audited" the process nor signed off on the estimated production costs. Not a smoking gun, but one more little warning bell.

Like so many rigs, there was enough in the Solv-Ex story to ring at least a little true. Solv-Ex really did have a bitumen-extraction procedure and leases on fields, and there actually was some aluminum, titanium, and gold in the representative core holes. The problem is that almost none of that added up to anything remotely close to a profitable business model. Solv-Ex counted on few investors with the wherewithal to analyze bitumen trekking up to the Athabasca region of Alberta, Canada, and for quite a while that assumption was right. Even *after* these developments and my reporting of them, the stock had a few nice runs.

And then I started to assemble the information that's vital to proving that a rig is in process. With the help of some sleuthing short sellers, I was able to draw a connection between a convicted felon named Samuel Francis and Solv-Ex's current CEO, John Rendall. It seems that in Solv-Ex's earliest days these two owned virtually all the company's stock. In fact, they co-founded Solv-Ex in 1980. The company took 4 million shares public shortly thereafter, and then issued a whopping 18 million more through private placements and offshore transactions. Those were no doubt issued to funds controlled by Rendall, Francis, and their supplicants. In 1990 Francis was indicted in Albuquerque for racketeering in the promotion of seven penny-stock issues. He was found guilty of securities fraud in March 1992. That's the kind of connection that emboldens a reporter or investor when he thinks he smells a rat.

Even after I disclosed some of these connections, Solv-Ex's stock hung in there. Investors were still entranced and had focused their attention not on the history of the management but on whether Solv-Ex could come up with the $30 million the company needed to fund continued operations.

It's tempting to assume complex rigs and oil-exploration investments would never find their way into the portfolios of conservative investors. But that's one of the elements that make

Solv-Ex special. It simply seemed impossible, given all the negative information on Solv-Ex now extant, that any right-minded investor would risk $30 million on the company. Solv-Ex's banker, a European firm called Fiba-Nordic, had been carrying on the search for funds for weeks. In early March 1996 Fiba-Nordic, which had already placed about $9 million in Solv-Ex shares with investors, found an investor willing to step up and buy another 1.1 million shares — $30.69 million! On March 11 Solv-Ex put out a press release citing the investment by Fiba's client as a "clear signal that Solv-Ex and its investors have the confidence and capability to ensure that the company has the necessary financial strength and support to carry out its plans."

So what had happened? A dashing London portfolio manager, Peter Young of Morgan Grenfell, had led some 90,000 shareholders in his unit trusts (British for "mutual funds") down the Solv-Ex path. It was Young who turned out to be the investor who purchased many of the shares Fiba-Nordic was selling. And it was more than "just" $30 million: Young invested about £100 million of his funds' money in Solv-Ex through a web of shell companies and kickbacks.

Peter Young — and six other senior Morgan Grenfell employees — were canned right after the allegations emerged. Within days, stories of his eccentric behavior surfaced: romps with buxom birds in the West End, bulk condom purchases, and a supermarket spree that featured Young's buying thirty jars of pickled gherkins. In September 1996 Rendall acknowledged a connection between Fiba-Nordic and the Morgan Grenfell funds Peter Young had been running. Young was hauled into court to face charges of conspiracy to defraud and showed up wearing a dress and what I'm told was a very nice purse as well.

Richard Geist, newsletter tout for *Richard Geist's Strategic Investing*, took CNBC to task for its "extraordinary attempt to destroy Solv-Ex and its management's credibility." In doing so, we had the rare trifecta: a promoter promoting the work of two other promoters:

1. Geist's newsletter, including his "buy" recommendation, was included in the Solv-Ex investor package sent to prospective investors.

2. Geist mentioned Charlie Maxwell, then a managing director at Morgan Grenfell. Maxwell's opinion carried weight because he'd worked at Mobil Oil (with Solv-Ex president Jack Butler, incidentally), but Maxwell's "letter," as Geist charmingly refers to it, was actually one of the better promotions in history. Titled "Classic Growth Stock of Our Generation," Maxwell declared, "Solv-Ex, between now and the year 2008, will be the fastest growing oil company in the world." He failed to mention that his firm not only owned $70 million worth of Solv-Ex but had purchased "as much as $40 million of common stock at a discount to the then prevailing market price in the U.S.," according to the class-action lawsuit later filed against the company. Add to that the *Financial Post*'s 1996 revelation that Maxwell did not disclose that he personally owned 100,000 shares of Solv-Ex and you've got a whiff of what was to come.

3. Then there's David G. Snow's "painstaking fundamental analysis." Snow is the Wayne, New Jersey–based head of "investment adviser firm" Energy Equities, Inc., which has been disciplined for, among other things, accepting "finder's fees" from one covered security and personal trading in recommended stocks. According to the SEC, which fined Snow $15,000, "between January 30 and March 13, 1996, Snow purchased 2,300 shares of Solv-Ex stock on the open market," failing to disclose this position to his readers.

The Solv-Ex aftermath:

- Amazingly, Solv-Ex hung in there till mid-1997 before plunging from a market value of close to $1 billion to zero, nada, nothing, zilch. It's been there ever since.
- Solv-Ex's suits against several short sellers and the engineering firm that challenged it came to nothing.

- Morgan Grenfell was fined £2 million, the largest penalty ever imposed on a British financial institution.

Rendall stayed on with the company through October 2000, resigning his post as chairman and CEO a few months before Solv-Ex filed a voluntary petition with the U.S. bankruptcy court in Albuquerque on February 1, 2001. Solv-Ex listed $2.9 million in liabilities and $560,000 in assets. It listed no income from operations.

In April 2000 Judge Bruce D. Black issued a ruling that Rendall and the company's vice president, Herbert M. Campbell II, had from 1995 to 1997 "engaged in a pattern of issuing fraudulent statements that created the false impression that each of three technologies being developed by the company were unqualified successes." Rendall received a minimal fine of $5,000.

Unlike most pure rigs, in this one the CEO may have actually been a true believer. While Rendall did lie and cheat along the way, it seems he also believed his company could one day produce oil from tar sands in a profitable fashion. But when Solv-Ex went bust, Rendall appears to have gone bust with it.

Unfortunately, the rig is just one of many types of fraud perpetrated on the investing public. Dozens of others are out there, each with its own warning signs.

Phony Sales

Perhaps the most frequent form of fraud occurs when a company simply lies about how much product it's selling by reporting sales numbers that are above the dollar value of the products that were actually purchased by customers. The SEC is currently investigating nearly 260 separate cases of accounting-related fraud, many of them at some of the nation's largest companies. But whether at small or large companies, the signs of phony sales look the same.

Emanuel Pinez committed one of the most blatant frauds in

RIG TIPS

- Keep an eye on how many shares are issued. Rigs tend to constantly enlarge the float (the number of shares outstanding), and these companies can wind up with truly astonishing equity values when you finally figure out how many shares have been issued. That's because the companies don't always publicly announce when they have sold stock. A company I followed for some time in the mid-nineties was Aura Systems. The company made magnetic valve actuators for the auto industry, but its real business seemed to be selling shares to anyone who expressed an interest. Every time a quarterly filing from Aura would come out, the share count would rise. As of May 31, 1995, Aura listed its total common shares at 45.4 million. A year later the share count had risen to 62.7 million. The stock never seemed to go much above $5, but as its share count rose, even a $5 stock implied a huge market value for a company with minimal revenues in an industrial business.

- Be suspicious of any company whose investors are tied to telltale locations (Caribbean islands with "business-friendly" accounting and bank secrecy laws) or that is involved in one of the telltale businesses (precious metals, fuel exploration, experimental drugs not yet submitted for FDA approval, medical devices, strange software).

- Be suspicious if the company has recently entered one of those businesses or a business that is generating some heat in the market. In April 1998 a company that designed and developed desiccant-based climate-control systems with the name ICC Technologies changed its name to Rare Medium and its business to that of providing Internet professional service. Rare Medium was not and is not a fraud. The change from climate control to the Internet, however, came at a particularly propitious time, and Rare Medium's stock price exploded from $3 to $80 over the next year. It now trades around 35 cents.

- Don't take too much reassurance when a big-name investor takes a position in a stock that looks like a rig. As we saw in Solv-Ex, a money manager who was actually involved in the rig dragged Morgan Grenfell's good name through the mud. And as you'll soon see, big-name investors can often be completely wrong.
- Don't underestimate the ingenuity of the rigger. I wear hats only at Mets games, but if I had one on when I discovered the following story, I'd almost have to tip it to the riggers who deployed it:

When a promote of a company called AgriBioTech began, people involved with it opened dozens of regular investor accounts at Fidelity. Whenever an investment fund or individual acquires more than 5 percent of a company's stock, a 13-D must be filed with the SEC. The 13-D indicates how much stock is owned and whether the buyer intends to be a passive investor or may take some future actions that try to influence management. The same goes for a group of related accounts — a rule the SEC implemented so that investors can't hold several accounts that individually hold less than 5 percent but cumulatively total more.

In the case of AgriBioTech, Fidelity filed a 13-D, indicating that more than 5 percent of AgriBioTech's shares were in its coffers. The promoters then had an official SEC document with Fidelity's name on it indicating that Fidelity was a big holder of AgriBioTech. What a great way to woo future investors. "Oh, by the way, Fidelity owns more than a five percent stake in our company." Sure, a close reader would see that it wasn't one of Fidelity's mutual funds that was backing the company. But that was the beauty of the setup: for a speculative flier like AgriBioTech, investors weren't necessarily reading that closely, and it was the SEC's own rules — designed to protect the small investor — that made this faux endorsement possible.

Talk about Dr. Evil–type brilliance. Reporting on these scams, it often seems as though guys smart enough to cook up these schemes could make a decent buck in the market without risking prison time.

modern times a few years back at Centennial Technologies. As CEO of this maker of PC cards, he took the company public in 1994 and then went to work making things up. It was a tour de force of tall tales. Pinez quickly booked $40 million in phony sales: shipping empty PC housings to customers, inventing nonexistent products and phony invoices, paying for products himself to give the illusion of sales growth. And it worked, until it didn't.

Centennial's stock rode up 450 percent in 1996, making it the best performer on the New York Stock Exchange for that year. When the fraud was discovered in early 1997, the stock took just a couple of days to travel from $55 to $3. Pinez was sentenced to five years in prison, but the order that he pay $150 million in restitution didn't do much for investors — even the SEC can't get blood from a fraudulent turnip.

Sensormatic Electronics (now part of Tyco) is a maker of security products like the plastic doohickey that stores attach to jackets and pants to prevent theft. Unlike Centennial, Sensormatic didn't go on a rampage of unreality. It's a real company with real products. But like many other companies trying and failing to make good on their promises to Wall Street, Sensormatic started fudging its numbers rather than admit the truth.

Sensormatic wore its thirty consecutive quarters of 20 percent or better revenue growth like a badge of honor. To maintain that pace, though, the company resorted to some truly bizarre contortions. On the last day of the quarter, for example, Sensormatic would stop its computer's clocks so that any additional sales would be counted as having been made within the quarter. The company also had a habit of booking revenues twice — once when it shipped product to the warehouse and again when the warehouse shipped the same product to customers. If need be, the company would simply ship some product to its own warehouse and call it a sale. The result? The stock dropped from $35 to $20 as hints of fraud started creeping into the market. Eventually the SEC slapped the company on the wrist, and Sensormatic settled with investors for $53 million, which didn't begin to cover the $2 billion loss in market cap from the spring of 1995, before the fraud was discovered, to its aftermath in the summer of 1998.

Then there's Informix, another outrageous phony-sales offender. From 1994 to 1997 the database-management company goosed its sales every which way: backdating sales agreements to pump sales into different quarters; cutting side agreements with customers to provide price breaks of longer payment terms; counting revenue from customers who could not pay; shipping unordered products to customers. The company inflated its revenues by $295 million and its earnings by $244 million while the stock shot from $8 to $36 between 1994 and 1996. It fell back to $8 when it was revealed exactly how Informix achieved its revenue growth.

MicroStrategy was a high-flying provider of business-intelligence software. Its founder and CEO, Michael Saylor, was deified in a *New Yorker* profile in which his ambitious charitable plans to further education in this country were given glowing reviews: the stock was hovering near $300. Saylor was worth well north of $6 billion, and he was planning on starting his own set of schools with a bit of that money.

MicroStrategy's CEO might have been better off teaching at the school for creative accounting than starting his own university. His company was fond of signing deals after the quarter and backdating them. It even worked out side deals in which it kicked back its "revenue" by purchasing products from its customers. In one deal — backdated, of course — NCR agreed to pay MicroStrategy $27.5 million to license its software. MicroStrategy then used its stock to buy an NCR unit for $14 million and a data-warehousing system for $11 million. The deals were clearly related, but on MicroStrategy's financial statement, it made out like a bandit. The company recorded $17.5 million in revenue for the quarter (more than its entire quarter-to-quarter revenue growth) and also got to add $25 million in assets to its balance sheet.

At its high, MicroStrategy had an equity market value over

$25 billion. A year later the stock was below $4 and the market value below $300 million. Saylor has yet to make good on his pledge of billions for education.

Bad Deal

A lot of frauds are uncovered around the time of a merger or acquisition. Either the due diligence before the merger uncovers it or the accounting firm from one company discovers something the others didn't see or chose to ignore.

HBO & Co., the health-software company acquired by McKesson in January 1999, would do just about anything to close sales at the end of a quarter in order to make its aggressive growth targets. It would make deals up to a week after the quarter and get customers to backdate them, in exchange for unlimited returns and HBO's buying its customers' products. In one deal, 17 percent of HBO's revenues came from a $25 million backdated deal that included — what a coincidence — HBO's buying exactly $25 million of products from that customer. When McKesson disclosed these activities — some occurred after the acquisition, but McKesson claimed its management was unaware of them — McKesson had to restate three years of financial results and its stock dropped from $64 to $24. It has yet to fully recover.

Phony sales aren't the only danger sign to look out for during a merger. Companies that grow rapidly through acquisitions are often Wall Street favorites. Not only do their activities fatten the wallets of investment banking firms, but buying other companies increases earnings and revenues. Unfortunately, all those acquisitions make such a mess of the balance sheet that the opportunity for sharp practices, if not outright fraud, multiplies.

Waste Management bought hundreds of companies during the 1980s and early 1990s. In 1998, though, after years of deflecting criticism about its accounting, it had to restate $3.5 billion in earnings covering a six-year period. Think about that for a moment. Three point five billion dollars! That's an awful lot of scratch. The company's admission that it overstated its pretax earnings by $1.43 billion from 1992 to 1996 stood as an SEC record until WorldCom. But despite that massive restatement, management was not prosecuted or even pursued by regulators. Arthur Andersen did pay the SEC a $7 million fine for its complicity in allowing Waste Management to make up its numbers, and the two companies paid shareholders $220 million to settle litigation. But that was it. Actually, one other group was punished: investors, who saw the stock go from the high 50s to the high teens between 1999 and 2001.

Although acquisitions can allow for favorable accounting treatments that make tepid growth seem somewhat stronger, there's another danger for companies that thrive on doing deals. Call it the bad-apple theory: when a company keeps gobbling up other companies, the likelihood that it will acquire a rotten piece of fruit increases. If you believe Henry Silverman, that's what happened to him when his HFS merged with fraud-ridden CUC. Insurance company Conseco kept buying and buying, until it bought Green Tree, whose balance-sheet problems brought the company to the brink of bankruptcy. If you live by takeovers, you can die by them, too.

Earlier, I mentioned that the promoters of the rigs must exit through sales of stock before that stock price comes crashing down. Another, perhaps even more insidious way for insiders who have run fraudulent companies to cash out is to sell them to another company too stupid or too in need of an acquisition to know better.

Such was the case when Mattel purchased The Learning Company (TLC) in December 1998 for $3.8 billion worth of Mattel stock. On the day the deal was announced, Mattel warned that it would not meet earnings guidance. That was apparently not enough to dissuade TLC from taking Mattel's deal, despite what promised to be an appreciable drop in Mattel shares due to the big earnings miss. Mattel's management, led by embattled CEO Jill Barad, was searching for something that could put the company on a new course. She promised that the TLC deal would "build a unique on-line connection with customers, enabling Mattel to educate and entertain children and their families around the world."

Turns out that Mattel could have used an education in TLC's business. The company might have gotten it had management spoken to some of TLC's competitors. I used to speak with the CEO of a company that competed with TLC. He would pepper me with rhetorical questions about how TLC could not possibly have the revenue growth it claimed, when much of its product was winding up in the discount bin at the local Kmart.

He had read TLC's financial statements, knew who its customers were, and apparently wasn't blowing smoke when he claimed it all didn't add up. Mattel found out the hard way. TLC never did create the "brand cross-leverage opportunities" (I kid you not, this is an actual sentence from the press release announcing the deal). It did create more than $200 million in losses before Mattel was able to jettison the unit to a private-equity firm. In return, Mattel received nothing. It gave away TLC. Was there outright fraud? It's still tough to say. But with a loss like that, it doesn't really matter.

HOW TO FIND OUT:
Spotting Phony Sales

It's hard to identify when companies are cooking up phony sales, because the whole point is to make them resemble real sales on the balance sheet (think Enron). Companies cooking the books usually do it to meet the Street's growth targets. As we will learn in "Delving Into the Balance Sheet" section in chapter 2, there are many techniques companies can use to pump up earnings. But many of those same things can at least be questioned if one sees them on a balance sheet.

In the case of sales that are simply made up, it is harder to find the truth. But some simple signs can be telling. A surprising number of phony-sales frauds can be deduced by simple logic. Ask yourself whether the company's story makes sense. Is it possible in light of the market conditions, the state of its competitors, even the tone of the economy that the company could be doing so well? Where is the company's growth coming from? If it sells something like barbecues and claims to be growing 50 percent a year, year after year, does that sound right? A grill is hardly a novel idea, and one doesn't wear out overnight. And it's not a business in which one manufacturer can easily gain such an advantage that it wipes out its competitors. That sort of growth was part of the story at Sunbeam, and it turned out that Chainsaw Al Dunlap's company was just shipping those grills to a warehouse and counting the shipments as sales.

Regulators let companies get away with so much in their financial reporting that if it smells bad, it probably is. AgriBioTech was so aggressive in accounting for acquisitions that it began consolidating with its own the results of a company it had no more than a handshake agreement to buy. It was sort of like an eager college student practicing surgery as soon as he receives a med-school-admission letter. The SEC made the company put a footnote in the financial statements detailing this policy, and footnotes about special accounting treatments often signal trouble down the road. It really does pay to read them.

And remember how *Spy* magazine would nail writers who had issued complimentary quotes on each other's book jackets? That sort of logrolling happens with phony sales. Reciprocal sales arrangements can signal cooked books. Both HBO & Co. and MicroStrategy goosed revenue with these kinds of deals, which usually take place at the end of a quarter and are publicized in self-congratulatory press releases. Global Crossing's quarter-ending swaps of capacity with other telecom companies may have artificially inflated Global's revenues. The SEC has awoken to such schemes and is investigating.

Watch the Watchers

When trolling for fraud, keep a close eye on whoever's paid to keep an eye on the company. The statements that public companies file with the SEC — 10Qs (filed quarterly) and 10Ks (filed annually) — or its glossy annual report are audited by accounting firms that sign their names attesting to the veracity of the documents. The prose is boilerplate under the heading "Independent Auditor Report": "In our opinion, the consolidated financial statements referred to above present fairly, in all material respects, the financial position of COMPANY ABC, Inc., and the results of their operations and their cash flow for the year ended December 31, 2001, in conformity with generally accepted accounting principles. Signed, KPMG LLP [or Whoever], Atlanta, Georgia, January 28, 2002."

Inspires confidence, right? Don't be too sure.

Most of the time, auditors simply miss fraud. (Repeat after Henry Silverman: "Fraud by its very nature is intended to be difficult to detect.") But sometimes the auditors have a motive to help the fraud along. The other services provided by the big accounting firms often put them into a conflict of interest: instead of blowing the whistle on bad corporate conduct, the auditing firm might get itself additional business by trying to fix it or even perpetuate it. The Enron debacle has awoken many investors to this conflict. As a result, each of the Big Four accounting firms has committed to cleaving its consulting business from its auditing functions if it has not already done so. That may help eliminate some of the potential for compromised audit work, but there are still plenty of opportunities for the auditor who doesn't rat out the company.

A study by the Investor Responsibility Research Center found that fees for nonauditing services were two and a half times greater than the fees paid for audits. The larger the company, the larger the percentage of fees paid for services other than actual audits. The Gap, for example, allocated 93 cents of every dollar it paid to its accounting firm for services that had nothing to do with an audit of its financial statements. With that kind of dough on the line, it's certainly understandable how its auditor might let The Gap get away with some strange accounting choices, such as the decision to take a special charge for paying income taxes that were higher than expected.

Enron was not the first company to compromise the work of its auditor. Before anyone had heard of Enron, Just for Feet, a sorry-ass, Super-Bowl-ad-running shoe-store chain, went from a market cap of $700 million to zero in three years with Deloitte & Touche's accountants on watch. Deloitte's consulting arm hit the company up for business to fix its internal-control problems. The comedian Jon Stewart has joked that some companies hire the consulting arm to show them how to a outsmart the auditing arm they also hired. Deloitte also made revenue-enhancing suggestions, such as recording the display booths donated by manufacturers as assets. The current trend to divorce accounting firms from their consulting business will help, but sometimes, a package deal is still expected.

That was part of the problem with our old friend Micro-Strategy. When it crashed, the SEC was looking into whether PricewaterhouseCoopers, the company's auditor, was encouraging MicroStrategy to pressure its customers and partners to hire PricewaterhouseCoopers consultants. Because the auditors and consultants are typically partners, the accountants benefit when the advisers get work. Not all that "independent" of an independent auditor.

One auditor-related warning sign can also come when an unknown firm audits a relatively large public company. The Big Four — Deloitte & Touche, Ernst & Young, KPMG, and PricewaterhouseCoopers — own over 90 percent of the auditing business for companies listed on America's major exchanges. This isn't meant to suggest a lesser-known firm is probably a scam, in the same way we know that a big name does not ensure that the books have been reviewed with a fine-tooth comb. But keep your eyes open when the auditor is a name you don't recognize, just as you would when the investment bank bringing a company public is unknown to you.

When a company seems too big or complex for its auditor, it may be a sign that fraud will go undetected. Although big firms clearly miss a lot of fraud, at least they have the weapons and the experience, if they choose to use them. The columnist Herb Greenberg picked out Family Golf Centers as an accident waiting to happen based in part on its decision to keep its original tiny auditing firm even after going public. As it grew larger and more complex, and its acquisitions became more frequent, Family Golf's books outstripped the firm's ability to detect fraud. It filed for bankruptcy at the end of 2000.

A sudden change in auditors can signal that the original auditor discovered something and would rather quit than rock the boat. Unfortunately, the resignation often occurs at the same time as (or, worse, after) the exposure of the fraud. Sometimes, however, the auditor resigns, everybody acts as if it's business as usual, and the new auditor blows the whistle. One of the most controversial Silicon Valley companies of the early nineties, California Micro Devices (CMD), replaced Price Waterhouse (which told the company and the world, through CMD's SEC filings) with Coopers & Lybrand in 1990. After several years of additional controversies, the company was forced to report that it had engaged in widespread accounting fraud. It engaged in just about every possible means of improper revenue recognition: booking revenue before shipment, shipping before customers requested, sending unordered shipments, faking invoices and customers, allowing unconditional rights of return, and creating bogus title transfers.

Big-Name Investors Get Stung, Too (and Sometimes Sting)

The Solv-Ex story shows how a fraudulent company can be buoyed by a respected financial company. When people associated with Morgan Grenfell put money into Solv-Ex and touted its prospects, ordinary investors felt they could trust the company at least to be honest, if not to prosper. Unfortunately, that's a dubious assumption.

When the chief geologist of Bre-X "fell" from a helicopter over the jungles of Indonesia, even the analysts who followed the Canadian gold-mining company started to worry. But by then it was too late. The cast of characters to get sucked in by what turned out to be Bre-X's completely fraudulent gold-exploration company includes splendid names:

- Fidelity Investments — by the end of 1996, Fido held 7.3 percent of Bre-X.
- Lehman Brothers rated the company as a "strong buy" and anointed the worthless Busang claims the "gold discovery of the century."
- J.P. Morgan was Bre-X's investment banker and introduced the company to mining giants worldwide.
- Esteemed Canadian mining firm Kilborn Engineering Pacific confirmed Bre-X reports that Busang contained 71 million ounces of gold.

HOW TO FIND OUT:
Auditor Changes

Whenever a company has a material development not covered by one of its periodic filings, it files a Form 8-K with the SEC. Companies have to file an 8-K to report "changes in registrant's certifying accountant." Numerous financial sites have some information from corporate SEC filings, but the best place to find 8-Ks is at EDGAR (www.sec.gov/edgar.shtml), which is operated by the SEC. Just punch in the name of the company and the type of filing you are looking for ("8-K") and you will see every such document going back to 1994.

Mark Twain said that a gold mine "is a hole in the ground with a liar on top." The Bre-X tale might have been worthy of a book from the great master. I can remember the final day of the hoax. Investors were lined up on both sides of one big question: was there an amazing 71 million ounces of gold at the Busang site, or none at all? One stark headline crossed Reuters: NO GOLD FOUND AT BUSANG SITE. The stock would never trade again. At that instant, nearly $4.5 billion of investors' money was deemed worthless.

Bre-X's mine contained no gold at all. The samples that Bre-X used to attract investor interest had been "salted" with flakes of the precious metal that had been mined from a site far away. John Felderhof, Bre-X's co-founder, is being sued by the Ontario Securities Commission on insider-trading charges. Like any good promoter, Felderhof managed to sell $55 million worth of Bre-X stock before the fraud was uncovered. Felderhof is not in attendance at the trial; instead, he is ensconced in his seaside home in the Cayman Islands, a place that does not have an extradition treaty with Canada.

The point: don't think that just because you invest alongside the experts your company can't be riddled with fraud.

After (badly) running Apple Computer, John Sculley signed on with Spectrum Information Technologies in October 1993. He was going to bring its new wireless technology into the big leagues. He apparently became CEO without realizing that the National Association of Securities Dealers had once delisted Spectrum and that the company had a close and continuing relationship with a notorious stock promoter who had been investigated by the SEC. Sculley resigned four months later, claiming he had been misled about the company's financial condition.

In April 1998 Michael Ovitz, once the most powerful man in Hollywood, and Roy Furman, principal of Furman Selz, invested in theatrical producer Livent. They knew its founder, Garth Drabinsky, had a controversial past, but the deal included options to buy stock at then current prices, so they took the company's performance at face value. Ovitz, one of the shrewdest deal makers in the entertainment industry, put up $20 million of his own money. Furman, who was Livent's investment banker, had access to plenty of info on the company — he apparently felt confident enough to pay $2 million for 250,000 shares. And, of course, each bought options. Up until August the stock was trading around $10. Then the new principals discovered widespread fraudulent accounting and restated three years of financial results. The stock fetched a few pennies a share when trading resumed in November, then stopped trading altogether later that month.

When Chainsaw Al Dunlap brought down Sunbeam with a wide-ranging accounting fraud, he was doing it under the noses of some very astute investors. Michael Price, value manager extraordinaire and a man *Fortune* magazine labeled "the toughest SOB on Wall Street," was Sunbeam's largest shareholder before Dunlap took over. Ronald Perelman, who has made a career of taking advantage of his own shareholders but rarely gets taken advantage of himself, sold camping-equipment maker Coleman to Sunbeam. In his infinite wisdom and apparent confidence in Dunlap, Perelman took payment in stock instead of cash. Big mistake. And good old Ronnie made sure to screw Coleman shareholders as well, since they were also left with worthless Sunbeam shares.

ICG Communications Inc., the telecommunications company led by dashing chairman and chief executive J. Shelby Bryan, attracted billions from regular investors and pros alike, all while its chief found time to suntan in France, squire *Vogue*'s Anna Wintour around town, and host a star-studded dinner in Hollywood for Al Gore's daughter.

ICG's largest investor was John Malone. The savvy chief of Liberty Media and everyone's favorite evil genius was neither smart nor nasty in this deal. Instead, Malone's Liberty Media was suckered in by Bryan's smooth talk. Liberty purchased $500 million worth of ICG's convertible preferred stock in February of

2000 with a strike price of $28. Also taken in: those gullible boys over at Hicks Muse, who were in for $230 million on the same preferred deal. ICG was bankrupt less than a year later.

Never in my career as a reporter have I encountered a person for whom more people reserve unmitigated enmity than Linda Wachner, who was the CEO of clothing manufacturer Warnaco. I have never met her. I've never even spoken with her, given her refusal to be interviewed on CNBC. She could be a saint. But judging from how many disparate, disconsolate, and disaffected people she's touched who in turn hate her, it is fair to say Wachner is despised.

It's unclear whether Wachner perpetrated fraud when she ran Warnaco into bankruptcy. She certainly did not tell the truth. And her decision to load up Warnaco with debt so the company could pay cash for another company that Wachner controlled certainly did not help matters. She made out well on that deal, pocketing a $50 million gain that she had the audacity to shelter by selling Warnaco stock she owned in order to generate a paper loss and reduce her personal income tax.

John Lattanzio is a legendary Wall Street trader who made his name running the desk at a wildly successful hedge fund run by Michael Steinhardt. But in an inexplicable act of gullibility and paralysis, Lattanzio, a warm, kindhearted man, hung on in Warnaco as Linda Wachner ran the company into the ground. Lattanzio lost almost his entire fortune by believing Wachner's promises that profit growth was just around the corner. Wachner also kicked sand in the face of some really rich and savvy investors such as Steinhardt, hedge fund manager Lee Cooperman, and Gary Winnick, chairman of Global Crossing. None of them took hits that even approach Lattanzio's mind-numbing losses, but lose they did after believing Linda's bullshit.

These were all professionals. These men made billions using the financial markets, all of them accustomed to playing in that busy intersection where business meets high finance. And still they did not avoid big, costly mistakes. They should have known better, but were victims of the same schemes and greed that ensnared ordinary investors. A chilling lesson.

Trouble with Regulators and Johnny Law

If a company is in trouble with its industry regulators, it could be hiding problems from shareholders, too. One of the biggest security frauds in recent history occurred at Oxford Health Plans in 1996 and 1997. Oxford presented itself as a giant, fast-growing health-services organization, and investors bid up its stock accordingly. No one (except the short sellers) seemed to wonder how one HMO could be so much more efficient and generate such higher margins than its competitors.

In fact, Oxford's internal billing and payment systems were so bad that the company could not process claims, collect money from customers, or pay claims to its member doctors and facilities. During one day in October 1997, the stock fell from $75 to $25 and then drifted down to $6 not long after. Astute investors were tipped off to the fraud in advance, however, by watching the problems Oxford had with the New York State Insurance Department. Nine months before disclosure of the fraud, the Insurance Department announced that it was targeting Oxford in looking at widespread reports of nonpayment to hospitals and doctors. Then in June the New York attorney general threatened to sue Oxford unless it settled the issue of late payments to providers. The Insurance Department and the attorney general made additional statements about the situation — not announcing the magnitude of the problem, just its existence and seriousness — in August and early October.

Accounting rules focus on when a contract is signed, a bill is sent, or goods are shipped. But if the company cannot collect the money, it is going to have problems down the road. This was exactly the situation with Oxford. Its premium receivables — premiums to which it was entitled but had not collected —

HOW TO FIND OUT:
Trouble with Regulators

No one expects you to follow the goings-on of each state's department of insurance just for the hell of it. But if you were an investor in Oxford, or if you were considering becoming one, a simple look through sources as obscure as the *New York Times,* which reported the regulators' activities, would have sounded the alarm. Sometimes, local papers are best for following the workaday stuff that matters to employees — and ends up mattering to investors. New Jersey's *Star-Ledger,* for example, often has the scoop on the pharmaceutical industry, as do the Detroit papers on the auto industry. The *San Jose Mercury News* is the leading newspaper of Silicon Valley and offers extensive coverage of technology companies. You could also regularly read a specialty publication covering the company — *Best's Review* provided regular coverage of Oxford Health's public news — but if you are already feeling spread thin by your financial reading, stick with a general financial site and a local paper.

ballooned between 1995 and 1997, from less than $100 million to over $420 million. Even as a percentage of revenues, earnings, or any other benchmark you care to name, Oxford was leaving a lot of money on the table. In addition, despite this phenomenal growth, cash flow from operations was actually declining. In the first two quarters of 1997, operating cash flow was negative. And as we will learn in chapter 2, that is often a key signal of trouble.

Oh yes — and while Oxford Health Plans hid its massive billing and regulatory problems, three top insiders sold more than a third of their stock for $50 million. These sales occurred well before the fraud was disclosed.

Weak (or Complicit) Boards of Directors

Bad boards of directors are all too common in corporate America, but their failures are almost always ones of omission. The board that's actually in on the bad acts taking place at a company is fairly rare. Still, it's up to you as an investor to pay attention to the composition of the board. Have the members been together on boards in the past? What are their connections to management, and will those connections make it tough for them to act in the best interests of shareholders? You also need to dig deep. The SEC requires only that management and board members furnish their history for five years, unless they have had bankruptcies. Management and their boards know this — it's not unheard-of for those intent on separating you from your investment capital to wait exactly five years before perpetrating their next fraud.

More often than a conspiracy among board members you get a group of lazy, self-interested directors who do not provide the oversight necessary to prevent or detect fraud. Between 1997 and 2001 Archer Daniels Midland (ADM) stock underwent a painful slide from $25 to $10. During that stretch the company fixed prices on certain food chemicals, paid $100 million to settle with the government, and saw some of its top executives go to prison.

ADM's 1995 proxy statement reveals seventeen board members. Four were members of the Andreas family (papa Dwayne has run the company since 1966). The Daniels and Midland families each held one seat. Two more members were current officers. Another retired from the company but stayed on the board. Happy Rockefeller served as a director, along with a Harvard agricultural professor who owned just 544 shares. One of the "outside" directors was an in-law of a management member of the board. This leaves five outsider-professionals, two of whom were power-broker lawyers (former Canadian prime minister Brian Mulroney and former Democratic Party chairman Robert

Strauss) with close ties to management. There was clearly no one in a position to question the schemes of Dwayne Andreas and his family.

Waste Management's problems might have been spotted were it not for a board packed with former officers, as well as members included for their influence-peddling acumen. The 1996 board — that's when the company was flying high and reporting phony earnings — had twelve members:

- 2 officers
- 3 former officers
- 2 lawyers with whom Waste Management did business and who served on ten other boards between them
- 3 included for window dressing or influence peddling, including Reagan chief of staff Howard Baker, former Secretary of Commerce Alexander Trowbridge (holder of *nine* other directorships), and former Energy Secretary James Edwards (director of four other companies)

That left two directors, Dr. Pastora San Juan Cafferty, a University of Chicago professor of cultural diversity, and James Peterson, who had been a director for fifteen years and was CEO of Parker Pen Company.

Waste Management racked up transactions — small companies, large companies, spin-offs, divestitures, acquisitions of minority interests — at an extremely rapid rate, each with a dizzying array of accounting artifices. Who in this group had the independence, qualifications, and plain old time to figure out whether the company was behaving in a fiscally responsible manner?

A Weak (but Sometimes Meaningful) Signal

As explained earlier, selling by insiders is a key to pulling off a successful rig. But you have to look for patterns that extend beyond the selling insiders undertake to fund their lives. Shareholders in Cendant were wary of Henry Silverman in part because until the shit hit the fan, Henry never actually bought a share and kept it. He made hundreds of millions by exercising options that he had been granted at substantially lower prices and selling the stock immediately. His claim was that he was still determined to get the stock price up because of his large position for future options, but it's also clear that his interests were not entirely aligned with shareholders', since his entry price was far below theirs.

HOW TO FIND OUT:
Board Composition

Every public company has to disclose certain information about its directors. The proxy statement, in which shareholders vote for directors and any other resolutions presented, is called a Form 14A. EDGAR goes back to 1994. The proxy provides the director's age, employment, and other directorships. It mentions for how long the person has been a director, along with his or her stock holdings. Another section of the proxy, just as important, is called "Certain Relationships and Transactions." That's corporate-speak for conflicts of interest. If the proxy statement is not handy (assuming you haven't saved several years of proxy statements to evaluate the changing composition of the board), you can find the information online by searching EDGAR.

Be especially wary of insider selling at new companies. When a company goes public, the insiders' shares are usually restricted from sale for only six months. But for what legitimate reason would the people who got the public to buy shares want to sell them just six months later? Many insiders and venture capitalists of those bygone Internet companies in 1999 and 2000 cashed out as soon as the six-month lockup expired. They were not frauds in the classic sense; rather, they were companies built on business plans that didn't have a chance of working. Keep a particular eye on the lockup expiration when the number of shares sold in the IPO is less than 20 percent of the total held. That means insiders, who hold the other 80 percent (or more), can flood the market.

The CD-ROM company Oak Technology went public in February 1995. As soon as the lockup expired in August, insiders sold $104 million in stock. By November the company disclosed not only slowing sales but also improper revenue recognition, phony sales, and inventory parking. The insiders got out between $18 and $30. The stock fell to $5.

Milestone Scientific created a dental tool called The Wand, but it didn't have nearly the potential it claimed. CEO Leonard Osser sold 500,000 of his 1.8 million shares between late 1997 and mid-1998. Osser owned 21 percent of the outstanding stock, so 500,000 shares (which he sold for about $5 million) was pretty substantial. And all that selling certainly didn't help his shareholders.

Pay special attention to the transactions of CEOs or other high-ranking insiders. Also look at the percentage of their shares insiders are releasing, particularly during secondary offerings, which are dilutive in any case. Michael Egan, chairman of TheGlobe.com, got $20 each for the 2.5 million shares he sold during his company's May 1999 secondary offering. That was about one-third of his position, and it was a smart trade — within two years the stock was under a quarter and had been booted to the OTC board.

I continue to be grossed out, even three years later, by what the gang at InfoSpace got away with. The Yellow-Pages-for-the-Internet company went public in December 1998, raising $75 million as part of the Blodget-induced updraft for Internet companies. In April 1999 they pulled off another equity offering. Of the $286 million raised, $144 million was from shares sold by insiders. In other words, four months after they went public, guys were cashing out.

InfoSpace founder Naveen Jain, in a follow-on offering, sold a greater percentage of his shares than any other insider — 10 percent of his stake, or 1.2 million shares — for nearly $100 million. That'll fund plenty of homes, gifts, tax liabilities, and college tuitions — and every other reason an insider gives for selling out. But Jain was barely started. A month later he sold 1.8 million shares for $100 million. In January 2000 he dumped another 781,000 shares for $113 million. Finally, during May and June 2000 he unloaded 3 million more shares, hauling in nearly $200 million.

Jain wasn't alone. From December 2000 to March 2001, InfoSpace fell from $15 to $2. Perhaps insiders and venture capitalists flooding the market with more than 17 million shares caused part of that run. Or perhaps they were positioned to know that the company's stock wouldn't hold up. Either way, ordinary InfoSpace investors would have done better to imitate the trading of InfoSpace insiders.

The United States has without a doubt the most transparent and egalitarian capital markets in the world. They are a blessing and a key force behind the innovation of American business. And still, there is plenty of fraud.

You should now feel confident in being able to recognize fraud, but although it's one thing to recognize fraud, it's another to put that information to use. Don't play the rigged game, just because you think there is a greater fool out there. Longs ought to stay away from frauds, and shorts can print money by correctly timing their downfall. But in the end, the smart investor realizes that there are too many good companies out there to play a game in which the crooks have the edge.

Lessons and reminders

- Watch out for unusual or unexplained transactions that increase the number of outstanding shares.
- Pay attention to the country of incorporation.
- Understand how the corporation became public and what firm underwrote its initial offering.
- Be wary of hot businesses of the moment. Remember industry areas where frauds are typically found.
- Question growth claims if they seem beyond reason.
- Examine balance sheets.
- Watch for a change in auditors.
- Be wary of consistent regulatory problems.

HOW TO FIND OUT:
Insider Selling

There are numerous sources for learning about insider selling, but not all of them are reliable, because they don't all furnish an accurate picture of what the executives control in terms of options.

Corporate officers selling stock have to file with the SEC regularly unless they sell stock back to the company to repay a loan. A document called a Form 4 discloses changes in their beneficial ownership. (A lot of officers file F-4s late.) You can search by company through EDGAR or in comprehensive financial sites. All insider dealings must be disclosed once a year in a Form 5 filing, which comes out too late to be of much help.

Ipolockup.com has a calendar listing exactly when each new company's lockup expires. Run your mouse over it to get the total number and percentage of shares outstanding that will become available. Pull-down boxes allow you to set any month you like. Unlockdates.com, affiliated with Thomson Financial, does essentially the same thing.

2

WHY I LOVE SHORT SELLERS

Short sellers are a bunch of nasty, misbegotten, morose people who've never seen an earnings report they couldn't criticize, a product launch they couldn't deem "hype," and a management they could stand. And I love them for it.

There's a vast machinery in place to sell stocks to regular investors ("longs"). Short sellers fight that machine with intellect, reasoned analysis, and hard-fought research. And that's why I really love them.

Everyone knows the proverb "Buy low, sell high." A short seller tries to do that, but in reverse order — sell high, then buy low. Here's a simple look at how a short sale works.

Step 1: Joe Investor does his homework and decides there's no way high-flying Juniper, which is selling at four hundred times earnings (in a ferociously competitive industry), can sustain its lofty price of $200.

Step 2: Joe borrows 100 shares of Juniper from his broker for a small fee. The key here is that he's borrowing shares and has to return them at some point.

Step 3: Joe immediately sells the borrowed shares, grossing $20,000 (less commissions on the sale).

Step 4: Over the course of the next few months, Joe watches the stock obsessively.

Stock Price Rises	Stock Price Falls
Step 5: Juniper demonstrates extraordinary resilience (or luck!) and rises to 240.	**Step 5:** Joe waits out Juniper's rise, riding the stock as it declines to $50.
Step 6: Joe decides he's taken enough of a beating. He buys 100 shares on the open market for $24,000. He repays his broker by handing over the shares. Since he got $20,000 for the shares he originally borrowed and then spent $24,000 to pay back the loan, Joe lost $4,000 plus two commissions and a borrow fee.	**Step 6:** Joe buys 100 shares on the open market for $5,000. He repays his broker by handing over the shares. Since he received $20,000 for the shares he originally borrowed and then spent only $5,000 to pay back the loan, Joe's profit is $15,000, less two commissions and the borrow fee.

The diagram above isn't some fictitious scenario designed to show shorting in its most favorable light. The fact is, on October 11, 2000, Juniper closed at $206. By October 16 Juniper's stock hit its all-time high of $244.50 — up about 20 percent in five days — exactly the kind of move that makes shorts rush to cover their exposed fannies. But by September 2001 the stock was below $20 — a huge gain in eleven months for those who had shorted the shares.

Reporters are generally not permitted to short stocks, and I wouldn't do so even if we were. It's too easy to be accused of slamming a company for personal gain. But the whole premise of this book — that the skills of a good investor are the same as those of a good reporter — are most clear when you look at the skepticism and contrary nature of the short seller.

Don't get me wrong. Selling stocks short is a dangerous game and I do not recommend that anyone make it the focus of his investment activity. What I do recommend is that investors make the techniques used by short sellers a part of their own investing discipline. Those practices are explained in this chapter and the previous one. These techniques can be relied upon time and again to save you from bad investment decisions. And they're always there should you choose to short stocks from time to time.

Most short sellers work at hedge funds, though there are a few mutual funds that specialize in selling short. The average hedge fund manager will both buy stocks and sell them short. There are managers who focus solely on selling short, as well as managers who buy stocks but have a talent for finding stocks that are going down.

Short sellers are in many ways the policemen of Wall Street; as with cops, there are a few dirty ones, but most are clean. They do tend to work in small groups, which leads to frequent but specious charges that they are somehow out to sabotage companies. That's simply not the case; they often work in groups to split up the detailed, time-consuming investigation and analysis that selling short can require. One short seller might be expert in researching the biographies of various managements, while another has expertise in dealing with and getting information from regulators. Still another might best serve by assessing the fundamentals of a particular short candidate. Still another may have close ties to certain reporters who can be told of the findings of this informal group. I have encountered no ethical difference between those who short stocks and those who focus solely on buying stocks.

Being alone in one's belief is instinctively unsettling. That's why believing in a company everyone hates takes some courage. But hating a company everyone loves, however, takes a different sort of constitution. Beyond the psychic torment, there's the stigma of rooting against the home team. There's something vaguely unpatriotic about short selling, akin to playing the DON'T

PASS line at a craps table. Some countries, such as Israel, don't even allow it; others, such as Japan, simply wonder what kind of wet blanket would do something so gauche. And the companies themselves, suspecting short sellers of spreading stories that hurt their stocks, ferociously punish such investors by ostracizing them, accusing them of rumormongering, or even suing them.

In addition to the me-against-the-world stuff that makes me naturally root for the short-seller underdog, shorts perform a valuable service. By reining in hype, shorts provide an antidote to unrealistic expectations, reminding investors that stocks aren't on some unending march to ever greener pastures. During the relentless ascent of the Nasdaq during the 1990s, that attitude seemed anachronistic. Not anymore.

Short sellers are frequently the first to tip investors off to fraud, which can save millions for longs who get out before it's too late. They perform another valuable service: providing market liquidity. Since the short sells his borrowed shares, he adds to the supply of stock available for sale. This benefits longs who want to begin a position, both by lowering the price of the stock and by reducing spikes in price created by a supply shortage.

So that's why I love short sellers. Personality issues aside, the work of a good short seller can be instructive for the average investor conducting research on a potential investment. Because those who short stocks are often barred from access to information from the company, they must rely on a shrewd reading of public documents and careful attention to subtle shifts and evidence of misdeeds by companies the market thinks can do no wrong. Whether you're short or long, these techniques are priceless for any investor.

In an efficient market, a stock will supposedly gravitate to its "right" price. That's why value investors buy stocks whose prices are temporarily deflated and why every mutual fund advertises its ability to hunt out bargains. But what about the other side of the coin? For every stock that sells for less than it "should," there's probably one that sells for more. Here's how to identify those opportunities.

Efficient market The theory holds that securities are "priced correctly," since pertinent information about an investment's prospects is well known to all. That's why insiders are forbidden to trade on information that's not available to everyone. It's a nice theory, but it is just that. Even with CNBC, not all pertinent information is available to all the people making a decision on a stock's price. If it were, few of the hedge fund managers I speak with would be spending their days searching for the informational edge that allows them to buy and sell securities before the information that motivated those transactions is widely disseminated.

Value investing Value is often in the eye of the beholder. So although this investing discipline began with very specific designs, many investors who don't adhere to those original precepts nonetheless call themselves value investors.

Professors David Dodd and Benjamin Graham developed the original method of value investing during the 1930s. Their focus was on hard assets, such as machinery, cash, and real estate: the elements of book value. Early value investors focused primarily on the balance sheet, specifically book value versus stock price. The analysis extended beyond book value, recognizing that certain assets were carried at unrealistically low values and that even if these companies never earned a cent, a simple sale of the company's assets would result in more cash per share than the stock's current price.

Value investing is now focused on those companies selling at p/e ratios (see page 212) that do not adequately discount their future growth. A company selling at seven times its earnings but growing those earnings at 10 percent a year would be defined as a value by most investors focused on such things.

Look for a Catalyst

If you take away one idea from this chapter, make it this one: never ever — ever — short a stock based solely on the fact that its valuation appears to be far in excess of the company's prospects.

That a stock is "way too expensive" may very well be true. But that alone won't keep it from quadrupling — and wiping out the shorts who stare at it with mouths agape and wallets empty.

When Amazon was on its historic mission to the moon in late 1998 with daily moves up of 20 percent, a hedge fund manager who was short a boatload would send me these detailed, passionately argued handwritten faxes proving that Amazon couldn't possibly justify its stock price. He listed the total number of books sold each year worldwide and demonstrated that Amazon would have to sell every one of them twice to equal half its market value. He had shorted the stock in the 20s, and by the time it climbed to $50 in less than six months, he was starting to lose it. Still he hung in there and shorted more, as Amazon kept moving up. He let emotion creep into his investment decisions, knowing that he was a rational investor in an irrational market. As *Star Trek*'s Mr. Spock said, "A sane man is judged insane in an insane world."

Market value The number of outstanding shares of a company multiplied by the price of each share of that company. GE has roughly 10 billion shares outstanding. If its stock price is $60 (one can always hope), GE would have a market value of $600 billion.

Enterprise value or total cap Market value plus the face value of all outstanding debt. GE's total cap would be its market value plus the value of its outstanding debt.

The hedge fund manager was finally forced to cover when his short position in Amazon threatened to crater his entire $400 million fund. If only he could have waited: two years later Amazon traded below $10 and a semblance of rationality had returned to the market. The hedge fund manager can only look on and wonder what might have been. His fund never recovered from the Amazon short, and I'm not sure his mind did, either.

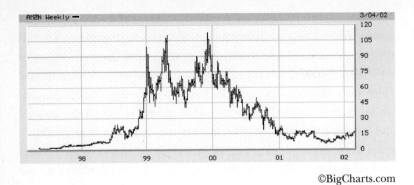

©BigCharts.com

The lesson: Just because a stock trades at twenty times revenue today doesn't mean it won't be at thirty times revenue tomorrow. And unlike a long investment, where your risk is capped at a loss of 100 percent, when you short a stock the risk is infinite.

Here's why.

UNLIMITED DOWNSIDE / LIMITED UPSIDE

Unlimited Downside

1. You short 100 shares of XYZ at $10 — you get $1,000 in cash.
2. XYZ soars to $50 — a common occurrence not too long ago.
3. You decide to cover before the carnage worsens.
4. You buy 100 shares of XYZ at $50 — which costs you $5,000.

Result: You lose $4,000 on a $1,000 investment — a –400 percent return. And if it went higher before you covered, it'd be even worse.

Limited Upside

1. You short 100 shares of ABC at $10 — you get $1,000 in cash.
2. ABC implodes to pennies per share — also a common occurrence not too long ago.
3. You cover and pat yourself on the back.
4. You buy 100 shares of ABC at 10 cents — which costs you $10.

Result: You gain $990 on a $1,000 investment — a nearly 100 percent return.

No one's sneezing at a 100 percent return. But the point here is that a guy who's short 100 ABC *and* XYZ ends up down $3,010, while a guy who's long 100 shares of both winds up with a gain of $3,010. Even if the stocks don't perform such dramatic three-digit moves, there's something scary about not knowing how deep the water is before you dive in. When you lose 25 percent on the long side, you've already taken a quarter of the haircut you could possibly face. A 25 percent loss on the short side, however, doesn't put you any closer to the potential limit of your losses.

There are investors who can take that kind of pain, and simply won't give in. They are almost always extremely rich, risk-taking investors who are managing their own funds, as opposed to those of people who have entrusted them with their life savings.

Carl Icahn, the corporate cage rattler, is one. Icahn is known for aggressive activities when it comes to pressuring corporate boards to do the right thing and create shareholder value and make him even richer in the process. But old Carl was just as tenacious when it came to shorting Internet stocks during 1998 and 1999. Carl was one of the founding shareholders of Lowestfare.com, so he had a certain inside knowledge of the business of selling airline tickets over the Internet. With that, he took to shorting shares of Priceline as the stock skyrocketed during the Internet bubble. Icahn, unlike many investors who did the same thing but couldn't take the pain, is incredibly rich and answers only to himself. He used each run-up in Priceline's stock to borrow more shares, shorting at $60, at $80, at $120, even at $160. And unlike so many other investors, Carl got richer as Priceline's stock finally crashed.

So how do you know whether to go long or short? Simple: the only time to short a stock is when an *event*, rather than a *perception*, can be expected to drive down the price.

The most common event that rewards a short sale is a warning from a company that it is unable to meet the expectations it has set for its earnings growth. Other events include the disclosure of a failed product, significant management departures, failure to win expected business from a customer, deteriorating credit quality, and the granddaddy of them all — fraud. Fraud is the toughest catalyst to anticipate. It's the hardest to find and, when found, can still result in a stock going straight up before the end comes.

In 1998 Cendant CEO Henry Silverman, who had been CEO of HFS International before its merger with CUC formed Cendant, announced that there were some problems with the way CUC had accounted for revenue. The stock took a hit, but not a knockout blow. A few weeks later Cendant dropped the bomb that would eviscerate its share price for years to come. The modest accounting discrepancies revealed weeks earlier were actually part of a much larger accounting fraud that had taken place at CUC for years previous to its merger with HFS.

On a conference call, Silverman detailed the devastation. He was clearly shaken and, unlike the previous call a few weeks earlier, was not joined by co-CEO Walter Forbes. I was on the call. Investors were angry — rightfully demanding to know how Silverman could say with a straight face that he had had no idea. What about due diligence? What about all those high-profile bankers to whom HFS investors paid a fortune — weren't they checking out CUC's books? What about CUC's "independent" auditors? Everyone was asking the same question: "How could you not have known?"

I'm no fan of Henry Silverman. But he made a valid point as the criticism rained down. By its very nature, said Silverman, fraud is intended to be difficult to detect. Clearly, he had been unable to detect it. And for that matter, so had the premier statesmen of American business.

When he was pursuing his due diligence on the deal, Silverman asked Walter Forbes for references. I'm told that Forbes furnished five of them. One from Bill Gates. One from Jack Welch. One from Henry Kravis. One from Warren Buffet, and another from Louis Gerstner. I don't think it would be possible to put together a better set of business references. And yet, while all those men were attesting to Walter Forbes's reputation, the company he ran was fabricating hundreds of millions in sales. No wonder Silverman is still haunted by his decision to merge with CUC. Had he consulted some short sellers, he might have saved himself a great deal of torment. Before the merger, and then after, while the stock was climbing, a small chorus of short sellers were on to CUC's shenanigans. They weren't able to pick up the scent of disaster from the company's income statement or balance sheet, since those numbers were made up. But those who spoke with customers of CUC had been getting an unsettling feeling. It seems that those customers didn't always think much of the company's products and had their doubts about the reported numbers. I spoke with several short sellers before the HFS deal. They could never quite break this company, could never quite prove what they suspected, but, boy, were they suspicious.

The average investor is not going to call customers, purchasing managers, and the like. But the point is valid. If the customer of a public company should offer you some insight into that company and it's not pretty, stay away from buying the stock. And if you should choose to do more research, perhaps you'll find the stock worth shorting. Let's take a look at what that research might entail.

Delving Into the Balance Sheet

Wall Street is so focused on earnings and revenue growth that many investors think the income statement is the only important document. But many shorts look to the balance sheet as a better indicator of a company's overall health.

Every company has a balance sheet, and all public companies file one with the SEC every three months. Every investor with an Internet connection can obtain a company's balance sheet in minutes.

Let's say you have some suspicions about a company and you decide to check out its balance sheet. What should you be looking for?

GETTING THE BALANCE SHEET

Unlike an income statement, which is typically included with an earnings release, a balance sheet — the detailed listing of a company's assets and liabilities — doesn't see the light of day until it's filed with the Securities and Exchange Commission (SEC), typically a few weeks after the income statement is released.

Not surprisingly, the companies tend to make the warts-and-all balance sheet trickier to obtain than the cheerleading income statement. The best places to look include:

- www.FreeEdgar.com has balance sheets and all SEC filings, all viewable for free online. If you want a downloadable copy, you gotta pay EDGAR Online to join.
- www.10Kwizard.com: This was my favorite until it started to change. It's free and easy to use and has virtually every filing you need. Each filing is broken into sections for easy viewing.
- Yahoo! Finance (http://finance.yahoo.com) is free and easy, but incomplete. Simply enter your company's ticker, then click "Financials" — *if* it's offered for the stock you pick, you're there. Problem is, the "Financials" option is not available for every stock.
- Hoover's (www.hoovers.com) has decent free info, but the really good stuff (and it is really good) is for subscribers only.
- Finally, you can always get a company's most recent balance sheet by calling the firm's investor-relations department and simply asking.

LUCENT: A CAUTIONARY TALE

Lucent. Just saying the name brings shivers down the spine of many a portfolio manager and individual investor. The great growth stock of the late 1990s, Lucent was America's most widely held stock after the largest spin-off in history separated it from parent AT&T in 1996. It was a feature in every growth mutual fund manager's portfolio. Some nineteen hundred institutions owned hundreds of millions of shares of Lucent in the spring of 1999, a time of flight and fancy for the stock. That flight would soon end in a crash landing.

Lucent was not the great growth company that its CEO Rich McGinn had made it out to be. I got to know McGinn rather well during the years he was at the helm. We had lunch at Lucent headquarters. We spoke off-camera during his frequent appearances on CNBC. He was charming. The kind of guy who made you feel as though he was telling it like it was. Unfortunately, he wasn't.

McGinn made some big promises to Wall Street. He boasted that Lucent would deliver a revenue growth rate of 20 percent or better each year and an earnings growth rate of more than 15 percent each year. When Lucent was first spun off from AT&T, those targets must have seemed like hanging sliders. The Telecommunications Act of 1996 had led to the birth of literally hundreds of telecom providers, each building networks on the back of billions raised by a Wall Street that was drunk on the banking fees it was raking in with each deal. All those companies needed equipment, and Lucent found itself selling telecommunications equipment in a boom.

But 20 percent revenue growth is tough to keep up even in the middle of a boom. The law of large numbers eventually catches up with the best of companies. When you've got $10 billion in revenues, you need to find only another $2 billion for the next year to keep your promise. But when you're a forty-billion-dollar-revenue company, it can be a challenge to find another $8 billion in revenues the next year.

McGinn relished his promise. One day, prior to one of his many interviews on CNBC, we were talking. McGinn asked me to guess how many companies with more than $40 billion in revenues had revenue growth rates in excess of 20 percent. I knew that one was Home Depot. McGinn was gleeful to inform me that the other was Lucent.

The problem was that Lucent was also a ticking time bomb of accounting gimmicks and dubious sales that was about to make a stinking mess of many a portfolio. And the thing about it is that it was all there in the balance sheet — every warning sign, every accounting crutch, every lever Lucent was using to help it meet revenue and earnings targets that were held sacred by Wall Street, but no longer attainable through plain old growth.

I attended a dinner with a dozen hedge fund managers in the summer of 1999, when Lucent was still riding high. Two of the attendees picked Lucent as their favorite short candidate. They had been looking at the company's balance sheet. They liked what it showed them — a company busting its hump with ever inventive ways of making the numbers. But by the end of the year, the stock was flying toward new heights, and many shorts covered their positions with sizable losses. They had made their bets too early, and the catalyst on which those short positions were banking had not yet arrived.

Earlier in 1999 Lucent developed a true enemy in the person of one Robert Olstein. The Bronx-born Olstein is a street-fighting kind of guy. He runs value mutual funds that can short stocks and he is a balance sheet's worst enemy. Olstein is a garrulous sort who doesn't give up easily — in other words, just the kind of personality one needs to sell short successfully.

Olstein had been telling me for months that Lucent was a big accounting game that would come crashing down. When Lucent reported its first fiscal quarter of 1999, which actually ended with December 1998, he sent me a detailed analysis of Lucent's balance sheet and all the ways the company was full of shit. The stock was $65 a share at the time.

The twelve points that Olstein made in his analysis of Lucent's balance sheet belong in the short-selling hall of fame. They read like a how-to checklist for any enterprising individual investor looking to uncover all the ways companies can inflate revenues and earnings. And so I reproduce Olstein's entire list here and then explain exactly what he was getting at and why it's important.

1. The company has written off $2.5 billion of "in-process R&D" over the last two years (fiscal year-end September 1998 and September 1997), giving a jump start to earnings. Watch out for more write-offs upon consolidation of Ascend.

Here, Olstein is making reference to two common ways that companies cut out operating expenses, thereby increasing margins and making operating earnings look better than they really are.

Write-offs for "in-process R&D" take place upon the acquisition of one company by another. In-process R&D refers to the cost of the research and development for new products. One company's acquiring another may hurt such efforts; therefore, those costs can be expensed through a separate charge that need not be run through the income statement. It was Olstein's contention that Lucent's in-process R&D write-offs were unusually large and may have included expenses that were of an operating nature and therefore should have been included in the income statement and applied against revenues. By writing off expenses that would be a part of its ongoing business, Lucent was not accurately representing its true profit margins.

On this note, another important accounting factor to watch out for is how companies treat certain capital expenditures. When a company buys new software or agrees to an advertising deal that extends over a number of years, it makes a choice on how to account for the expense. It can record the entire expense at one time, or it can choose to capitalize the expense, which is a method that incurs the expense over the presumed life of the asset. If a company buys software that it will be using for what it estimates to be five years, it might choose to amortize the cost of that software over five years rather than expense the entire price of the software on the day it was purchased.

Some companies take the full expense for software or advertising up front, and others choose to capitalize the expense: it's a judgment call. But beware of companies that choose the latter to the exclusion of the former on most occasions. By capitalizing such costs, companies can make near-term earnings shine. But that decision can come at a cost in future quarters when similar expenses arise, but cannot be capitalized because the life of the asset proved shorter than anticipated. If a company expensed the cost of new software over six years but found itself needing a software upgrade after two, it might have a harder time convincing its accountants to capitalize the expense yet again.

I know one short seller who has a sophisticated software program to identify companies that make liberal use of capitalizing costs. It's his belief that such companies may become ripe for an earnings miss in the near term, since their decision to capitalize many expenses may be a sign of a need to stretch to make the quarterly earnings projection. Lucent was not guilty of such activities.

As I explained, acquisitions allow for writing off in-process research and development. It was Olstein's belief that Lucent would use the closing of its deal to buy Ascend as another occasion to beef up operating earnings by writing off expenses that were actually part of operating its business.

As we'll see in chapter 6, companies that grow aggressively through acquisitions sometimes lean toward accounting that masks true operating results. All those acquisitions create write-offs, reserve accounts, pro forma (instead of actual) accounting of results, and layers of complexity that can obfuscate the real results of operations. It is not a coincidence that many of the big stock-market collapses of the past several years — Cendant, Rite Aid, Tyco, and WorldCom, to name a few — have involved companies that grew (and became Wall Street darlings) through acquisitions.

2. Year-end (September 1998) backlog dropped ($9.9 billion 1998 vs. $12.1 billion 1997).

Backlog is a simple concept. It's the amount of orders that have been taken but not yet filled. It can be a sign of a company's long-term health. Though not always a reliable indicator of future demand (since orders can be withdrawn), backlog does give some sense of revenues in future quarters. In this case, Lucent's backlog dropped appreciably from one year to the next — a potential sign that demand for its products was waning.

3. Retained earnings increased a cumulative $.80 per share between FY 1996 and FY 1998, significantly below inferred reported recurring earnings.

Retained earnings are profits that are not paid out in dividends but are instead retained by the company to reinvest in its business or to pay debt. Therefore, net income minus dividends that were paid and share repurchases should roughly equal retained earnings. The retained earnings number being less than "inferred reported recurring earnings" implies that the actual net income for Lucent is less than the number reported, since it didn't carry through to retained earnings.

4. The company's restructuring reserve at fiscal year-end September 1998 was depleted to $251 million from $1.3 billion at fiscal year-end September 1996.

Keep an eye on things like reserves. Much of the information concerning reserves and write-offs is in the footnotes to the balance sheet, so don't forget to read them. In this case, Olstein made the point that a reserve account Lucent had created for a restructuring was almost out of money. The implication was that Lucent either would be forced to add to the reserve, depleting cash in the process, or would be unable to tap the reserve in the future to pay for expenses that might then come out of operating expenses.

5. The company pension plan has been the beneficiary of the stock market resulting in pension expense credits to income

over the past few years. We view pension credit benefits as nonrecurring contributions to income. Pension credit in FY 1998 $558 million, pre-tax operating income $3.8 billion. The pension credit represents 15% of operating income.

This is a big one. During the bull market, the pension funds of many companies grew at a rate greater than that of their actuarial assumptions. That meant they were overfunded, and any overfunding in a given year can be credited to operating income under accounting rules. In Lucent's case, the company credited $558 million from its pension fund's gains in fiscal year 1998 to its operating income. Olstein was right. You can't view that kind of contribution as though it's going to happen again, so it probably should not be included in operating income. A company that does so may be stretching to make the numbers. In this case Olstein realized that a whopping 15 percent of Lucent's operating income from 1998 was not from operating its business and couldn't be counted on in future quarters.

It's essential to look for this sort of thing in companies' annual and quarterly reports. Ryder, for example, used income from its pension plan to boost earnings in calendar year 2000. Management didn't mention this in its conference calls, but if you go to page twelve of Ryder's September 30, 2000, 10-Q, the quarterly SEC filing, you'll learn that "pension income recognized for full year 2000 will be approximately $35 million to $40 million greater than that recognized for full year 1999. Based upon preliminary estimates as of October 2000, the Company expects pension income in 2001 to be comparable to that recorded in 1999 and thus significantly less than pension income recorded in 2000." For a company that earned a modest $61 million in the first nine months of 2000 to acknowledge that $35 million–$40 million of that was not from repeatable operations — seems that it should have been on the front page, not the twelfth page, no?

In fact, many of the same companies that were benefiting

from overfunded pensions now face the opposite. This is an issue of concern for investors in General Motors, which also benefited from an overfunded pension. Many companies may be forced to take non-cash charges against earnings in order to deal with pension funds that have suffered as a result of the bear market.

6. We calculate that an accounting change, a lower percentage allowance for doubtful accounts, and a lower tax rate accounted for 19 cents of Lucent's first quarter 1999 $0.20 per share recurring increase ($1.06 vs. $.86). Expect accounting change on pension plan to contribute an additional $0.13 for the remainder of fiscal '99.

You may on occasion encounter the term *quality of earnings.* That's what Olstein was getting at here. In fact, that's what he was getting at with the entire memo, and here he describes a couple of the most frequently employed mechanisms companies use to show earnings growth when there isn't any.

In this case, Olstein noted that Lucent was devoting less to its reserve for nonpayment despite an increase in revenues and what turned out to be an increase in what the company was owed (receivables). The point is that Lucent might well have been underestimating how many of its customers would fail to make payments. By cutting back on its doubtful-accounts allowance, Lucent allowed operating earnings to increase.

Keep another eye out for lower-than-normal tax rates. They are usually caught by analysts on a company's quarterly report, but using a tax rate to advantage can be another sign that a company is trying to hide something. Without the aid of a lower tax rate, a smaller allowance for doubtful accounts, and the pension fund accounting change, Lucent would have shown no year-over-year earnings growth. For a beloved growth company to have no real earnings growth would have been death. It was lucky for Lucent that most investors didn't care to read the balance sheet.

7. Internal sales growth is slowing down. Reported up 5.0% first quarter full year 1999 (quarter ended December 1998). Our analysis indicates up 3% after eliminating a reconsolidated joint venture; $800 million of deferred sales are offset by purchase accounting on $1.5 billion of acquisitions.

Internal sales growth refers to the growth of the core business. Olstein was saying that Lucent's core business was not growing that fast and that the results were manipulated to look more positive by using one-time gains, accounting and financial maneuvers, and acquisitions.

8. Accounts receivable (up 43%) and inventories (up 46%) increased rapidly compared to sales (up 5%) in first quarter 1999 (ended December 31, 1998).

These are two of the most important line items in a balance sheet. If receivables (what a company is owed) and inventories (what it has yet to sell) are moving up together and at a greater pace than revenues, trouble is usually not far behind. This condition can mean any of the following:

- shrinking ability of customers to pay
- more aggressive placing of merchandise (sometimes in an attempt to make it appear as though more is being sold than really is)
- simple lack of demand

Not all imbalances are equal. It's one thing if a company hasn't yet been paid by the U.S. government or General Electric. But if you're Scient — a consulting firm for Internet companies — and your customers are dot coms, rising receivables is a harbinger. Sometimes receivables indicate good margins, since customers that don't pay up front usually pay full price. (Depending on finance plans, they might even pay more.) But when you start seeing companies with lots of receivables *and* low margins, you're looking at trouble. Profit margins and a reference to a company's largest customers are normally available in a company's annual report and quarterly financial statements.

When Lucent fell apart eighteen months after this memo was written, it acknowledged that in addition to being unable to meet revenue and earnings growth expectations, the company had also improperly recognized as revenue sales that never came to fruition or were booked before their proper time. (The SEC is still investigating whether Lucent improperly booked $679 million of revenue during its 2000 fiscal year.) Lucent employees, under severe pressure to meet expectations for earnings and revenue growth that were unattainable, had fudged things a bit.

If there are any signs that can clue in an investor to the potential for improper recognition of revenue, they can usually be spotted on the inventory, receivables, and revenue lines.

Your own personal finances, and the finances of most small businesses, operate on a cash basis. If you own a restaurant, you recognize income when it comes into the register. If a customer says, "I'm going to eat lunch here every day," you don't count a lifetime of lunches from that person in your restaurant's current income. But accounting rules allow public companies to recognize revenue in many instances before they actually receive the cash, and plenty of companies abuse this rule.

Customarily, public companies recognize revenue when the product is shipped to a customer. If the customer never pays, the company later takes the revenue off the books, charging that doubtful-accounts reserve referred to above.

If simply shipping the product counts as a revenue event, a company intent on impressing the Street may push customers to take products they don't want. They'll cut prices, offer unlimited return policies, sell by whatever means necessary — especially at the end of the quarter, when pressure to make expected numbers mounts.

Sunbeam shipped millions of dollars in grills to warehouses

and called them sales. In March 1998 the stock traded at $50. By July these revelations helped drag the price to $10. Chapter 11 followed in February 2001. As an investor, you might not have known about these warehouses. But the proof of Sunbeam's future demise was there in the numbers, where both receivables and inventory were growing quickly.

9. Despite a first quarter increase in sales, cost of goods sold decreased. The 4% increase in gross margin aided year-to-year comparisons by 18 cents per share. The company's first quarter 10Q warned that "... although gross margins are expected to increase this year, gross margin spread would narrow." Thus, the company expects first quarter gross margins to be nonrecurring.

The cost of goods sold is just that — the amount of money Lucent spent to make the product it was selling. In this case, Lucent's cost declined, which is somewhat strange. In fact, the company warned that this situation would not recur. If any analyst or investor had bothered to read this paragraph in the company's quarterly filing, she would have found that assuming gross profit margins would remain at the same level would have been incorrect. Hence, any projections of future earnings based on the current gross margin would have been wrong.

10. Other assets increased $0.06 a share, net of taxes in the first quarter.

At big companies, the "other assets" line on the balance sheet can get fairly large. At the end of 2000, Microsoft reported "other assets" on its balance sheet of some $2.23 billion. Those assets are real and in most cases comprise things owned by businesses that have been acquired, but they are classified as "other" because they are not a part of what the company does and therefore not related to why you would buy the stock. In Lucent's case, other assets may have included a golf course the company was building near its headquarters. When such assets are producing income that is essential to the company's earnings growth, it can be a sign that its core business can't generate the growth on its own.

11. The company has become responsible for financing customers. The company has commitments for $3.2 billion in credit to customers at the end of December 1998. Short-term debt increased $1.5 billion in the first quarter of 1999.

In noting this item, Olstein was particularly prescient. Financing customers is unusual, though it did become somewhat prevalent among the telecom-equipment suppliers in the late 1990s as they extended credit to upstart telecom companies so that those companies could buy equipment from them. It seemed like a good idea at the time.

Lucent was owed some $700 million by WinStar, a telecom upstart that filed Chapter 11 in April 2001 with $4 billion in debt. WinStar was purchased for $42 million at year's end. Lucent didn't get a dime. Companies such as Nortel and Cisco, in competing with Lucent for customers, also extended loans to and guaranteed debt of their customers.

Olstein also noted a large increase in Lucent's short-term debt obligations. It's not necessarily a sign of trouble when a company's short-term debt rises a great deal, but it does raise questions about why it needed the money. In this instance, Lucent may have been borrowing short-term to finance its customers long-term. That kind of banking activity isn't exactly what investors in a telecom-equipment company are expecting.

12. Cash flow after capital expenditures (but before $1.5 billion in acquisitions) was a negative $250 million in FY 1998 and a negative $1.4 billion in the first quarter of FY 1999.

Olstein's final point is the most salient. Cash flow is the lifeblood of a company. How much cash the company is producing, or losing, is often a key to whether it has a thriving business. After Lucent was done spending money on things like plants and equipment, it was in the hole. And performance in 1999's first fiscal quarter was a whole lot worse than the preceding year, when cash flow was also negative.

A couple of years after Olstein's note was written, Lucent would post an operating loss for its first fiscal quarter of 2001 of some $1.7 billion, and a similar loss for its second fiscal quarter of 2001. Every sign of trouble he spotted in 1999 was a precursor to a growing malignancy.

So, how do you spot cash-flow trouble? Start by looking hard at the line "cash flow from operations." Obviously, if it's negative or declining, that's bad news. And it is bad news regardless of whether net income is rising. In the post-Enron world, where investors are once again examining balance sheets, they are also starting to ignore net income in favor of cash flow.

Cash flow is a useful short signal even for companies that aren't in what's known as "going concern" danger (when a company doesn't have enough cash for twelve months), especially when it consistently trails earnings growth. Occasionally this situation makes sense: the company has a new product that is selling great, but it's going to take a few quarters to pay down the expenses it took to develop the product. But when cash flow *always* trails earnings growth, however, look out.

I know this is tough stuff. I don't expect you, dear reader, to understand every nuance of what we've just gone over. Most investors — including plenty who are paid handsomely for their services — don't even bother with balance sheets or annual reports.

But that's the point. With so few people really reading the numbers, it can pay off big-time for those who do. So don't be afraid to look at a balance sheet and read the "notes to financial statements" and the footnotes as well. And if after reading all that, you fail to understand either a company's business or how it makes its money, a decision not to invest is probably wise.

Enron and On and On

Investors in Enron have plenty to complain about and plenty of people to blame. I do, however, wish some of them would extend that blame to include themselves. I hate to seem unfeeling. The collapse of Enron was a travesty, and the thousands of employees and investors who were hurt by that collapse are justified in being angry.

Unlike Lucent, in which every gimmick being employed to increase earnings growth was readily identifiable, no such disclosure was coming from Enron. Even if you suspected that Enron's earnings were a fiction, it was nearly impossible to prove that theory using the audited financial results the company provided the investment community. It was tough to build an investment case for shorting the stock beyond your gut instinct. But that's one of the key things I hope this book helps you develop — the gut instinct to know when things don't add up and the sagacity to know when to stay away.

There were plenty of wild men shorting Enron's stock on a hunch and a few others who managed to build a strong investment thesis using information that was not likely available through public sources to buttress their claims that Enron's numbers were a sham. But I wouldn't expect you to be among them. What I would hope is that you took notice of a few things that didn't quite make sense.

As Enron transformed itself from an energy company into a trading house, its financial statements became more and more opaque. Much of the investment community, including virtually every analyst who followed the company, proved happy to take management's word that it all made sense, that the earnings growth generated by trading was real growth, even though the company's return on capital was anemic and its underlying cash flow growth did not match the growth in its revenues.

A small, dogged group of short sellers kept asking management about those discrepancies. The short sellers were intrigued simply because the company's numbers didn't seem to add up. If trading was so profitable, how come Enron's cash earnings didn't seem to show it? And why was it so damn hard to understand this company's balance sheet? Goldman Sachs is a trading house, and its balance sheet is not hard to follow. Instead of answering these questions, Enron's management insulted the questioners and moved on to another softball from an analyst.

This was before anyone knew that Enron might have to re-state earnings and before anyone knew that members of management were profiting personally from those off-balance-sheet partnerships. It was even before anyone really knew there were any off-balance-sheet partnerships where Enron was secreting debt that should have been on its own balance sheet while generating profits that were a fantasy. Still, the pattern was there.

When things don't add up. When it's hard to understand how a company makes its money. When the analysts are unanimous in their praise and lackeys for management. When management dismisses tough questions without answering them. When you have all that, you may have nothing, or you may have another Enron.

Enron may have been a criminal enterprise. That's something for the regulators and courts to figure out. But even with all its deceptions to keep investors from understanding the truth, the signals of something rotten were there.

What might have prompted smart investors to stay away or even go short started in the same place that led Bob Olstein to short Lucent: the balance sheet.

History: A Guide to the Future

As George Santayana said, those who cannot remember the past are condemned to repeat it. For investors, the lesson holds in a slightly different form. Those who fail to adequately investigate the history of a management team and a company may be doomed to suffer losses or may end up missing a great opportunity to profit from a short sale.

With the Internet allowing for quick and fruitful searches, there is no excuse for not checking out the history of management and the board of directors of suspect companies. And while you're at it, check on the pedigree of the company itself. Who took it public? How did it become a public company?

Consider the following.

ANTs software inc. claimed in 1999 that it developed software that could make computers run a thousand times faster. Then-CEO Fred Pettit explained how: "Due to software design methods that go back to the start of computers, software forces hardware to spend over 90 percent of its time doing nothing; and when it gives the hardware something to do, it uses huge amounts of unnecessary tasks. ANTs has been designed to eliminate this wasteful waiting time and unnecessary work."

The company sprang from the Over the Counter (OTC) Bulletin Board at less than a dollar a share in early 1999 to trade as high as $40 in February 2000. Its market capitalization reached nearly a billion dollars.

ANTs founder Donald Hutton was a stock promoter on the Vancouver Stock Exchange (VSE). (Not a bad idea to look a little harder whenever you see the words *Vancouver Stock Exchange*.) ANTs, in fact, started as CHoPP Computer in 1984. In 1985–86 it traded on the VSE, rising from 40 cents to $120 (Canadian). Its shtick was to build a supercomputer ten times faster than Cray's. It failed. Its corporate publicist was censured, fined, and banned from the brokerage industry in 1995 by the National Association of Securites Dealers (NASD). Hutton changed the company's name and started trading on the bulletin boards in February 1999. It didn't take much snooping to find this out, but do you think many people bothered? Certainly not those who were buying ANTs at more than $40 per share — shares now traded in the single digits. And while it's all too clear now, it's also too late.

One of my scoops demonstrated the benefits of looking beyond the chief executive for a history of unsavory behavior. Short sellers were lining up to borrow shares of Nutrition for Life, a homeopathic multilevel marketer that became a Wall Street darling in 1996. What tipped off the short sellers? It was the principals and the dubious connections between them.

Nutrition for Life CEO David Bertrand had been president of Seagold Products, which went bankrupt in 1981. He then started Consumer Express, another multilevel marketing (MLM) operation. The executive vice president of Consumer Express and Drax Ventures (a shell company that acquired Consumer Express) was Jana Mitcham, who happened to be Bertrand's sister-in-law. (Mitcham is now the executive vice president of Advanced Nutraceuticals, another MLM nutrition company, of which Bertrand is currently president.) The pair also controlled a Louisiana corporation called Elegant Cosmetics, which entered into an unwritten agreement with Consumer Express, wherein the latter acquired all the former's inventory for $45,000, as well as the rights to market and distribute its line of products. Ronnie Meaux — the name alone should have rung alarm bells — was the controller of Consumer Express. He's also married to Bertrand's niece. And then there's Kevin Trudeau, Nutrition for Life's master marketer. I broke the story that the telegenic Mr. Trudeau was also a twice-convicted felon who had done a couple of bullets in the clink.

These things were all knowable, with bankruptcies and convictions leaving a public paper trail. The average investor may not turn up all these intricate connections, but even one trail that leads to a former bankruptcy or the fact that a company insider did jail time should be enough to warrant staying away, if not making a bet on the short side.

Certain underwriters show up time and again when one traces the roots of bankrupt or corrupt companies. Notice what firm underwrote the initial public offering of a company. ANTs, for example, did its underwriting through a small Arizona firm. Sometimes the underwriter can be all the evidence a short seller needs to target a stock for future shorting possibilities.

Sometimes there isn't even an underwriter — also a sign of potential trouble. Some companies do a series of placements using Form SB-2, which allows stock to be sold with fewer restrictions and less transparency. Other companies back into the public markets by acquiring all the shares of a dormant publicly traded company, known as a shell, trading at pennies with virtually nothing but a ticker symbol — thereby allowing them to begin life with a minimum of disclosure . . . a big help when trying to perpetrate a fraud.

It also helps when an unsavory underwriter is joined with a history of management ineptitude and promotion of a product that doesn't have a real audience.

The case of Milestone Scientific is emblematic. Milestone makes The Wand; a high-tech local-anesthetic delivery device that the company claimed would soon replace the dentist's needle, given its ability to deliver Novocain painlessly.

Milestone had two prominent fraud markers. Its underwriter was a company called GKN Securities, a brokerage with a specialty of underwriting the IPOs of companies that later ran into trouble. And its management and board had a checkered history, to say the least.

GKN contacted one of my hedge fund sources, hoping to stir up interest in buying Milestone shares. But when they reviewed the history of other companies that GKN had brought public, they went to work on the short side. The reputation of the underwriter was the clue that set them off to other discoveries. And this is the kind of thing any investor can check out pretty easily.

A quick visit to Hoover's, for example, showed that of seven companies listed as having been brought public by GKN — blue chips like Firebrand Financial Group and the Millbrook Press — none was trading over $3.40 and most were under a buck.

My short sellers started by reading the company's proxy. By now you've learned that selling short requires reading. Balance sheets, quarterly filings, annual reports, notes to financial statements, and proxy statements are all available and highly recommended for consumption. A proxy lists a company's board of directors and gives a brief history of each board member's accomplishments, current position, age, and length of service on said board. In the case of Milestone, it was worthwhile reading.

It seems that Milestone's CEO, Leonard Osser, had a colorful background that included a position at a brokerage that specialized in bringing companies public, all of which later filed for bankruptcy. Osser also had a stint as a director of Geri-Care, a manufacturer of incontinence products that had been sued by the U.S. government several years before for Medicare fraud.

Those admissions were not part of Mr. Osser's bio, but what he did list led to a number of unsavory connections. One of the guys promoting the stock, Robert Gintel, had a long history of ties to companies that eventually ended in the toilet — C-Cube Microsystems and Fantom Technologies Inc., for example. I don't expect you to come up with all the stuff that my sources were able to unearth or that I can find when digging. On Milestone, for example, my assistant and I called dozens of dentists all over the country — not many investors' idea of a fun afternoon.

But again, even a sign of dirt can mean there's a whole lot more where that came from. If there's one bad sign in the background of management, a link to a questionable underwriter or some of the balance sheet shenanigans we've discussed, chances are that a short seller is taking a hard look.

It doesn't always take a history of management fraud to sit up and take notice. Some CEOs aren't criminals, but they find a way to ruin one company after the next just the same.

To give you a sense of the tough work that short sellers do, I've included a memo one short seller sent to me detailing the background of Leonard Osser. The memo was dated April 13, 1998.

Osser's obscure bio, which by the way is pretty difficult to find in recent financial filings, talks about his association with U.S. Asian Consulting Group . . . a "work out and turn-around" consulting firm. Then it discusses such activities including companies engaged in "waste disposal . . . medical devices . . . and securities."

The waste disposal company appears to be Wastemate, a San Diego based company involved in "water powered waste disposal." His involvement included his investment-banking role at a firm called Mostel & Taylor which appears to be some kind of penny stock bucket shop. I looked at all the other deals Mostel & Taylor were involved in . . . all bust . . . all B.S. Mostel & Taylor had lots of problems with the NASD and apparently went out of business. Wastemate looks like it had all kinds of other problems.

The most interesting connection is his involvement in Geri care (aka Geri-Care). So far I found his name on a lawsuit involving Geri Care having to do with unfair termination and business tort. According to people I located (the plaintiffs who represented the California officers/managers of Geri Care), Osser had a significant role and told them he "ran the operation." Geri Care and its titular officers . . . were indicted for Medicare fraud. I don't know the outcome.

Lastly, one of these same people was involved with another "Osser deal" called Sonics Research. Sonics also went bust. Osser was apparently involved with NY investors called the "Stuart Brothers."

I spoke to one of the main operating officers of Sonics (Robert Bush); he confirmed that Osser played a major role in both raising money for and effecting certain operations of Sonics. He then told me as an afterthought that Osser and [Milestone attorney Stephen] Zelnick tried to merge Sonics into a Canadian company called EmFax and a Canadian named John McBean. I'm pretty sure it is the same

John McBean that was busted by the Alberta Stock Exchange for fraud.

A week later, the short seller sent me a follow-up memo, which I have edited to protect the identity of people named.

> I have included excerpts from a Geri-Care offering prospectus and some financial history of Osser which he provided through his attorneys.
>   Osser lists holdings in three companies:
>   Geri-Care (a medicare fraud)
>   Sonics Research (a company which he and Zelnick tried to merge into EmFax with John McBean, a Canadian stock fraudster)
>   Aquanetics: a company which ended up as an involved party in a securities fraud RICO case.
>   Coincidence? 3 companies, 3 frauds. With Abe "magic marker fraud" Salaman as a 144 seller in WAND. I don't think so.

What I love about these memos are the connections. Everything ultimately leads to someone who went to jail for securities fraud. The final reference to Abe Salaman is the kicker. Salaman was an early seller of Milestone's stock in a private placement. How he got the stock is unclear. But the fact that he had is very telling, because Salaman is a well-known stock swindler from way back who served probation for a famous rig in the early 1970s known as the Magic Marker Corporation.

My file on Milestone is three inches thick. Filled with notes from interviews with dentists and former employees of the companies associated with Leonard Osser. And yet I never did one story on Milestone. By the time I was certain the company was bad news, other journalists had decided the same thing, and stories on Bloomberg and TheStreet.com began to proliferate.

As a journalist, I had a window in which to break the story. But as an investor, there was still time to make money on the short side before Milestone collapsed — that is, if you could borrow the shares. Because in the same way other journalists beat me to the ultimate punch, investors can get beaten to the punch by other short sellers.

The Borrow/The Squeeze

One of the key challenges in shorting stocks is simply finding shares to borrow. Since many of the juiciest shorting situations occur in low-float stocks (those with few shares available for trading), often no one has any shares to lend. And if you are late on a situation that other investors have already piled into, you're probably going to be without a short position. Do you get in before you've finished your research? Many short sellers actually check the borrow situation before they begin the heavy lifting of research. (Certain brokers are more likely to have shares to lend than others. Goldman Sachs and Morgan Stanley are two of the better firms from which to borrow shares because they pride themselves on their ability to search out stock to loan.)

Earlier in this chapter, I spoke of always having a catalyst in mind when shorting a particular company's stock. But even then, danger lurks.

Since shorts eventually have to cover, each share that's sold short can be thought of as a future buy order. As a stock rises, short sellers are tempted — even forced — to cover their positions by buying shares. All that buying drives the price still higher. The lightning speed with which this can occur makes this episode, known as a short squeeze, one of the more excruciating an investor can experience.

The short squeeze can happen for a number of reasons:

- positive news, such as earnings that beat forecasts
- a big lender of the stock suddenly wanting his shares back (which he's free to do at any time)
- a positive rumor getting traction

There are even some investors who target heavily shorted stocks to create a short squeeze. Jeff Vinik had the buying power to snap up shares of heavily shorted stocks. He'd target those with small floats, and his buying alone — along with carefully leaked word that he was buying — would be enough to stimulate upward movement. Shorts would start buying shares to run for cover, driving prices higher, and in turn other panicked shorts — as well as longs who buy on any upward momentum — would start buying. By selling the shares he'd bought, Vinik would actually unload his position to the very people whose pain he'd caused!

At least part of Krispy Kreme's phenomenal rise in 2000 can be attributed to short sellers rushing to cover in August and September, creating demand for an already scarce stock that exaggerated the rally. EToys, now out of business, had its fall arrested by a short squeeze in the fall of 1999. The stock was 50 percent off its high, but still well above its IPO price from May 1999. In September and October eToys rose from $30 to $70. The shorts that covered at a loss lost out on the bonanza when the company and its stock collapsed only a few months later. But that was one of the characteristics of the Internet bubble: underwriters chose not to issue many shares, and rather than being traded on fundamentals, shares of these companies traded on scarcity value, only enhanced when people shorted.

The squeeze is even worse when the company itself participates, agitating shareholders into reducing the supply of stock that can be loaned by encouraging longs to take their shares out of margin accounts, or the so-called street name. When that happens, the brokers have what they call a "buy-in," whereby they force investors who've borrowed shares to return them because the stock is no longer available for loaning. The buy-in creates a short squeeze that further frustrates the shorts.

The buy-in can be generated by investors, too. In July 2000 Irwin Jacobs, who owned roughly 5 percent of insurer Conseco's shares at the time, took out full-page ads in the *Wall Street Journal* and the *New York Times,* calling on shareholders to take their shares in-house — that is, out of circulation for lending to short sellers. Irwin's efforts succeeded in taking much of Conseco's stock off the Street. And Irwin, perhaps drunk on the success of that effort, decided to branch out. In his new career as a short buster, he attacked analyst Colin Devine of Salomon Smith Barney for his negative stance on Conseco, again with huge ads in major newspapers. But Devine had been correct: Conseco shares collapsed in the months following Irwin's attack.

At least in the case of Conseco, there was general disagreement on the fundamental value of what was a sound company. It was after Conseco that Irwin found his Waterloo. He chose to defend a small health-care-related software company called AremisSoft from what he said were unfair attacks from short sellers. Irwin told me at the time that he had done a great deal of research and was certain that AremisSoft, contrary to the claims of those who shorted the stock, was clean.

Irwin was utterly wrong. And if he had had any idea how a typical rig worked, he might have saved himself a pretty penny, not to mention his reputation. AremisSoft had all the markings of a fraud, from the place of its incorporation (Cyprus) to the inside dealings of its management (which controlled another company that AremisSoft had paid big money for) to the place of its supposed contracts (Bulgaria and India). The SEC is currently investigating AremisSoft's accounting practices, and the company is also the subject of a criminal probe by the U.S. attorney's office. AremisSoft says it's still trying to determine who in management was at fault for its apparent inability to keep accurate books.

In the spring of 2001 MicroStrategy and its CEO, Michael Saylor, purchased ads advocating that investors remove their shares from accounts where they could be lent to short sellers. That move puzzled me, since shorting a stock below $5 a share is rarely done. At the time, the once mighty MicroStrategy's stock price had gone from over $300 a share to $3. Saylor was actually trying to engineer a short squeeze rather than protecting future investors. And that, in my opinion, is wrong. CEOs who spend time worrying about short sellers, rather than operating their business, are probably doing it because they have something to hide.

In early 2001 Harland Stonecipher, CEO of Pre-Paid Legal Services (subject of more than a dozen class actions), encouraged his sales force to contact attorneys about filing class actions against short sellers. In late April Pre-Paid's VP of corporate development followed up with a letter to all of Pre-Paid's selling associates.

> During these days of heightened interest in our stock, it might benefit every independent associate to review the role short sellers play:
>
> Short sellers sell stock they don't currently own by borrowing shares from a broker, promising to return — or cover — the shares at a later date. The ideal scenario from a short seller's perspective is to have the price of the borrowed stock take a substantial dip. A variety of tactics are often utilized by the short sellers to drive down the price — negative press reports, etc. Once the price has bottomed out in the mind of the short seller, the shares are then purchased (covered) by the short seller and given back to the broker.
>
> **Important note:** short sellers may borrow this stock from shareholders like you!
>
> Shares of stock you own that are registered in your broker's name are, in all likelihood, being used by short sellers. Your broker stands to benefit financially by lending the stock to the shorts. This is entirely legal and occurs without your knowledge.
>
> How can you combat this from happening? You need to call your broker immediately. If your broker has used your stock in this way, ask that it be returned, or covered, immediately. Furthermore, ask that your stock be taken out of the broker — or street — name and, instead, placed into your cash account — your name. You will still own the stock and your ability to hold or sell the stock will be unaffected.
>
> However, by doing this you've eliminated the short seller's access to borrow your stock. Only after obtaining

YOUR PERMISSION could a broker send YOUR STOCK to a short seller.

In a remarkable coincidence, just a few days after this memo, Pre-Paid said it received a letter from the SEC questioning the practice of booking three years of commission expenses as soon as each new customer is signed.

Pre-Paid's memo is accurate in what it describes. But it's also telling in one line. In all likelihood, shares of stock registered in your broker's name are *not* being loaned to short sellers. Far from it. In the case of Pre-Paid, however, they were. That's because Pre-Paid is a company that was using curious accounting which the SEC was questioning. In other words, Pre-Paid would do a lot better addressing the demand for shares to short than the supply.

It's my experience that companies that focus on combating short sellers are typically good candidates for shorting. I disagree with what Irwin Jacobs did regarding Conseco, but Irwin was simply a shareholder, not part of management. When managements spend their time taking on short sellers, it is likely time not well spent. They attack because they have something to hide and are trying to maintain whatever scam they're perpetrating a little longer so they can keep selling stock. Which leads me to another warning sign: insiders selling en masse.

Any number of sites, such as Yahoo! Finance or CNBC.com, detail the buys and sells executives and board members must file with the SEC through Form 4s and Form 144s. I don't view the trading by company insiders as a crystal ball. There are too many unknown variables — maybe one guy has kids starting college at the same time another guy, bullish about his company's future, is adding a wing to his house. When *all* the insiders are bailing at the same time, however, take note.

Consider AgriBioTech, which in August 1998 held a conference call claiming that the company's falling stock price was the result of short sellers' false rumors. Within six months the CEO was selling stock to meet margin calls and had to resign. After trading as high as $29 in June 1998, the company filed for bankruptcy in January 2000.

Then there's Dan Borislow, former CEO of Tel-Save (now on its third corporate name, Talk.com), who wins the award for shooting himself in the foot while aiming at short sellers. Back in 1998 Dan sued Deutsche Bank for shorting Tel-Save shares. He then conducted a destructive stock buyback to shrink the float. The buyback burned the company's cash, which he remedied by selling stock, which was then trading at a fraction of the buyback price. Borislow resigned to breed racehorses and become the professional gambler he clearly was to begin with.

While I've spent a good deal of this chapter on low-life companies, others with no discernible patterns of dubiousness or balance-sheet mayhem are also quite capable of producing negative results. Happily for the short seller, there are several ways to predict these disappointments. Let's look at three of them.

1. THE TECHNOLOGY MIGHT NOT BE AS IMPRESSIVE AS HOPED, OR HAVE AS MUCH DEMAND AS ASSUMED

Motorola's launch of Iridium started with the largest private placement in history. As a public company, Iridium traded as high as $72 in May 1998, five months before its satellite-telephone company went live. The telephone equipment was too large and heavy, and could be used only outdoors. The company's marketing partners were never properly organized, and there really wasn't a market there to market to anyway. It turns out that few people had any interest in paying $3,000 for the equipment and $7 per minute to use it. When those costs were halved, Iridium still could not find customers. Before going bankrupt in the summer of 1999, Iridium obtained only 5 percent of the subscribers projected.

As we've discussed, there's so much pressure not to be negative that *any* negative out-of-consensus call is worth paying attention to. This is particularly true when evaluating demand — the analyst allegedly covers the industry and is well positioned to ask the kinds of "what if this *doesn't* work?" hypotheticals of would-be buyers.

There was plenty of time to short Iridium before it fell out of orbit. And its ultimate demise brings up another important signal worth watching. While Iridium's share price was still fairly healthy, the price of its bonds was not.

Keep an Eye on the Debt

Companies such as Iridium, which incur massive amounts of debt in order to build networks, have more than one constituency of investors to deal with. And often it is the holders of a company's debt who are better informed as to its fiscal and strategic health.

In the spring of 2001 I focused a great deal of my reporting on the ongoing collapse of the emerging telecommunications companies. In order to help finance their plans, these companies sold billions in debt to various institutional investors in the form of various classes of bonds. And as the companies proved unable to generate enough growth in their cash flow to meet capital-expenditure needs and interest payments, the price of those bonds deteriorated. So, too, did the price of these companies' bank debt.

In many cases, that price erosion began prior to a true collapse in share price, a precursor to the fear and ultimate reality of bankruptcy that would befall such companies as WinStar, Teligent, ICG Communications, 360 Communications, PSINet, Exodus Communications, Excite@Home, and Global Crossing.

It doesn't have to be a telecom company, either. Clothing manufacturer Warnaco took on a great deal of debt to finance acquisitions, and the price of that debt began to deteriorate before the company's share price collapsed and it, too, was forced to file for bankruptcy.

The trading of bonds and bank debt does not take place in a particularly liquid market. Prices can be deceiving. However, you can get your average stockbroker at a major firm to call his fixed-income or distressed-debt desk and quote you some prices. If a company's bank debt is trading well below 100 cents on the dollar, clearly someone doubts the company's ability to repay even its most senior creditors. And if the company's bonds are trading below 50 cents on the dollar, at least one class of investor is dubious about its prospects of getting paid back in full, if at all. If your broker quotes you prices like these for a stock that's still in double digits, you may have a short-sale candidate on your hands.

2. THE TECHNOLOGY MIGHT NOT EVEN EXIST

This *is* the kind of thing that sends people to jail. You may notice that a number of the companies in this shorting chapter would be equally at home in the chapter on fraud. That's not an accident.

The only real breakthrough of some of these companies is a well-oiled hype machine. Quigley Corp. graduated from the penny market to $21 per share in December 1996 on the strength of a product — zinc lozenges — it claimed reduced the severity and duration of the common cold. Quigley still claims that, but the stock trades at $7; independent studies have undermined Quigley's claims and the medical community has thumbed its nose at the theory.

Bogus products aren't the only thing to worry about. As mentioned earlier, management quality and stability can be major signs of underlying strength or weakness. Of course, a high-ranking executive leaving a firm is pretty standard — it happens. But when several managers depart within months of one another, it might be time to worry. Not the CEO necessarily, but the guys deep in the B section of the *Journal,* the guys who actually run the company.

The best recent example of how management defections can precede operational trouble is at AT&T. As the largest company in the fastest-changing industry, it was particularly susceptible to an exodus about the time C. Michael Armstrong became CEO. First, Alex Mandl, president and COO, left in 1996 (even before Armstrong took over) for the top job at Teligent. Joe Nacchio, head of AT&T's consumer long distance, departed late that year to helm Qwest. One of the men who succeeded him, Dan Schulman, exited in 1999, becoming the new president of Priceline.com. His successor, H. Eugene Lockhart, fled for the CEO job at the New Power Co. Dan Hesse, a senior VP and CEO of AT&T Wireless, said good-bye in March 2000 for Terabeam, taking at least four top employees with him. Three consecutive presidents of AT&T Business Services, the company's largest division, have waved adios since 1998, having gone on to at least briefly run their own shows at Gateway (Jeffrey Weitzen), Global Crossing (Robert Annunziata), and ADC Telecommunications (Richard Roscitt). With that kind of management exodus, important decisions are delayed, and in a dynamic industry, delay means trouble down the road. It's no coincidence that when AT&T's stock collapsed in 2000, it was the failure of its business services unit to execute and deliver growth which surprised investors, not the sharp but expected decline in revenue from consumer long distance.

Obviously, division heads of giant companies will always defect to run companies, especially when passed over for a vacant top job and especially when fistfuls of options and a bull market are involved. GE has seen some of its top guys head to leadership positions with Home Depot (Robert Nardelli), 3M (James McNerney Jr.), and Conseco (Gary Wendt), and it wasn't a sign of corporate decline. But a rush for the exits at a company as troubled as AT&T should ring bells. Many of AT&T's defectors quarreled about operations with Armstrong, and their departures signaled a double whammy: difficulty in executing the operating strategy, and a loss of quality leaders.

Sometimes even one person can make a big difference. After

Disney lost its number two, Frank Wells, in a tragic helicopter crash in 1994, the company was not the same for years to come. CEO Michael Eisner struggled to replace Wells, resulting in a series of damaging missteps, including the expensive fiasco of hiring and firing Michael Ovitz and an ugly feud with Jeffrey Katzenberg.

Lesson and reminders
- Never short purely on perceived overvaluation.
- Learn to understand the nuances of a balance sheet and read them.

A STOCK STORY:
Xerox

A short-seller pal of mine was onto the office-supply companies — Ikon, Xerox, Danka — before their breakdowns. Here's how he knew, and pay attention — it incorporates many of the elements I've been talking about.

Back when he was a banker, he noticed that Ikon had a lot of people questioning its numbers. They were known for having very tricky, aggressive accounting. GAAP (generally accepted accounting principles) leaves a lot of leeway, and Ikon had a separate line for "repositioning costs" (one-time charges taken to exit a particular line of business) — not just once, but nearly every quarter. It seemed to be constantly buying companies. As a result, its earnings were excellent, growing 30 percent a year, but like a lot of companies that serially acquire, it was tough to see what portion of that growth was real and what was due to all those added operations.

My friend went to see Ikon in Pennsylvania. Like a lot of hedge fund investors, he's not only a short seller, he'll go long if the story merits it. In Ikon's case, inventories were climbing, along with accounts receivable. But with earnings going up, the market didn't care. Here it paid to consider who it was that owed Ikon money. A lot of the receivables were actually on the books of the companies

Ikon acquired, and the reason they had to sell out was that they were having such a hard time getting paid. In other words, Ikon owed itself money but mentioned only that it would be paid, not that it would also be the one paying, canceling out any gains.

Then my friend discovered that the salesmen got their commissions on revenue, not on collected money. This almost always indicates focus on the top line more than the bottom line — a mind-set that often catches up with a company.

The macro situation was going bad, too. About the same time, 1997, Danka paid $600 million for Kodak's copier business. Even the folks at Ikon — which basically bought everything not nailed down — said that Danka way overpaid: "We looked at that co. and passed." In addition, the Ikon sources were telling my friend that Xerox, which Ikon sells to and services, was in terrible shape: "They're financing their customers, their receivables are even worse than ours," and so on.

The sweet thing about this short was that everything led to everything else. It wasn't obvious that Xerox was a basket case, but finding Ikon led to Danka and Xerox. A trip to Xerox in Rochester led to Kodak; a local guy mentioned to my short-seller friend how brutal things were getting in Rochester. Calls to a couple of buyers at Kmart and Sam's Club revealed that Kodak was discounting film even as it said it was not. The whole group turned out very profitable for shorts. And very painful for longs who missed the warning signs.

Interestingly, in early December 1997 Prudential Securities analyst B. Alex Henderson said $60–$75 was a reasonable target for Danka — this just after Danka had paid $600 million for Kodak's equipment-service business and was trading at $30. When it hit $6, I did a story saying the company might be forced to file for bankruptcy. Pru had been Danka's underwriter, and Henderson felt compelled to attack me in a report the very next day. I kept the report and called Henderson, promising to exact my revenge when Danka went bankrupt. The company has stubbornly hung on ever since, avoiding bankruptcy but not penny-stock status. At one point it was 28 cents, but a new management team has brought the company back from the brink.

SOME GROUND RULES OF SHORT SELLING

In addition to unlimited downside risk and squeeze vulnerability, know these potential pitfalls before you plunge.

- *The uptick rule.* The SEC artificially protects troubled companies by forbidding shorts from piling on when a stock is plummeting. That means a short sale can occur only at a price higher than the previous trade. No big deal, but it means you might not get your position the instant you call your broker.
- *Dead money.* When you borrow your shares and immediately sell them, you're sitting on a pile of cash. Unfortunately, many brokerages don't pay interest on that cash to individual investors, and you're not allowed to spend it all on other investments, since you're required to keep that cash as margin — collateral so you don't just ditch whomever lent you the shares.
- *Dividend payments.* If the company pays a dividend during the time you're borrowing the shares, you've got to reimburse the owner for the money he didn't collect. This seldom comes into play because sizable dividends usually connote slow-moving, stable stocks that don't make good short candidates (troubled utilities providing an occasional exception).
- *Taxes.* Short positions are usually held for only a little while, which means you'll face the short-term capital-gains rate. That's equivalent to your rate on normal income, rather than the new 20 percent maximum you'd pay on a long held for more than a year.

- Check the history of management and what companies they have formerly worked for.
- Check the history of the company — what firm brought it public and how it became public.
- Don't be afraid to make phone calls when doing so can turn up valid information.
- Check on whether shares are available for borrow on potential short candidates.

- Be dubious of companies that spend time combating short sellers.
- Keep an eye on sales of stock by insiders.
- Watch out for heavy debt loads.
- Watch out for a series of management departures.

3

WHY ANALYSTS ARE IRRELEVANT

I sat next to Eliot Spitzer, New York's attorney general, at an awards ceremony I hosted in late 2002 for my former employer, *Institutional Investor*. We made an odd pair. Spitzer had gained renown over the previous six months for his attack on the conflict of interest between investment banking and Wall Street's research. I had been a critic of analysts for many years, heartily denouncing from my perch on CNBC's *Squawk Box* every morning the nonsense published by Wall Street investment houses. I had also published a book in early 2002 (the one you're reading) that examined in detail why analysts couldn't be trusted.

The awards to be delivered that evening were bestowed on analysts who had been elected to *II*'s "all-star team." Election to that team had once been the highest honor in the world of research, resulting in contractually obligated bonuses for those selected that frequently exceeded a million dollars. No more. Despite the attempt at festivity, the evening was weighted down by the knowledge that for those in attendance, the good times had surely passed.

Spitzer, never one to shy away from a fight, made that clear when he used his keynote address to attack the stock-picking

ability of the analysts who would receive *II*'s awards. He was not warmly received. I used my time as emcee to vigorously question Spitzer. Although his effort to curb the influence of investment banking on investment research was bearing fruit, Spitzer had done little to confront the conflicts beyond banking that severely compromise the integrity of research.

For all the magazine covers Eliot Spitzer's face has now graced and for all the column inches his crusade has generated, intellectual honesty is still hard to find on Wall Street. And even when they are honest, analysts are still far too often wrong. To understand why, one must not only understand the now de rigueur excuse of investment banking but look beyond it to conflicts that still have not been made a cause célèbre.

The aim of a stock analyst is the same as it has been since modern securities analysis came into existence roughly twenty-five years ago: know everything there is to know about the companies within a particular industry sector and about conditions that affect the sector itself. The automotive analyst's job is to determine how well GM's cars are selling and how much profit GM is making on each car. That requires a detailed knowledge of things like the cost of raw materials, labor conditions, currency exchange rates, and all the other things that can have an impact on the profitability of a company that makes cars. Ideally, the analyst gleans this information just as a reporter would. He visits the manufacturers, interviews suppliers and customers, and pores over the company's accounting statements and other sources with keen instincts, a bunch of experience, and a finely tuned ear for bullshit.

The analyst then writes a report explaining what's up with the company and/or its sector, detailing why he thinks the stock will rise, coast, or, in those rarest of imagined circumstances, actually go down. He writes a report that also includes a short- and long-term rating of the stock and a target price.

The analyst's research report is communicated to clients by the firm's sales force and by the analyst on the firm's company-wide speakerphone (known as a squawk box). Analysts communicate

upgrades and downgrades to their firm's sales force on the "morning call," which typically begins at about 7:00 A.M. or so. The sales force then transmits that information to the firm's big institutional clients while the analysts get on the phone with selected clients. The retail guys — the friendly stockbroker you opened your account with — have no hope of speaking directly with the analyst (unless they are one of the firm's huge producers), and in turn there's about no chance they'd take the time to speak with you.

Earnings estimates are the most widely followed part of an analyst's work. The numbers are reported to First Call and/or Multex, companies that compile the estimates of many analysts to produce the "consensus earnings estimate" that so many of us rely on as the barometer of quarterly success. But an analyst report is a reliable source for any number of baseball-card-like stats — the company's revenue growth rate, the size of the market, the company's market share, stuff like that. The reports give many investors the numbers and the models that can help them compare one company with another in a variety of ways, and they provide the all-important estimates of profit a company is expected to earn in the year ahead. When news on the sector or company surfaces, analysts gets on the squawk box and try to explain the meaning and effect of that news on the companies they follow.

In any given week, the stock analysts of Wall Street issue hundreds of reports on the companies they follow, either to update shareholders on news that affects those companies or to offer a new opinion on a company. On many occasions the stocks mentioned react to those "research calls" by moving up or down, depending on whether the opinion stated is positive or negative. Often the stocks move because of the news, not because of the analysts' commentary on that news. Still, not a day goes by that some company's stock price is not noticeably affected purely by the opinion of an analyst. In late February of 2003, for example, an upgrade of the semiconductor sector by Morgan Stanley helped send the group up over 3 percent — not bad in a bear market.

The Best Call

Plenty of fund managers are in constant contact with analysts, looking for insights, info, and gossip. In these conversations, analysts speak freely about the stuff they know but can never share publicly. It might be what they heard from a CEO who asked them for an opinion on takeover candidates. It might be a negative take on the management of a company they just met with.

The information flows in both directions. In April 2001 I was surprised to see Goldman Sachs's well-regarded auto analyst Gary Lapidus publish a detailed research report on the then rather abstruse topic of General Motors' pension fund. Lapidus focused on the fact that GM might have to shore up the pension fund with an infusion of cash, thus hurting the company's credit rating. Not two weeks earlier I had received a similar and detailed analysis of the same topic from a money manager I speak with. It seems that he also speaks with Mr. Lapidus and was successful in convincing this influential analyst to spread the word, thus incidentally helping the manager's short position in GM stock.

There is a common perception on the Street that the firms generating the greatest amount of commission dollars get what we refer to as the "best call." They're big traders, so they have the juice to get analysts on the phone. Such firms can be helpful for the analyst as well, since analysts like to know who is trading a particular stock. Steven Cohen's hair-trigger day trading firm, SAC Capital, has been known to account for more than 1 percent of a day's volume on the Nasdaq and the New York Stock Exchange. As one of the ten biggest commission generators on Wall Street, Cohen's firm throws its weight around with analysts. Cohen is an incredible trader, truly gifted with some sort of otherworldly sense. But it doesn't hurt to get the best call — which he does on a daily, sometimes hourly, basis.

The best call rarely has much to do with what the analyst puts in print or releases to the general public. It might be an early read on breaking news that could have a secondary market ef-

GET THE INFO:
Ratings Changes

- **Multex.com**

Enter a ticker symbol and select from a variety of reports by about 250 research departments, ranging from white-shoe (Salomon Smith Barney, Morgan Stanley, Merrill Lynch) to gym-shoe (Red Chip Review) to extremely specialized sources (Jardine Fleming, Nomura). A few of the reports are truly free; lots more are free to those who agree to be marketed to by the brokerage that wrote the report.

- **FirstCall.com and Zacks.com**

These are the two official scorekeepers of the analyst community. They track ratings; ratings changes; consensus revenue and profit forecasts for the quarter, year, and beyond; revenue and earnings surprises (in each direction).

- **Yahoo!'s Earnings Calendar**

Go to http://biz.yahoo.com/research/earncal/today.html for a company's next earnings report.

- **CNET's Investor Section**

For a list of recent analyst upgrades, downgrades, and commentary (not complete, but still useful), go to http://investor.cnet.com. Enter any ticker and select any "broker reports" for a list of recent changes.

- **Nasdaq**

The web page http://earnings.nasdaq.com/earnings/analyst_activity. asp lists stocks with the most analyst activity during the past week — not just for Nasdaq-listed stocks. You can also access earnings surprises, analyst forecast changes, and a decent, if uninspired, earnings calendar.

fect. In such a situation, a timely call from an analyst who knows the relative strengths of all the players in a sector can be helpful for a quick and profitable trade. And the best call is not confined to research. It can also come from a trading desk trying to woo future orders from a large commission generator. When an institution moves to sell or buy a large position in the stock, it often gives a trading desk working the order a sense of how much stock is left to sell or buy. That is supposed to be privileged information, but Wall Street firms routinely let their best clients know who's selling and buying, which can give them an edge in their own trading.

When Jeff Vinik was running Fidelity's Magellan, the world's largest mutual fund, banks had obvious reasons to curry favor with him. Fidelity's size (and its Magellan Fund in particular) is marketed to mutual fund investors as one reason to invest there, the reasoning being that Fidelity has not only its own crack research team but also — being the biggest — the best access to Street research.

In the case of Magellan, the only person truly benefiting from the fund's size may have been its manager. While it's true that Magellan's massive ability to generate commissions had banks bending over backward to service Vinik's every research need, a fund of Magellan's size cannot possibly benefit from an early research or trading call: it can take months to accumulate or shed enough shares to make a difference to a portfolio worth over $50 billion. But good old Vinik was happy to get everyone's best idea and everyone's first phone call when a profitable trade could almost be guaranteed. He used Magellan's power for his own benefit, making personal trades on the information he received. It's one of the perks of the job since mutual fund managers aren't nearly as well compensated as their peers in the hedge fund world. In fact, Vinik racked up huge trading profits in his personal account (PA in Street lingo) while Magellan languished after Vinik made a poorly timed purchase of Treasury bonds in the belief that the stock market was overvalued. Eventually, a richer Vinik and a wounded Magellan went their separate ways.

Sorry to say, you're probably not Jeff Vinik, or at least don't have his bank account. Most individual investors, who never hear from analysts without the filter of a salesman, must rely on written analyst reports for guidance. Those reports are of little use in picking stocks. Why? Three big reasons:

1. Conflicts of interest
2. Unrelenting optimism
3. Congenital timidity

Let's take a look at each.

1. Conflicts of Interest

In 2002 the conflict created by investment houses that peddled "objective" research while providing investment banking services exploded into the investing public's consciousness. Although strides have been made to eliminate that conflict, it is only one of many and is still one that should be fully understood by investors, given its deep roots in the culture of Wall Street.

Nearly every stock analyst you've ever heard of works for an investment bank — Morgan Stanley, Merrill Lynch, Goldman Sachs, Salomon Smith Barney, etc. These banks might keep a few bucks in the house from individual investors who value the "exclusive" research the analyst produces. But that's nothing compared with the trading commissions generated by institutional investors. Best of all, the bread and butter of these firms is the banking fees they receive for arranging and advising on transactions. Analysts who cement corporate relationships, create buzz, and entice a buying public for these deals usually find themselves promoted and highly paid. Analysts who don't usually find other work.

It wasn't always this way. Back in the 1970s, securities analysis was an almost professorial discipline. Analysts worked in the distant bowels of their firm's offices, dissecting balance sheets and making lots of phone calls. Back then, research departments were headed by strong-willed directors who policed their analysts. Talk to some old-timers and they'll be sure to point out that research directors wouldn't let an analyst get away with shoddy projections or publish reports clearly intended to please the corporation being discussed. And the old-time analysts insist they never felt any pressure to boost a recommendation, sugarcoat a warning, or let the truth slide.

Although analysis was never a profit center, it stimulated enough trading to earn its keep. Then deregulation hit the industry on May 1, 1975, and the discount brokerage was born. Before deregulation, Wall Street firms charged clients about 28 cents per share on trades. At that rate, stimulating trading in either direction was worthwhile to the banks, and honest analysis that revealed real reasons to trade provided its own reward.

But discounters started offering investors trades for much less, sometimes only a few pennies per share. At the same time, the exchanges, particularly the Nasdaq, cracked down on the spread between the bid and ask price on a stock that used to add up to big money for the banks' market makers. Both of these changes cut deeply into the profits these firms made whenever a trade — buy or sell — was made. If they were to maintain or increase their rate of growth, Wall Street firms would need to rely on another source of revenue. They found it in investment banking, an area in which the firm's analysts would prove invaluable in converting their existing relationships with companies into cold, hard cash.

Boy, did they ever find it. Consider this: in the fourth quarter of 2000, the nation's largest retail brokerage, Merrill Lynch, brought in $1.1 billion in revenue from its investment banking department's underwriting and advisory services. That's 17.5 percent of the firm's total revenue for the quarter, at a firm that more than any other on Wall Street still relies on old-fashioned stock brokering for a lot of its profits. During its 2000 fiscal year, Morgan Stanley's securities business made $4 billion in *profit*, much of that generated by advising on mergers and acquisitions and underwriting offerings of stocks and bonds, where profit margins are very high.

How high? Consider this: in a typical initial public offering, the underwriters can share as much as 7 percent of the net proceeds as their fee, with the lead underwriter taking the lion's share of that 7 percent. (The Justice Department has been inves-

---

Bulge bracket This refers to the top echelon of investment banking firms, particularly in underwriting — the usual suspects include Goldman Sachs, Merrill Lynch, Salomon Smith Barney, J.P. Morgan Chase, and CS First Boston. Following a successful stock or bond offering, the underwriting group places a self-congratulatory ad in leading financial publications, usually including the *Wall Street Journal*. (These ads are called "tombstones.") At the bottom, the entire underwriting group is listed in order of the amount of securities each sold in the underwriting — the ones at the top constitute the "bulge bracket."

---

tigating this apparent price inflexibility). If technology company Y sells $500 million in stock to the public, its underwriters get to split $35 million. In larger deals the percentage devoted to the underwriters' fee falls, but only because the numbers get so large.

The total amount of cash generated by this process is staggering. In the year 2000, investment banks issued $73.1 billion worth of brand-spanking-new stocks to the investing public. Those 458 new issues generated some $5 billion in fees for the underwriters, with Morgan, Goldman Sachs, Merrill Lynch, and Credit Suisse First Boston (CSFB) garnering most of it.

Mergers-and-acquisitions advisory is a similarly high-margin business. CommScan, a firm that tracks Wall Street deals, reports that for the nine months ended mid-February 2001, deals over $5 billion resulted in an average of $23 million paid to the acquirer's adviser. By way of example, CSFB received a $23 million fee for its work on advising Firstar in its $21 billion takeover of U.S. Bancorp. CIBC and Bank of America split $35 million for advising JDS Uniphase on its acquisition of SDLI. Merrill Lynch reaped a $20 million fee for successfully getting Pepsi to prevail in a bid for Quaker Oats. J.P. Morgan Chase would have received $25 million if GE had been able to purchase Honeywell.

Let's consider the Quaker deal for a moment, as though it were still in process. Pepsi is buying Quaker with roughly $14 billion of its own stock. Suppose Merrill's food analyst thinks that the price is far too high and that the deal doesn't make strategic sense. His stinging report on the deal would surely send Pepsi's stock south, which could force Pepsi to issue more shares to make Quaker shareholders whole. In some circumstances, a negative review of the deal could get Pepsi shareholders in a tiff that would result in their voting down the deal.

If you're Merrill and have a $20 million fee on the line, is there any chance you would run the slightest risk of that happening? I think not. And so does Merrill. You can imagine the pressure the bankers bring to bear on an analyst who might jeopardize those banking relationships with negative assessments.

So, too, for a stock issue. No company looking to sell stocks or bonds is going to send millions in fees to a firm that is not totally enraptured by its every move. In the initial public offering of Kraft, CSFB and Salomon Smith Barney, as the co-lead managers, split the bulk of a $245 million underwriting fee. In a tough year, that's the biggest fee either firm might see. So there's not a chance those firms' analysts won't be positive on both Kraft and its parent, Philip Morris, especially with the prospect that down the road Morris will spin off its remaining stake in Kraft to its shareholders, generating yet another fee.

In the Kraft deal, Goldman Sachs learned the hard way that even a firm playing a minor underwriting role can pay a price when its analyst is less than positive. Goldman was part of the larger underwriting group for the deal. A month before the shares were brought public, Goldman's food analyst apparently felt compelled to publish a report that included less-than-favorable things about Kraft's assumed value after it was public. CSFB and Salomon did not allocate Goldman, among the most powerful firms on Wall Street, a single share for its clients. Not one. If you were an investor who traded through Goldman and wanted a piece of the Kraft deal, you were out of luck. Payback for an analyst who made the mistake of speaking her mind.

Year	Deals	Value (in billions)
1991	1,877	$ 71.2
1992	2,574	$ 96.7
1993	2,663	$ 176.4
1994	2,997	$ 226.7
1995	3,510	$ 356.0
1996	5,848	$ 495.0
1997	7,800	$ 657.1
1998	7,809	$1,192.9
1999	9,278	$1,425.8
2000	9,602	$1,395.5
2001	8,231	$ 702.8

(*Source:* mergerstat.com)

Underwriting volume has similarly skyrocketed from the early 1990s.

Global Debt, Equity, and Equity-Related Underwriting	
Year	Industry total (in billions)
1991	$ 914.7
1992	$1,196.9
1993	$1,657.3
1994	$1,303.0
1995	$1,267.2
1996	$1,842.4
1997	$2,351.6
1998	$2,909.7
1999	$3,405.0
2000	$3,267.9
2001	$4,013.2

(*Source:* Thomson Financial Securities Data)

As commission dollars continue to decline, the deals keep increasing. The pace of U.S. mergers-and-acquisitions activity set records in almost each of the past ten years, until the bear market set deals back in 2001 and 2002.

Before they were forced by regulators to change their ways, the Chinese Wall between a firm's investment bankers and stock analysts was completely fiction. Of course, just about every senior manager at a Wall Street firm still pasted on a straight face and said otherwise. Six years ago, then president of Smith Barney Jamie Dimon hauled me in to lambaste me for constantly belittling the analysts at his firm. It was an amazing performance, given that Jamie must have known the truth.

The market's steep descent and the Enron scandal painfully brought home the fact that firms, through their analysts, had been bullish on loser after loser. As a result, many firms are trying to bring back a semblance of integrity to their research product. For a firm such as Merrill Lynch, which relies on retail investors for the bulk of its profits, it's imperative to regain their trust. It won't be easy. Merrill has made a point of firmly separating its research and banking departments. It's trimmed its ratings system and encourages analysts not to be afraid of saying "sell" (or in Merrill's case, "reduce"). And it managed to get great publicity on a largely symbolic policy that bars analysts from owning shares of companies they cover. But such efforts won't prove successful in helping investors pick stocks. Analysts know they will be considered stars only after they help bring in the banking business. And despite the efforts of Eliot Spitzer, that dynamic remains at every investment bank on Wall Street, waiting to rear its head during the next bull market.

The subtlest expression of an analyst's conflict is not what rating to assign a company but the decision whether to cover a company at all. Analysts can't cover every single company in their sector. One might expect that the coverage decision favors whatever companies are most useful to the most clients. One might also expect world peace.

Indeed, analysts typically do end up covering the most significant companies in their sector. But their criteria for coverage often begins with which companies hold the most promise for future banking business. In fact, it is an ongoing frustration to executives at many companies that they are incapable of garnering the attention of Wall Street analysts unless they've got securities to sell. I can't tell you how many times a CEO or CFO of a midsize company has bitched to me about not being able to get any coverage from Wall Street analysts. And as I'll explain in a later chapter, there are some funds that don't buy stocks of companies that lack ample research coverage. Make no mistake, coverage is a potent currency.

The lack of coverage for many companies is becoming a significant problem in the current environment. Many firms have vastly scaled back their research efforts since they can no longer tie banking to research, which has resulted in fewer analysts covering fewer companies.

Analysts automatically cover companies that their firms have brought public or with whom they've done other banking deals — secondary offerings, bond deals, mergers-and-acquisitions advice, and so on. Although they don't spell out this relationship, it's understood that part of the package that comes with the banking business is coverage — favorable coverage.

If you don't believe me, just keep an eye on the "tombstone" advertisement after a big deal is concluded. The underwriters are listed in descending order of importance. You can bet that almost every one of those underwriters is carrying a "buy" or better on the stock in question. And if not, companies have no trouble being vindictive and excluding them from the next deal.

The same game plays out in mergers. Morgan Stanley and Salomon were the two banks in on the AOL Time Warner merger from the beginning. For that hard work, Morgan Stanley netted $12.5 million upon the execution of the merger agreement, another $47.5 million when the merger closed, and up to $15 million more based on post-merger value. Since that last piece relies on stock price, you can see why Morgan Stanley and Salomon would want their analysts to show some enthusiasm for the deal.

In fact, Morgan's Internet analyst Mary Meeker, whom I will discuss in more detail later, was fully compromised from the start on AOL Time Warner. Meeker, sources at Morgan tell me, was asked to give both companies her take on the deal before it was made public. Her take, imparted during meetings with AOL and Time Warner management the weekend before the deal was announced, was — not surprisingly — a very positive one. What's wrong with that? Meeker's job is to objectively analyze and assess the merits of the transaction from the outside. Her job should not entail meeting with those companies' managements prior to their merger and offering her opinions as to what they should do. Certainly it is helpful for the banking clients to speak with the leading Internet analyst about the biggest (and, as it turns out, final) Internet deal of all time. But if the separation between banking and research is real, those conversations should not take place.

Morgan does have a media analyst who doesn't always toe the line for investment banking. His name is Rich Bilotti: I don't know him well, but Morgan's media and telecom bankers are scared shitless of this guy. He has the audacity to criticize companies the bankers are calling on for business and has more than once laid waste to a potential fee with a stinging report on an industry or company. Morgan's bankers, being a rather smart bunch, also use Bilotti's reputation to help them score clients. And while Bilotti does have that independent streak, he is also willing to take one for the team (see Comcast example, page 103). Still, when it comes to industry research, he is one of the few analysts worth paying some attention to.

Even analysts who don't shrug off their objectivity, such as Bilotti, are expected to at least make introductions. Longtime analysts know the CEOs and CFOs of the companies they cover, and their firms expect them to open those doors for their brethren bankers. Many times those relationships can pay off after a deal has been put together. Companies involved in transactions often hire additional "bankers" after the terms of the deal are already in place. These additional bankers tend to be — surprise, surprise — analysts. The companies call these "advisory services," even though they don't really need any advice since the transaction has already been negotiated and announced. So why bother? Because in doing so, companies ensure that the brokerage firm's analyst will be positive on the prospects for the combination.

It's a bribe, no two ways about it.

Banks brought in after a deal is announced don't receive fees anywhere near those of the lead banks. But it's still more than worth it to the secondary banks to sign on, and not simply because of those fees. The score in the world of mergers and acquisitions (M&A) is kept by "league tables" that track the relevant players in a deal — transaction size, investment banks, law firms. A banker added after the deal gets rolling gets credit on the league tables, which are expressed in both number of deals and dollar value. These rankings are critical for recruiting new business, determining banker bonuses, and stroking the all-important ego factor.

So although Morgan Stanley and Salomon were the main banks involved in the AOL Time Warner deal, AOL also brought in Merrill Lynch and Goldman Sachs while Time Warner brought in Wasserstein Perella to "advise" on aftermarket support. These firms received a "small" fee, less than $10 million, in return for their analysts' support of the transaction — and they got their money's worth with lots of outrageous estimates on cost savings and "synergies" from the firm's analysts. But more important, the firms get credit for the biggest deal of all time in the league tables. A few weeks after Merrill signed on to the deal, two of its highest-profile analysts at the time, Henry Blodget and Jessica Reif Cohen, issued "You've Got Upside: Analyzing AOL Time Warner," a glowing report on the prospects for a merged AOL Time Warner, sending both stocks higher by more than 10 percent. It's been a long, steep descent for the stock ever since.

Powerful analysts such as Reif Cohen can find their support of a transaction promised by fee-hungry bankers without their knowledge or consent. Consider the following e-mails sent by a Merrill banker to the management of a company looking to sell a large media property. E-mail #1: "We want to be named co-advisor on the transaction and there is no doubt that Jessica will support the deal. She can publish on the deal as soon as it's done." E-mail #2 gets a bit more desperate: "Need to be a part of this deal . . . happy with small fee . . . would spare us a big slap in the face and can insure Jessica's support."

In the summer of 2001, when, after months of planning, Comcast made its unsolicited bid for AT&T Broadband, people close to Comcast and its president, Brian Roberts, were perhaps most pleased by the fact that Comcast had hired both Morgan Stanley and Merrill Lynch to advise it. The two most powerful analysts in the cable television world worked for both firms: Rich Bilotti in the case of Morgan and Jessica in the case of Merrill. Their unquestioned support of the deal would now be expected, and people in the Comcast camp were giddy at the prospect.

For Bilotti this meant some quick backpedaling. Only a few weeks before Comcast made its bid and began using AT&T Broadband's pitiful operating margins as a key part of its argument as to why it could do much better, Bilotti had been telling investors that those same margins were understated because of things beyond poor management. Luckily for him, he didn't put it in writing, but he did share those thoughts with some of my hedge fund sources, who took notes of the meeting. When I told Comcast that I knew Bilotti's true opinion, they were not pleased. They probably got poor Rich on the phone at once and told him to shut up — which, under intense pressure, he apparently did.

Want another example?

Friday, October 27, 2000. Tom Rogers, former chairman and CEO of Primedia, announced a deal to buy About.com. Primedia's stock got crushed, down 25 percent on sixteen times normal volume. I called him a few days later, with Primedia's price having barely budged from that shellacking. "Tom, that was pretty ugly." Tom, whom I consider a very capable guy, trotted out the usual blather, telling me what a great deal it was and how he had expected the market to respond unkindly. He added that Merrill Lynch's Henry Blodget was going to come out and say how great the deal was. I was surprised that someone as sophisticated as Rogers put so much weight in an analyst's opinion.

"Blodget doesn't have it anymore," I told him. "He's been too positive too long, and now he's largely ignored."

"Then whom should I be going after?" he asked.

I nominated Holly Becker as the hot name of the month, because she'd been kind of negative. I figured if she gave it a thumbs-up, what with her somewhat skeptical bias, investors might give the deal a more sympathetic look.

"Let me write that down, we'll call her right away."

It was clear he was going to bring her in to sell her on the deal. Apparently, he was not successful — Holly never did endorse it, and was right not to have done so, given Primedia's poor performance since.

BIG, BIG CONFLICT

Jack Grubman never expected to become a household name. He spent the eighties as a telecom analyst at Paine Webber, toiling in relative obscurity in the days before analysts were superstars. He had worked for AT&T, had gotten to know different managements, and was well regarded by different companies. And he had made a couple of good calls — on AT&T, for example, he was correctly negative early on, probably because he had insight into the bureaucracy of the Bells.

The true metamorphosis of Jack Grubman must have occurred the day he met Bernard J. Ebbers. Ebbers was this bearded, backwoods guy down in the swamps of Jackson, Mississippi. He landed in the States after flunking out of the University of Alberta in his native Edmonton. Following a stint as a gym teacher, he got into the long-distance business almost by accident after a group of friends chipped in to start LDDS in 1983.

In Bernie, Jack smelled a man whose ambition and megalomania rivaled his own, and the feeling was clearly mutual. Jack became Bernie's champion as LDDS morphed into WorldCom, using its ever rising and ever promoted stock to buy up company after company — some seventy acquisitions in all.

WorldCom (WCOM) always represented the ultimate conflict for Grubman. On one hand, Grubman has been WorldCom's banker, advising Bernie on almost every single deal. Most investment bankers go back to being guys you never heard of as soon as the deal's done. But analyst-banker Grubman would finish a deal and then immediately revert to being the telecom analyst at Salomon Smith Barney, from where he had the balls to trumpet what a great deal — the very deal he had just advised Ebbers to do and been paid to help execute — it was.

Example: WorldCom buys MCI, with Grubman as part of WorldCom's advisory team. The difference in price between what WorldCom is paying and MCI's current price is large: a clear sign that investors are worried the deal may not close. In addition, WorldCom's price has fallen significantly since the deal was announced, depressing the deal's overall value. So here's a guy who's been telling WorldCom how great the deal is and how much the Street is going to love it. How to make that happen? Start digging.

Grubman tunnels back under the Chinese Wall and writes about this beautiful deal. An investor would be tempted to dismiss this obviously biased opinion, but Grubman has numbers and projections that others don't. He's got the inside dope on true synergy numbers, cost savings, growth rates. Hell, he'd better know those things — he put the deal together! He can give voice to things that the execs can't afford to comment on — that he's not worried about antitrust regulators blocking the deal, for example, or the level of confidence that the deal will be consummated.

You already know the rest of the story. The deal was announced on October 1, 1997. It was completed on September 14,

1998. Salomon Smith Barney walked away with more than $45 million in banking fees. And if you had bought WorldCom that day, on Jack Grubman's recommendation, you would have made money — briefly. Though the stock moved higher for another nine months, it topped out at $60, before going to zero when the company filed the largest bankruptcy in U.S. history in July 2002. Jack stayed positive during the entire trip.

My dad always told me, "Press your advantage." Grubman pressed his. He was Mr. WorldCom, Mr. PSINet, Mr. Global Crossing. Grubman made the conflicts faced by the analyst-banker so easy and clear to understand. He stuck by WCOM, relentlessly promoting it to his sales force as the telecom sector crashed and burned. He stood by Global Crossing from $60 to $1 and PSINet from $40 to bankruptcy. As ICG Communications went bankrupt, Dr. Grubman was at its side, lowering his opinion only when the patient was clearly terminal.

Perhaps my favorite Grubman moment occurred amid the proposed Global Crossing–US West deal. I deal with the transaction itself at length in chapter 6, but this little nugget bears mention here. The deal was coming unglued after Qwest emerged with a competing bid. Banker Grubman, smelling a fee going up in smoke, raced to strap on his analyst hat. To objectively weigh the bids? Yeah, sure. Here was Grubman on the merits of his client's bid: "We view [Global's] deal as a financially elegant way to unlock value for both US West and Global Crossing." (Why stop at "financially elegant" — how about "brilliantly innovative" or "ridiculously clever"?) Qwest's bid ultimately prevailed despite Grubman's sentiments.

Grubman's final undoing came with what he did on AT&T. After years as a banking whore, he held on to a scrap of credibility by being neutral to negative on the biggest fish in his sector, AT&T. And he was right. But in December 1999, after years and years of being negative on AT&T, Grubman suddenly professed to having seen something new. Suddenly AT&T was an incredibly undervalued asset, and the growth rates from its broadband business were clearly not appreciated. This after years of telling everyone what a piece of shit the company was, staying with his negative stance even when new CEO C. Michael Armstrong came on board and a new strategy was born. After years of being right, Grubman upgraded AT&T from a "neutral" to a "buy" and slapped a big target price on it. And he did so with aplomb. No snickering, no winks, just flat-out, previously undiscovered love.

By making his move, Grubman got on AT&T's good side, and sure enough, Salomon Smith Barney secured a lead-manager position in the upcoming offering of stock in AT&T's wireless subsidiary. (When the upgrade occurred, I said as much on *Squawk Box.*) The IPO of AT&T Wireless would weigh in at $10.6 billion, the largest IPO in U.S history. One can only imagine the pressure on him. Armstrong sits on the board of Citigroup (Salomon's parent), and Citigroup's CEO, Sandy Weill, holds a seat on AT&T's board. Weill had been quietly pressuring Grubman to upgrade the stock for a long time. How much pressure was the subject of a long line of inquiry by New York attorney general Spitzer, which did not find enough overt acts to go after Weill.

In the end, Salomon received in excess of $70 million in fees from that IPO, and Grubman received a percentage of that fee, and likely a bonus to boot.

A couple of months after the AT&T Wireless offering, I ran into Grubman at the annual Robin Hood Foundation gala. We schmoozed for quite a while, and at the end of the night he hugged me good-bye. This is a guy I had savaged. I looked at my wife and raised my eyebrows. But that's the way it worked for Jack. He knew exactly what he was doing and why. Jack Grubman made a decision years ago to go where the money was on Wall Street. It finally got him fired, but not before he drank copiously from the banking trough, amassing a net worth that is probably near $100 million. His biggest mistake may well have been the same one of so many investors. Jack overstayed his welcome. When the bear market took hold and culprits needed to be found, Jack was still at his post — the perfect whipping boy for politicians looking to build a career and investors looking for restitution.

Grubman's got lots of company. In fact, although he was the

highest-profile analyst-banker at his firm, he's only one egregious offender. Talk to brokers at Salomon Smith Barney and they'll be happy to trash Grubman. But they also reserve unmitigated enmity for a duo that wreaked havoc on them: health-care impresario Benjamin Lorello, who ran that sector's investment banking at Smith Barney (and then Salomon Smith Barney) for fifteen years, and his analyst sidekick, Geoff Harris. In the years these guys worked there, they shoveled more shit than Grubman could imagine: Integrated Health, Mid Atlantic Medical, MedPartners, US Oncology, HealthSouth — just a few of the names this pair foisted on the equity markets for Salomon Smith Barney in the nineties, all the while relying on the firm's brokers to put these dogs into the accounts of their clients. With great bitterness, Salomon Smith Barney's brokers can reel them off like so many battlegrounds in a lost war. So can some of Salomon's clients.

Sources at Salomon tell me the firm's capital-commitment committee finally had had enough and cut back sharply on how much capital they would let Lorello use to secure new business. Soon after, the duo found a new home at UBS Warburg, from where they are once again aggressively peddling health-care stocks. Oh, and don't fret for Ben and Geoff. Lorello received a three-year, $70-million contract to join UBS, while Harris bagged $26 million for the same three years.

QUEEN MARY

Nowhere are the priorities of the analyst-banker more in evidence than during the process of an initial public offering. Mary Meeker was a respected analyst covering PCs in the early 1990s when she embarked on a new sector of coverage that she would help create — the Internet. After placing a "buy" on AOL in 1993 — at a split-adjusted 52 cents — Meeker got some early momentum and, with the capital markets just starting to warm up to the word *dot com*, put her ass in gear.

Priceline.com, Akamai, Ask Jeeves, Redback Networks, Ariba, Women.com, Broadcast.com, CNET, Drugstore.com, Expedia,

FreeMarkets, Homestore.com, Ingram Micro, Intuit, Marimba, Scient, Tickets.com, VeriSign, Vignette, and Ziff-Davis are just a fraction of the companies for which Queen Mary marshalled the forces of Morgan Stanley to sell to the public. That's in addition to countless debt, secondary, private-placement, and M&A events, such as Healtheon's merger with WebMD, not to mention AOL Time Warner. Queen Mary's efforts paid off for Morgan Stanley. Thomson Financial Securities Data reports that between 1998 and 2000, Morgan Stanley took in $480 million in fees from Internet IPOs and follow-on offerings, so you won't be surprised that her firm forgives the unbelievably poor performance of nearly every company Mary helped price at many times what it's trading for a couple of years after its debut. God bless the Queen. And if the blessing wasn't enough, she got a reported $15 million a year for her services.

It's not just the distraction from her research duties, however, that compromises Meeker's analysis. That she remains positive on these companies after they're born keeps her from down-grading, no matter how unhealthy they look. At the time the Internet crash began in April 2000, Meeker had a "buy" on all fourteen of the Internet companies she covered and she had never issued anything close to a "sell." Not one. Ever.

Mary did try to make a research call that would have restored some semblance of credibility to her name, only to be beaten back by Morgan's bankers. In late 2000, when Yahoo!'s stock had yet to reflect the collapse of online advertising, Meeker alerted her bosses that she planned to downgrade shares of the blue-chip Internet name.

Morgan Stanley has offices for most of its analysts and bankers that are enclosed largely by glass. You can't hide from prying eyes. Sources at the firm tell me that when word got out that Meeker was planning a Yahoo! downgrade, a contingent of bankers were dispatched to her office. Eyewitnesses report a meeting between bankers and Meeker in her office. Meeker did not downgrade the shares of one of the few Internet companies that might still bring Morgan a fee in the future. Meeker shared her concerns about

Yahoo! in her report, without changing her rating on the stock. In the months that followed, Meeker adopted a much lower profile on Yahoo!, rarely offering comment on the company.

The reason these companies flock to Meeker's door is that they know she is going to come out with a "buy" rating. Does that mean Queen Mary accepts banking business only from companies she believes in? Yeah, sure. That's why the biggest name among Internet analyst-bankers brought dogs like Drugstore.com, Women.com, and Ask Jeeves — all of which were catastrophic failures — to the table. To her credit, she has occasionally lost subsequent banking business (Ask Jeeves and Redback are two examples) from companies dissatisfied with the number of reports she put out on them following the IPO.

The analysts didn't just bring the company to the table and let the bankers take over. The analysts were actively involved in drumming up hype for the IPO. They rode along with the companies on the pre-IPO presentations known as "roadshows." The lead underwriter always has its analyst in the room as it talks up the deal to clients. Many times the analyst chimes in to answer questions about valuation, projections, or industry comparisons. The analyst also travels with company executives to key one-on-one meetings. The buy-side guys realize that the level of BS is inevitably higher with an analyst participating in the conversation, and some, including Fidelity, do not permit the analyst in the room when questioning company executives. But most play the game, probably figuring that no matter what they pay for the initial shares, the individual investor will be convinced by the analyst to pay even more.

Sell side/buy side The *sell side* refers to the brokerage firms and investment banks that sell securities. The *buy side* refers to the institutional buyers of those securities, typically mutual funds, pension funds, and hedge funds.

According to a survey of CEOs and CFOs who took their companies public in the 1990s, 75 percent cited the quality and reputation of the research department as key factors in selecting a lead underwriter. (*Quality* and *reputation* will probably join *down on all fours* and *spread-eagled* in *Roget's* any day now.) In fact, when bankers detail their capital-raising plan to companies, the most important part of the presentation is from the analyst, who explains how he would sell the story to the Street.

Unbelievable.

Former Securities and Exchange Commission (SEC) chairman Arthur Levitt has spoken of the "web of dysfunctional relationships" that exists among bankers, analysts, and the companies they deal with and follow. "In many respects, analysts' employers expect them to act more like promoters and marketers [for the corporate finance division] than unbiased and dispassionate analysts." Nicely put. The "Wall Street settlement" has ostensibly ended this practice, but it remains to be seen how long that will last.

THE CORPORATE FINANCE SHUFFLE

It's been put on hold by regulators, but mark my words: if a bull market returns to Wall Street, so will something I like to call the corporate finance shuffle.

I thought maybe a step-by-step account of how that dance works would help.

When AT&T announced a plan in late 2000 to separate its remaining components — broadband services, business services, and consumer long distance — the investment banks went ga-ga over the fees such a split would bring their way. And the analysts at those investment banks put on their dancing shoes.

It works like this. The most senior banker calls a meeting in the boardroom. The room is connected to the chairman's office, so the boss can poke his head in and give support. Twenty people sit around a thirty-foot table. The bankers present their internal pitch books, detailing how they'll present the transaction to AT&T and what their bank is positioned to bring to the table. The size of potential deals and the resulting fees are thrown around. The senior banker announces that this is the most important transaction for the firm this year.

Meanwhile, the telecom analyst sits in the corner, cooking up something positive to say about AT&T. He whips out his HP 12c and starts to calculate how big the fees might actually be to his firm and to himself. The analyst realizes that his book of banking clients has shrunk dramatically during the slowdown that settled in after the dot-com crash in the spring of 2000. He needs some banking fees. More important, after bonus time, all smart analysts try to re-up their contract, and bonus time is right around the corner. The analyst cannot be seen as an impediment to AT&T, or his contract will not be renewed. What would you expect him to do? So everyone loves AT&T in spite of its deteriorating fundamentals. (In the early part of January 2001, we actually saw the start of that rush to upgrade. First CSFB and then Morgan Stanley showed AT&T some serious love, hoping that some love would get thrown their way when the underwriters were chosen for the various AT&T spin-offs and exchange offers.)

In February 2001 Lucent (LU) was reeling. Its lines of credit were days from expiring, which would further weaken the company's already bad credit rating and suck sparse cash into interest payments. Personal pleas at the last minute from chief executive Henry Schacht and chief financial officer Deborah Hopkins led about thirty banks to the lending table, including Bank of America, Bank One, and Barclays Capital.

Also stepping into the lending breach were Morgan Stanley, Deutsche Bank, and Bear Stearns. They did so in order to secure a place in the underwriting of Lucent's planned spin-off of its optical electronics company, Agere Systems. Lucent, in what is likely a sign of things to come in corporate finance, linked participation in the profitable underwriting with willingness to lend it money. Goldman Sachs, Lucent's banker for its 1999 purchase of Ascend, didn't step up to the lending plate — so it was left out of the Agere offering. Same with CSFB — no dough, no go. But the banks that did pony up did so in a big way, and Lucent showed its appreciation. J.P. Morgan Chase was one of the companies that helped out when LU needed it. And it found itself with a lucrative co-managing chunk of the $3.6 billion Agere IPO. But just in case that might not have been enough to help snare the business, J.P. Morgan Chase sent its telecom-equipment analyst to the meeting to help pitch the deal, and no doubt offer the prospect of favorable research coverage. That analyst made $14 million in 2000. He was thirty-one years old.

There's a reason I've made a point of mentioning the astronomical compensation of analysts — and it's not just to make you angry. It's my contention that the girls and boys who become analysts do so more for the promise of vast riches than for the opportunity to satiate a passion for analyzing companies. And that's why I believe efforts by Wall Street firms to instill some integrity into the research process once again will fail.

Wall Street research simply does not generate enough revenue on its own to justify the compensation levels accorded analysts. Unless firms can figure out a way to eviscerate the current compensation structure but still attract smart people, research will continue to be poor: either because it's tainted by banking prejudice or because it's written by idiots.

The analyst-banking compensation structure on Wall Street is not a casual arrangement. Former analysts who won't let me use their names have told me how it works. The analyst gets a percentage of the fees generated for deals in his or her particular industry or sector. This includes equity business, high-yield debt offerings, and mergers and acquisitions. Those departments are often separate, so different groups pay off the analyst out of their own fees. In an M&A transaction in which a covered company is advised by the firm, the M&A group earmarks part of its fee for the analyst. These aren't handshake agreements; we're talking about contractually defined direct-percentage participation. Sometimes, in place of the spelled-out contracts, a "black box" algorithm is applied, under which fee generation, trading business, sector importance, and client votes on such surveys as the all-star list in *Institutional Investor* magazine each October are weighed to come up with a percentage participation. If an analyst is instrumental to winning a piece of business, he or she might get 10 percent of the fees generated. If the bankers do all the work and are the ones who have the relationship, then hand the analyst a deal to promote after it's set, he or she might get 5 percent. If the analyst brings the deal in and is the major force in selling it, he or she might get as much as 15 percent.

Example: A $100 million IPO with fees of 7 percent — $7 million. If a co-manager gets 50 percent of the IPO fees, that's 3.5 million bucks to the firm. The analyst could get anywhere from $100K to $400K for being involved. As deal size increases, the percentage falls, but there's plenty of money to go around. And the IPO loop is a self-generating cash cow. Some banks even bribe certain favored investors with offering-price IPO shares while demanding artificially high commissions from others for the same access.

It couldn't be clearer that an analyst whose pay depends on the number and size of deals he pushes through will inevitably create analysis that's directed more at deal making than at forecasting which stocks will move and why. I've seen the unseemly process at work, whereby younger analysts learn how the game is really played.

Jeff Schlesinger was an analyst at the no-name firm Unterberg Harris. He'd call me all full of excitement, saying, "I got some G-two for you." G-2 is military code for classified information. Very often that G-2 was a piece of negative news. The wireless industry was just beginning the transition to digital and there were lots of technical questions about which systems would work and which wouldn't. There was money to be made from figuring it all out. Schlesinger would make outgoing calls to people in the industry, and it was refreshing to hear an analyst speak his mind, regardless of the consequences. Ah, but he was so naive. He would soon learn better.

Young analysts at smaller firms often feel freer to speak their minds. When Schlesinger was at Unterberg, he seemed to have no idea he wasn't supposed to be negative. "Ah, these guys are full of shit, those guys are full of shit," he'd say. As his career progressed, Schlesinger became less and less useful. He left Unterberg in 1995 to become the wireless analyst at UBS Warburg. Not surprisingly, the larger his firm, the more he was prevented from saying anything negative about a company, at least to me. "You know I can't say anything bad about Motorola," he'd explain. "They do huge banking business." Last time I spoke to Schlesinger, he was asking me to get him on TV to speak positively about Motorola in the hope that such sentiments would put him in good stead with the company. At Unterberg he could say whatever he wanted about Motorola, because he'd never get their big-money banking business. At Warburg, he's got much less G-2 to share.

2. Unrelenting Optimism

The optimist proclaims that we live in the best of all possible worlds; and the pessimist fears this is true.

— *James Branch Cabell*

At the pinnacle of the bull market — just when a clear "sell" signal would have done investors the most good — the consensus among analysts had only 3 percent of stocks rated "sell" or "strong sell."

We've already discussed the main reason analysts are blessed with perpetually rosy outlooks: their employers and the analysts themselves won't jeopardize the potential for lucrative banking business. But there are other factors behind the permanent smile. Let's look at a few.

MONEY MANAGER PRESSURE

The managers of the nation's large mutual funds want stocks to go only one way: up. When analysts issue a downgrade, chances are they won't hear directly from the investment banking department, since that pressure is applied quietly. But there is nothing quiet about the ruckus that money managers make when an analyst with some power decides to downgrade shares of a company that's in their portfolio.

As opposed to the threat of lost banking business, mutual fund and hedge fund managers use the threat of taking their trading business elsewhere if a firm's analyst is negative on a stock they own. It's a simple and effective threat. "Downgrade that stock and I'll make sure we don't do another trade with your firm for six months." A big mutual fund can generate an awful lot of commissions in six months' worth of trading. So though the threat may be somewhat overstated, many analysts don't want to take the chance.

BIG PIMPIN'

I'm pretty sure I coined the verb "Blodgeting," which means to place a price target on the stock of a company with no earnings or other conceivable basis for justifying that price. I've already mentioned the word's namesake, one Henry Blodget, the apple-cheeked optimist who "analyzed" Internet stocks for Merrill Lynch.

Blodget is retired now. He took a multimillion-dollar buyout offer from Merrill and happily departed to spend more time with his new wife and new child in their new Greenwich Village town house. The Internet boom of the late 1990s minted thousands of millionaires, but few of them kept those millions as the dot-com bubble burst. Henry was an exception. In his five-year career as Wall Street's leading cheerleader for the Internet, Henry earned at least $25 million. That kind of money can make for a nice retirement at age thirty-four.

Blodget almost literally came out of nowhere — after a history degree from Yale, he'd been a go-fetch-'em at *Harper's* magazine and then an intern on CNN's *Moneyline* before wandering into a training program at Prudential in 1994. He landed at CIBC Oppenheimer in 1996, not the best balance-sheet reader by a long shot but a better writer than most and a couple of days ahead of his elders regarding comfort with technology. When the Internet exploded, Blodget was ready.

On December 16, 1998, Henry Blodget strolled into Oppenheimer's morning call with a time bomb in his backpack (he was, after all, only thirty at the time). Amazon.com was nearing $250 a share, having rocketed through the $150 price target he'd set just two months earlier. He waited through five seemingly monotonous presentations from old-line bottom-up guys, stuff like ten minutes on Rubbermaid's new inventory accounting in China. And then it was Henry's turn.

Four hundred dollars. That was the price Henry thought an owner of a share of Amazon would soon command for stock in a company that had never earned a cent. A company that by Blodget's own estimate would lose more that year than the last and more still the next year. He called the stock, which had closed at $242 and change the day before, "incredibly expensive," "scary to buy," and "extremely volatile." But he still thought it would go much higher.

Blodget was right on all counts. Amazon *did* lose more in 1999 than in 1998. Amazon *was* incredibly expensive, scary to buy, and extremely volatile. And goddammit, Amazon *did* go to $400. Up almost 20 percent the day of the Blodget call, the stock crossed the $400 mark on January 6 and soon after that would trade a full 200 points higher than Henry's price target. Amazon's market cap shot from $12 billion at the time of Blodget's call to $30 billion, or about $6,600 for every customer using Amazon's service that year.

Blodget's Amazon call was so absurd and so clearly calculated to generate publicity that I decided not to refer to it on the air. Sure enough, my colleague Maria Bartiromo mentioned it, and then I felt compelled to cover the pandemonium. Instantly, Blodget became a name. Being a name had some big rewards. And Blodget used his sudden fame to land a bigger job.

Meanwhile, a few months before, Merrill Lynch's then Internet analyst Jonathan Cohen on September 1, 1998, issued a report titled "Amazon.com: The World's Leading Internet Company Is Too Expensive" and slapped a "reduce" rating alongside his price target of $83.75. He referred to the "Gordian knot" Amazon faced: "the company may have to choose between running its business in order to maximize its long-term value or in a way more consistent with the near-term expectations of the public equity market." Gordian knot? Clearly, this was not the kind of wet blanket who was going to help bring Merrill the kind of Internet banking deals Morgan Stanley, Goldman Sachs, and CSFB were getting.

What's interesting about the Blodget/Cohen thing is the way their respective points of view led them to and from the spotlight. At Smith Barney, his first employer, Cohen came out as the voice of reason on the Internet.

Cohen slapped negative ratings on what were then the big 'net stocks of the day — PSINet, Netscape, Netcom, and others. He made a name for himself by standing above the herd, refusing to believe the hype. Unfortunately, in the short term, he was utterly wrong — they all quadrupled on him. Still, he used the notoriety from these bold calls, even though they were wrong (temporarily), to land his job at Merrill. Once there, though, Jon didn't change his point of view, and by the end of February 1999, Cohen was out and Blodget was in. Merrill gave its new star a staff of seven full-time, report-generating acolytes and set the analyst-banker loose on a sector drunk on his Amazon divination.

As it turns out, Blodget's bullishness was completely wrong from almost the day he started at Merrill. After Merrill lead-managed the IPO for Pets.com, Blodget could barely wait out the quiet period before he came through with a near- and long-term "buy" on March 8, 2000, setting a price target that was exceptionally modest for the two-fisted analyst — $16. Not modest enough, it turned out. After failing to rise above its $11 IPO price on the day of its debut, Pets.com was at $7 when Blodget first rated it. He didn't downgrade it (neither did the two analysts at UBS Warburg, which co-managed the IPO) until August, when he hit the buck-fifty stock with a "near-term accumulate." Even that proved too generous; by election day, Pets.com was out of business.

Analysts who expect great things from companies get famous and rich. They may not be great at predicting the future, but they can read the writing on the wall. Take a look at all the Blodgeting that took place during the two-week period following the master's Amazon homer. On December 20, 1999, a few days after Blodget's shot in the dark, David Garrity, the auto analyst at Dresder Kleinwort Benson, put a $1,000 price target on Commerce One, for which he forecast great things via business-to-business cost savings on auto parts and inventory management. Virtually overnight, a little-known analyst who'd been covering autos for fourteen years at a little-known bank was a household name. "We highly recommend that investors jump aboard this train," wrote Garrity. What he lacked in writerly grace he made up for in prescience and gall. Five trading days later Commerce One was knocking on the door of a thousand. A week after Garrity's call, December 27, Walter Piecyk at PaineWebber called for Qualcomm, then at 503, to hit 1000, even though it was already up more than 1,800 percent for the year. The stock gained 31 percent on his call. And so on . . .

- 1/3/00: Carolyn Luther Trabuco at First Union Securities raised Yahoo!'s target to 600.
- 1/4/00: Arthur Newman at Schroder did the *exact same thing!*
- 1/4/00: Jordan Rohan of Wit Capital raised his price target on DoubleClick to 325 from 140.

Hey, it pays to be positive. Analysts willing to sell their souls to the bankers can see their bonuses skyrocket alongside their celebrity. And the calls themselves do work in getting the analysts the attendant publicity that can also become important to their ability to land future banking business or future jobs. Sometimes these prophecies are self-fulfilling — the buzz generated by the call drives the stock higher. That's why I'm predicting this book will sell 11 million copies. But there's a flip side to analysts' boosting stock prices of companies that are actually losers. Sure, some people who had bought Amazon at $24 made a lot if they sold at $400. But what Blodget was saying was that if you bought Amazon at $300 or $350, you were smart and would make money. As any current Amazon shareholder will vouch for, losing your shirt on Amazon has been the rule, not the exception.

CONSEQUENCES FOR THOSE WHO DON'T PLAY

True story: Looking for a synonym, I entered the phrase *notorious optimist* on Google. The first forty results included two stories about — guess who? — Henry Blodget. If fame and fortune are the analyst carrot, then what's the stick?

Analysts and the companies they follow enjoy a symbiotic (some would say parasitic) relationship. Stock analysts rely on access to insiders. Since the whole value-added premise is that they can get information the average guy cannot, they're dead if they can't get their calls returned by the management at the companies they follow. For example, many analysts have come to depend entirely on a company's own guidance for an indication whether their estimates are in the ballpark. If his calls aren't returned, the ostracized analyst risks not only being unable to provide valuable insights but being outed as someone who cannot even do his job.

In the event that you're an adult, you probably can't imagine companies being so childish that they'd actually banish analysts — and their clients — simply over a difference of opinion. Rest assured, I'm not going to have to resort to hypothetical companies X, Y, and Z to drive this point home. To wit:

- In the fall of 2001, Merrill analysts Jessica Reif Cohen and Henry Blodget made a surprising (given their banking relationship) downgrade of AOL Time Warner to "neutral" from "buy." AOL's CFO at the time, Mike Kelly, responded by cursing at them and then shutting them out. The analysts' calls were not returned, and meetings between the analysts and AOL management were canceled.

- Outspoken Donaldson, Lufkin & Jenrette (DLJ) bank analyst Thomas K. Brown "resigned" right after DLJ hired a whole new investment banking team that didn't like his tendency to be honest. Brown made a name for himself in 1990 when he got bullish on BankAmerica, when most investors thought it was going out of business. It wasn't. Brown was also bold when it came to being bearish. He nearly came to blows with First Union Corporation CEO Edward Crutchfield at an analyst meeting when Brown questioned Crutchfield's strategy.

- America Online banned Cowen's permanently negative Jeff Goverman from a party for analysts.

- Owens-Corning dropped Smith Barney from a $200 million bond offering after analyst David Dwyer raised justified concerns about asbestos-liability costs.

- NationsBank (NCNB at the time) suspended all trading through Kidder, Peabody because Charles Peabody made repeated "sell" recommendations.

- Conseco canned Merrill Lynch as lead underwriter for a $325 million bond offering after analyst Edward Spehar lowered his rating.

- Conseco threatened Smith Barney's Colin Devine with cutting off all business unless he retreated from his downgrade.

- Morgan Stanley's global analyst, David Roche, received threatening anonymous calls in the middle of the night from his own firm's investment bankers, angry about his stance on foreign currencies.

- First Union stopped trading bonds through Bear Stearns after bank analyst Sean Ryan made negative comments.

▪ Prudential canned bank analyst George Salem *twice*. The first time was in 1983 for saying the LDC (lesser developed countries) debt crisis would choke U.S. banks (correctly, as it turned out). After being rehired some four years later, he was fired again in 1994 after negative comments about BancOne (right again), a big buyer of Prudential's asset-backed securities.

Perhaps the most publicized of such cases was Marvin Roffman versus The Donald. Roffman analyzed stocks for a small firm called Janney, Montgomery, Scott. He was dubious of Donald Trump's ability to service the debt load at his Taj Mahal casino in Atlantic City and said as much to the *Wall Street Journal*. Trump threatened to sue the brokerage unless it fired Roffman, which it did. Shortly thereafter, the casino declared bankruptcy and Roffman collected $750,000 from his brokerage for wrongful termination.

In April 2001 Merrill's Jessica Reif Cohen made an obvious but surprisingly public admission on the firm's morning call. Cohen was assessing the near-term prospects for radio giant Clear Channel Communications. She was quite negative in her outlook but, despite her view, was not downgrading the stock from her "buy" rating. On the call, she was peppered with questions from Merrill brokers asking why, given how bad she was predicting business would be for Clear Channel, she didn't downgrade the stock. And then Cohen made a startling admission. If she downgraded the stock, she said, Clear Channel management "would cut her off." Cohen didn't elaborate on what she would be cut off from, but the conclusion is obvious: from information and banking business.

Merrill offers its brokers a taped replay of the morning call throughout the day. But when I searched that replay for Cohen's comments, they had been deleted. No trace of her honest admission would be left. As I reported on CNBC that day, Cohen was forced to apply similar honesty when it came to her rating on Clear Channel. Not long after making her remark on the morning call, she was visited by Merrill's head of research, Andy

Melnick. A twenty-minute meeting ensued and, presto, Clear Channel Communications stock was downgraded by Merrill Lynch from a "buy" rating to a "neutral."

BAD MATH

In 600 B.C. the Greeks cooked up some enduringly elegant stories to explain observed phenomena. They didn't know that the reason it was cold in winter had to do with the angle of the earth's axis. So they figured that Hades had tricked Persephone into eating six pomegranate seeds in the underworld, causing her mother, Demeter, to lay the ground fallow for half the year.

That's pretty much how it works for many analysts, who simply suspend disbelief. "It's trading where? Sure!" And then they work backward to justify the price. In a January 1999 report called "Trying to Justify Valuations," Warburg's Michael Wallace wrote: "Yahoo is trading at 150 times our 1999 revenue estimate (693 times $.60 earnings per share [EPS]), and 107 times our 2000 revenue estimate (555 times EPS). Absurd? Absolutely. But it was absurd 100 points ago, and 200 points, so we will not be stupid and change the rating." Wallace's analysis turned out to have ignored the possibility of a slowdown in advertising spending, not to mention the possibility that banner ads and the like were still an untested format that might fail to attract a long-term buying audience. Wallace, by the way, kept a "buy" on Yahoo! long after it peaked.

That's the way it's worked for the sectors of the market that were Wall Street's greatest fee generators: dot com and telecom. Bad business plans be damned — we can make it shine. First assume a revenue number in five years given today's growth rate. Then take that revenue number and discount it back to the present. Apply a multiple to the revenue that's based on the standout performer rather than the median or weakling in an industry. Print it and run. And that's why the retail investor gets screwed — you get the broker reading from the report. You don't get to be on the phone with the analyst and hear the sarcasm and self-deprecation.

The analyst's main form of doing what appears to be impressive valuation work is the discounted cash flow model (DCF). Theoretically, this is a pure enough way to value companies, but it generally suffers from the same flagrant manipulations as those described above. Analysts employ ridiculously high valuations to current companies in order to impress management and nail down an underwriting. They'll then use the DCF model to prove that valuation. But the numbers are wacky. Absurd assumed growth rates, monstrous end multiples, and ass-backward assumptions that call for a company never to miss an earnings projection in ten years.

Equity analysts don't like to spend much time thinking about balance sheets or dissecting them. But on the fixed-income side of the business, analysts do focus on balance sheets to the exclusion of much else. That's because fixed-income analysts are servicing clients who buy and sell bonds — and those bonds move up or down in price based largely on the perceptions of the company's ability to adequately pay interest and principal on its debt. Fixed-income analysts can often be more dispassionate about the companies they follow and are less afraid to spot signs of trouble. But when there's banking involved, fixed-income analysts can be just as untrustworthy as their equity brethren. Lehman Brothers was the lead underwriter for many issues of equity and debt from Globalstar, the satellite-based telecommunications system. In September 1997 Lehman's high-yield research team released a report recommending purchase of Globalstar's bonds.

Lehman's outlook for Globalstar was definitely out of this world. Its projections called for Globalstar to have 1.6 million subscribers by 1999 and 3.2 million by 2002. Globalstar never got much beyond 36,000 subscribers and filed for Chapter 11. So much for fixed-income analysts being messengers of truth.

OVERWORK

With the unprecedented level of interest in the stock market, and a load of potential banking out there, you've got analysts who are, quite simply, overwhelmed. Most analysts, to increase their visibility and have the best shot at banking business, feel that they've got to have coverage on as many companies in their sector as possible.

And since these banking clients expect coverage after their deals — indeed, they feel they've paid for it — analysts are stuck cooking up reports on more companies than they can actually analyze. The result: analysts seldom call anyone other than the companies themselves.

It's also not an accident that something like the beverage sector, with few competitors, moderate growth, and a lesser need for capital, produces smarter and more thorough analysis than hotter sectors, whose analyst-bankers have other things on their minds. If nothing else, beverage analysts have more time, as evidenced by the ninety-seven-page analysis of country-by-country operating-profit projections for the beverage companies followed by Morgan Stanley's Andrew Conway. Perhaps this also gives analysts in that sector more balls: Conway downgraded his sector's behemoth, Coca-Cola, at 68 in December 1999. It was in the mid-40s three months later.

But time isn't everything. Telecom-equipment analysts take on fifteen to twenty companies, all of which might have banking business with their firms. They've got to be visible on JDS Uniphase, Corning, Ciena, and Tellabs, not to mention giants such as Cisco and Lucent. They're looking at complicated, quickly changing companies that must be covered in case a secondary offering or merger appears. No one has time to do detailed analysis beyond checking in with the investor-relations directors at the companies they follow. In terms of workload, they're like overworked detectives who only have time to ask the prime suspect if he's guilty. But the analysts in a volatile sector also have to deal with the fact that lots of deal making is going on, which means more pressure to say whatever it takes to get a chunk of the deal commissions.

In fact, companies are technically prevented from saying too much to their old friends. The rules go under the name Regulation FD. The FD stands for "fair disclosure," and the rules took effect on October 23, 2000. They're worth quoting at length:

> [The Securities and Exchange Commission has] become increasingly concerned about the selective disclosure of material information by issuers. As reflected in recent publicized reports, many issuers are disclosing important nonpublic information, such as advance warnings of earnings results, to securities analysts or selected institutional investors or both, before making full disclosure of the same information to the general public. Where this has happened, those who were privy to the information beforehand were able to make a profit or avoid a loss at the expense of those kept in the dark. . . . Investors who see a security's price change dramatically and only later are given access to the information responsible for that move rightly question whether they are on a level playing field with market insiders. . . . Issuer selective disclosure bears a close resemblance in this regard to ordinary "tipping" and insider trading. In both cases, a privileged few gain an informational edge — and the ability to use that edge to profit — from their superior access to corporate insiders, rather than from their skill, acumen, or diligence.

Now wait just a minute. The SEC suspects that the analysts get their info from privilege of entry rather than "skill, acumen, or diligence"? My heavens.

One more tidbit.

"Regulation FD is also designed to address another threat to the integrity of our markets: the potential for corporate management to treat material information as a commodity to be used to gain or maintain favor with particular analysts or investors."

The SEC could hardly be clearer: information that is not available to the public and can be expected to move the stock is not to be used. It's a good, fair rule and it removes a key barrier for the individual investor who's trying to scratch for info on the same terms as a Wall Street analyst. (By the way, Regulation FD in no way affects a company's communication with the press — I can pursue my reporting as aggressively as ever.)

The way it worked in pre–Reg FD days was simple. The analysts bounced their estimates off the companies, who in turn "gave guidance" about the numbers. In other words, they told the analysts to trim the expectation or add to it, usually leaving a little room to exceed the number by a couple of pennies in hopes of an earnings announcement bounce.

But anyone hoping that the Reg FD requirements may force analysts to actually start doing what their job title implies had better think again. As one hedge fund manager said to me when I asked whether Reg FD might be a force for real analysis, "It's not like they haven't been able to do real work before Reg FD, so why would they change now?"

NAIVETE/GULLIBILITY/THE FOLLY OF YOUTH

A friend of mine recently took over as chief strategist at one of the most prestigious investment banks. In that role, he visited with every one of his firm's 120 analysts, many of whom he noted are not yet shaving or menstruating. They had never seen anything but a bull market.

One woman he met covers an emerging technology area — B2B or some such — for the bank and was excited to sit down and talk. She greeted him by saying, "To understand my industry, you have to understand art." My friend, a broad-minded, liberal-arts kind of guy, was happy to hear this, thinking she might just be one of those rare analysts who had some creativity. She then proceeded to say, "In my industry, the CEOs are all like van Gogh." She believed, in other words, that every CEO she covers is a genius. My friend kindly informed her that van Gogh died a pauper in an insane asylum with one ear. She looked at him blankly and meekly answered, "I had no idea."

The difficult markets of 2000 and 2001 forced many Wall Street firms to trim their payrolls. But even when firing analysts, most of the firms are stuck paying them out on enormous guaranteed contracts. The art lover, who was barely out of college, made a million dollars in 2000. A twenty-eight-year-old who covered the discount brokerage industry for CSFB made $4 million that year. A twenty-seven-year-old analyst at Salomon Smith Barney who covers the cable television sector is receiving $7 million a year for his efforts.

3. Congenital Timidity

September 5, 2000. Ashok Kumar downgraded Intel. Although he kept his revenue and earnings estimates intact, he claimed to be worried about "demand weakness" and margins. His call and the news that followed helped take the stock from $71\frac{1}{16}$ to 41 exactly one month later. It was precisely the kind of analyst prediction that can really benefit investors.

Kumar is good at his job. He's shown some courage in making unpopular calls about important and well-supported companies, such as Intel and Dell. But we treat him as though he's an analyst god. The fact is, Kumar's only doing something that most analysts did twenty years ago. And for that, he's a hero. After his Intel downgrade, we brought him on CNBC. We congratulated him, paid our respects. But Kumar wouldn't explain why, if he was so negative, he downgraded it only to a "buy" from a "strong buy." Since the stock continued its slide (30 by year-end), wouldn't a "sell" or at least a "hold" have been more reasonable?

Look, I shouldn't complain about Kumar, because not a single analyst backed the man up. Amazingly, they lined up to take shots. Prudential's Hans Mosesman contradicted Kumar's analysis point by point. ABN Amro's David Wu turned it up a notch, accusing Kumar of a sort of reverse Blodgeting, "trying to grab some attention." He stood by his carping throughout the collapse, raising Intel to a "buy" from an "outperform." Others, such as Merrill Lynch and Credit Suisse First Boston, cut ratings, but not until October.

And that's nothing compared with the reception Salomon Smith Barney's semiconductor analyst John Joseph got when he made what was arguably the best call of 2000. In the late spring and before Kumar, Joseph became increasingly less positive on the chip sector. In the summer he became downright negative on it and the many huge companies, such as Intel, Texas Instruments, and Micron Technology, that he covered.

It was a wonderfully prescient research call from a veteran of the field who was clearly going against the prevailing sentiment. Many of the stocks in question declined the day Joseph went negative, and I reported his move on *Squawk Box*. But did investors pay heed? Some hopefully did. But in a shameless reflection of the "see no evil, hear no evil" mentality of Wall Street at the time, individual investors rushed to condemn Joseph in chat rooms and other forums. He received death threats. He was forced to pay for protection.

Let's review the price for being negative. You get cut off by covered companies, threatened by bullish money managers, glared at by your own firm's bankers, have your bonus shorn by lost banking opportunities, whaled on by colleagues at other firms, and, if you're really good, get your life threatened.

What Can I Do?

It's not all darkness. What I said at the beginning of this chapter bears repeating: analysts can be quite helpful to the individual investor even when he completely ignores their stock picks. If you're looking for the total revenue of the U.S. specialty-chemicals sector over the past five years, an analyst can tell you. Need the market share of the top five airlines? An analyst can tell you. And he can at the least give you some of the important developments to watch out for in a particular industry sector.

The fact that analysts cannot reliably predict the future doesn't mean they serve no purpose. Their research into their sectors is often the most thorough and detailed treatment available. They offer a lot of basic information, which can help you make investment decisions. Here's how they can help.

RECOGNIZE GREAT CALLS WHEN YOU SEE 'EM

There are countless examples of good calls — as Tony Soprano observes when his capos complain about Uncle Junior, even a broken clock is right twice a day. The trick is to distinguish a lucky call from one founded on signs and information.

Perhaps the most useful of all analysts are the ones least mentioned. The guy with the great call who few have heard of and nobody votes for on the all-star lists of the *Wall Street Journal* or *Institutional Investor*. Such research boutiques have begun to proliferate, but their research is not always available to the general public. On June 5, 1997, Anne K. Anderson, an analyst at tiny Atlantis Investment Co. in Parsippany, New Jersey, published a report on Oxford Health Plans. She had found discrepancies between the numbers the company was giving the public on membership and premiums. Anderson issued that rarest of all ratings: "sell." She stood alone. Fifteen of Oxford's nineteen analysts big enough to be counted by First Call rated the health-insurance giant as either a "buy" or "strong buy," with four "holds" sprinkled in for good measure. It took a while for reality to assert itself, but as is always the case, eventually it did. On October 27, Oxford plunged from 70 to 25⅞.

The point is not that this one analyst is some sort of prophet. But this particular call was the result of carefully poring over the numbers and talking to doctors who were grumbling about late payments from Oxford. Moreover, the fact that Anderson wasn't a big enough cheese to merit courtship by Oxford worked to her advantage. She asked the questions that no other analysts would, such as how Oxford could be so much better run than the other HMOs that its margins justified multiples many times the group's average. And it goes without saying that Oxford, the Tiffany HMO, wasn't doing any banking in Parsippany, New Jersey.

PAY MORE ATTENTION TO CERTAIN ANALYSTS: IGNORE OTHERS

Put more faith in analysts whose firms don't do investment banking. Even a banking firm's analyst who's not currently doing banking for a company cannot be considered totally impartial, since it's impossible to know whether he's positive only because he hopes to land some future banking business. Purer research tends to come from firms like Sanford Bernstein and, more recently, Prudential, whose analysts are good enough that the firm's investment clients will subsidize the expense.

Sanford Bernstein's Ron Mandle, for example, is the man in banking analysis. Five years ago he wrote that Chemical and Chase should get together. And they did. And on August 31, 2000, he said the same thing about J.P. Morgan and Chase, calling them a "good fit." Two weeks later it happened. He's willing to be thought-provoking, and when he talks about merger activity, one doesn't look behind the curtain for ulterior motives. Unlike a Mary Meeker, who is privately asked to validate existing merger plans, Mandle just points out deals that make sense.

Bernstein analysts still face some of the usual pressures — companies don't like to see negative things said about them and can cut off access or fall mute. But a guy like Tom Wolzien, a former TV news producer who covers media, will speak his mind. And when Steve Galbraith was at Bernstein, his books on the food industry were required reading among the sector's CEOs. Unfortunately, places without banking arms tend not to have retail arms, either, since no retail operation is needed to support the deals the bankers put together. That means that as an individual investor, you have to know someone at the firm who can send you reports from analysts at places like Bernstein.

Another thing to consider: the tendency to herd is as powerful among analysts as it is among sheep (or penguins!). That makes out-of-consensus analyst calls inherently interesting. But pay closer attention to out-of-consensus negative forecasts than positive ones. Since analysts are punished by companies for downgrades and low estimates, the analyst who's brave enough to go low deserves consideration.

NOTICE PATTERNS FOLLOWING THE MOVES OF CERTAIN ANALYSTS

Looking at an upgrade or downgrade, consider the clout of the analyst from two different perspectives. Obviously, if the analyst is widely known as someone close to the company, expect the stock to move more than it would were its rating changed by someone not well associated with the company. Rick Sherlund, the software analyst at Goldman Sachs, has been following Microsoft since his firm brought it public. When Sherlund makes a move on Microsoft, his long history with management must be accounted for. But sharper distinctions can also be drawn. Bigger firms have larger sales forces, so the pronouncement ripples more forcefully. However, the bigger firms are also less likely to say something off the beaten track, given the likelihood they either have banking business or hope to someday. There's a reason guys like Jack Grubman are well regarded for their contacts and knowledge but can barely budge stocks. It's the same reason that a positive rating from an analyst whose bank led an IPO triggers less buying than does the same rating issued by an analyst whose firm didn't participate. So don't overreact to an analyst who hasn't shown an ability to move stocks.

SPOT THE CONFLICTS WHENEVER POSSIBLE

Many analyst conflicts of interest are not knowable. You can't tell if the reason an analyst is positive is that he hopes to land future banking business. But you *can* tell if his firm does banking with the company. Since the lead banker(s) on a transaction or IPO will be listed on the prospectus that's filed with the SEC, go to EDGAR and search for the company's "plan of distribution." Deal prospectuses also list the number of shares purchased by each investment bank, sometimes beneath the "Underwriters" heading. The add-on bankers are not as easy to determine.

LOOK FOR CLUES BURIED WITHIN PRINTED REPORTS, AND NOT IN THEM AT ALL

We covered in detail why analysts feel they must maintain a positive view on the companies they cover. But the investigative investor digs deeper than the analyst's public stance, cutting through to what the analyst *really* thinks. Ideally, the investor would speak to the analyst privately, in person. That's tough to arrange even for investors with huge accounts at the analyst's firm — these guys are in high demand. If you can't get an in-person one-on-one, try to get the analyst on the phone, and if you can't do that, at least try to judge with your own ears how enthusiastic and genuine the analyst sounds on the morning calls when he discusses the company. Your broker might be able to arrange for you to listen when a stock he knows you follow is going to be discussed. Failing all else, try to judge an analyst by the way he sounds when he questions a company on their conference calls. Also remember to read deep into any analyst's report that is of interest. Although the analyst may remain positive in the report's headline, one or two sentences buried in the report can often be enough to signal that the analyst is really not positive. Look for them.

GET TO KNOW YOUR FAVORITE ANALYSTS' RATING SYSTEMS

Remember, different banks use different terms for their ratings systems. As you recognize an analyst who might be worth paying attention to, develop a feel for both the terms that his or her firm uses and the frequency with which the analyst seems to use each. Even if you don't have an account with a broker, you can call the firm's research department and ask for details on its rating system.

USE ANALYSTS AS CONTRARY INDICATORS

Legendary sports bettor Lem Banker has a nifty shortcut to picking winners. The guys on the sports page consistently come out below 50 percent. So whatever they say, do the opposite. (True, you'll need 52.3 percent to cover the juice, but you get the idea). There is no reason not to bet against an analyst you've come to suspect is wrong most of the time.

GET THE INFO:
Conference Calls

When companies make big announcements — quarterly earnings, transactions, and unusual events — they often broadcast the proceedings to investors, analysts, and journalists who cannot attend. Many of these calls are now open to the public over the phone (the company provides a number for you to call in — sometimes toll-free) or on the company's website. Happily, there are also a number of websites that stockpile and catalog calls, as well as alert you to upcoming calls. These sites include:

- www.vcall.com
- www.broadcast.com
- www.ccbn.com

This often works not just for a single analyst but with clumps of analysts.

On Thursday, August 31, 2000, four firms downgraded shares of The Gap — Salomon Smith Barney, PaineWebber, CSFB, and BancAmerica. They did so on Wednesday's closing price: $25.44.

As is often the case, the downgrade wasn't exactly prescient: The Gap had been having obvious problems for months. Weeks earlier, for example, the company reported logistical problems at its Old Navy unit and said sales would fail to meet expectations. But the analysts had kept their "buy" rating as the stock slid from the year's high of $54.

This for a company that is the easiest to research. In Manhattan, not far from any of these analysts' offices, are literally hundreds of Gap outlets, not to mention plenty of Banana Republics and Old Navys. An hour observing customer traffic, speaking with store managers, and watching what sold and what didn't could have offered numerous clues as to whether the company was going to fall further or start to improve.

I guess they're too busy to take a walk.

On the day of the downgrade, I sent an e-mail to my co-writer: "We should remember this price — $21." That's where The Gap fell to on Thursday on the early post-downgrade trades. My feeling was that the analysts marked at least a short-term bottom. I don't promote myself as a stock picker. But that time I was right. When the analysts finally said sell, The Gap started rising, and it rose for the next nine months, during which many of the analysts who had downgraded it began to upgrade the shares. Once they all agreed that The Gap was a good deal, the stock started slipping again. During the summer of 2001, The Gap's numbers showed no improvement, and the stock sank to new lows. And guess what: the analyst downgrades followed.

Lesson and reminders
- Check for banking relationships, particularly as lead underwriter or mergers-and-acquisitions adviser, when considering an analyst's opinion.

- Favor analysts' calls from firms with no banking business.
- Ignore whether or not analysts own shares in a particular company.
- Give less credence to positive calls, more credence to negative calls.
- Ignore ratings. Read deep into research reports to find details of analysts' actual thoughts. Check for increases or decreases in earnings estimates. Note the direction of the rating change.
- Use mass upgrades and downgrades as a contrary indicator.
- Keep track of analysts' previous opinions and use their good or bad track records to help you in deciding to go long or short stock.

4

THE TRUTH ABOUT YOUR BROKER

The retail broker is hard to kill. Like Indiana Jones or James Bond, he's been written off as dead time and again, only to return and thrive. The last greatly exaggerated report of the retail broker's death came at the end of 1999. That's when the nation's largest brokerage house, Merrill Lynch, reversed a long-standing policy and allowed clients to trade cheaply and online. If Merrill was willing to cut out its own brokers, the firm's lifeblood, certainly this had to be the true end of the full-service broker.

But less than three months later the Nasdaq began its long, frightful fall from 5000, and the S&P began its brutal slide. Investing got a lot tougher and not nearly as much fun. And although their overall business got hurt, retail brokers once again became relevant.

Before the year 2000 was over, that relevance would be underscored. PaineWebber would be sold for more than $10 billion to UBS Warburg. UBS paid a rich premium for the right to control a brokerage force that was nine thousand strong. In capturing this so-called distribution, UBS was simply following the lead of Morgan Stanley and Travelers, which years earlier had also seized on retail brokerage operations as a key to growing their profits. Clearly, the retail broker, with an ability to sell dozens of products to millions of clients, is valuable. And that value derives from one thing: a relationship with investors.

For you, the decision to become part of that vast "distribution" and make a full-service brokerage the hub of your financial life presents both an opportunity and a risk. The opportunity comes from the convenience and smarts you can access when you hook up with a broker who understands your needs and will fight for your portfolio. The risk? These guys often prove less savvy than the investors who are entrusting them with their money.

I have covered the big brokerage firms — the full-service firms, the experienced discounters, and the new online brokerages — enough to give you some tips about how they work, how you can take advantage of their services, and, most important, how to keep them from taking advantage of you.

The Three Species of Brokerages

In the beginning, old-time retail brokers — Merrill Lynch, PaineWebber, Smith Barney, and defunct firms such as E.F. Hutton and Kidder, Peabody — had their commissions fixed by the SEC. Because firms could not compete on price, there was no such thing as a "discount broker." The firms marketed similar services and tried to distinguish themselves on the basis of their research (can you imagine?) and their probity.

Marketmaker A middleman between buyers and sellers of Nasdaq stocks. On exchanges with physical trading floors, such as the New York Stock Exchange (NYSE), this function is performed by a "specialist" who stands in the trading pit and matches the orders of buyers and sellers. Marketmakers can be retail brokerage firms — such as Merrill Lynch or Charles Schwab — or firms that exist solely to match up buy and sell orders. Knight Securities is the largest such public company.

May 1, 1975, will forever be known in the brokerage business as May Day, the day the SEC ended the practice of fixed commissions. The goal was to encourage price competition, which indeed occurred for institutional stock trades. But for retail customers, most firms actually increased commissions. Charles Schwab and a few other mavericks saw an opportunity. They slashed trading costs, leading to the birth of the discount brokerage industry. The discount brokers competed with the full-service brokers on price, claiming that a broker can't do much more for you than execute trades. Full-service brokers struck back by claiming that they provided valuable services to investors.

Their marketing was also a key. Merrill Lynch proclaimed itself "bullish on America," a nice sentiment for sure, but somewhat anachronistic given its use during the brutal bear market that prevailed through much of the seventies. (Not the first disconnect at Merrill; my partner Joe Kernen has lambasted the bearishness of the firm's strategists through much of the nineties bull market.) E.F. Hutton pushed its stock-picking prowess with the famous phrase "when E.F. Hutton talks, people listen." Meanwhile Smith Barney stressed its industriousness using the power of John Houseman's now famous intonation: "At Smith Barney, we make money the old-fashioned way: we earn it."

With the development of trading on the Internet, there are now three types of brokers: full service, discount, and deep discount. Full-service firms charge plenty for their services (though much less than even a couple of years ago) and offer such things as proprietary research (as you know, I recommend that you accept this "service" with a fair amount of skepticism) and money-management services, which can range from analyzing portfolio diversity and risk tolerance to serving as an intermediary between the client and professional money managers.

The discount brokerages are firms such as Charles Schwab, Fidelity, and Quick & Reilly. Commissions are less, but these companies also trade on name recognition and trust. Consequently, they feel they can charge a little more than rock-bottom prices, and they have to offer some services, both to justify the price and live up to the marketing. They may not have in-house analysts, but they cut deals with other firms to make research available. They also have physical branches, so you can do in-person tasks in a more hands-on environment: opening an account, depositing funds, dealing with customer-service issues. They try to provide some advisory services, such as giving you an opportunity to define your investment goals and allocate your portfolio, and offer products beyond stocks. Fidelity, for example, is all about mutual funds, and Schwab's acquisition of white-shoe U.S. Trust gave the discounter entrée into the lucrative arena of high-end private banking.

Ameritrade and E*Trade are two of the deep-discount brokers. You log on, make your trades, and pay a paltry five or ten dollars in commissions. To compete with one another and the discount brokers (along with the encroachments of the full-service brokerage firms that made a mad dash into online trading), the deep discounters have tried to dress up their web sites. They now provide some data — Value Line or Standard & Poor's summary reports on companies — and offer automated "advice" on portfolio allocation. But basically they're there just to process trades.

Which Kind of Broker Is Best?

I wouldn't be writing this book and you wouldn't be reading it if you wanted a full-service stockbroker to make all your investment decisions. The increasing availability of corporate information, along with the growth in media outlets to help people make sense of that information, has made the investing world seem less alien to the individual investor. Prosperity, individual retirement accounts, and books like this one provide investors with both the means and the need to exert more control over their investments. But that does not mean you should dismiss a retail broker out of hand.

Amazing as it might seem, retail brokers can provide a value that exceeds their commissions and fees. It isn't from giving good stock-picking advice. The best broker is the one who keeps you from failing rather than makes you a success. As seductive as it may seem to pick someone because he gave a friend a hot tip that rode from $5 to $50, you will end up poorer if you select a broker that way. After all, the gap between what you know and what a broker knows about companies has disappeared to almost nothing, and if you've read most of this book, chances are that you know more than the average broker. Every SEC filing is online. Just about every conflict is readily apparent. While it might seem sexier to have a pal on the "inside" calling you with sure-fire advice, those guys are usually wrong more than right.

No one would call a broker a hero if he kept you diversified in 2000 and you lost 5–10 percent. But with the S&P down 12 percent, tech portfolios down much more, and dot-com and telecom stocks down 90 percent or out of business, a 5–10 percent loss is terrific. You've got that much more cash to invest if and hopefully when the market's riding back up. Any broker who did that for you, allowing you to keep some of those gains from 1995 to 1999 (when the S&P 500 went from 460 to 1400, the Dow Industrials went from 3900 to 11500, and the Nasdaq went from 750 to 4000), earned his keep. Even if you make all your own investment decisions, you can benefit from a broker who provides a sounding board on such things as asset allocation and risk tolerance and makes available (without cramming down your throat) the full range of products his firm offers.

Your best course is to consider taking advantage of both kinds of brokers. Be informed enough about your investments to make your own decisions. By all means save money on your trades — but keep in mind that even the deep discounters can blindside you with hidden costs. If you can park some money in a full-service account, you can get the benefits of a broker: advice on allocation and risk, access to research, access to certain financial products. Again, you have to keep an eye out for abuses, but if you commit some resources to both kinds of firms, hear everybody out but make your own decisions, you can save money and make smart decisions.

Only you can judge just how much TLC you need from a broker, but make sure you get the amount you're paying for: a full-service broker who doesn't return your calls certainly isn't worth the extra commissions. Conversely, if you don't want to spend tons of your own time and money on research and other things, you may be better off with a full-service firm. I can't tell you which kind of broker to choose. But I've spent enough time with executives in the brokerage industry and seen enough of its shortcomings that I can tell you some things to look for and some things to avoid.

How the Brokerage Business Works

Like the rest of Wall Street, the brokerage business is about selling. You make transactions — stocks, bonds, mutual funds, options, insurance — and the brokerage firm makes money facilitating those transactions. Actually, it can profit twice: by charging a commission for conducting the transaction, and by making money on the transaction itself — for example, by selling you shares of a stock you want from its own supply, rather than buying them for you on the open market. The possibilities for conflicts of interest are limitless, but the brokerage firms are getting better at giving their customers a fair shake. The best individual brokers hold their firms at arm's length and try to protect their customers from such conflicts.

Brokers are the foot soldiers of the firms, and are their most visible representatives, so the big firms take some care in selecting them. Once a brokerage hires you, you study for the Series 7 exam, administered by the National Association of Securities Dealers (NASD). The six-hour, three-hundred-question test requires a 70 percent to pass and focuses on product knowledge, securities law, and math — essentially, a bar exam for brokers. If you fail, you can usually count on the brokerage firm giving you the boot.

Once the broker passes, he is considered a "registered rep" and can legally transact securities business. At this point, the firm conducts its in-house training. The big brokerage firms conduct three to four weeks of training at a home office or training center. The training focuses on teaching the new reps about all the products the company sells or trades — unit trusts, municipal bonds, mutual funds, insurance, estate planning, and money management.

The brokerage business is still largely a commission-driven business. Typically, a broker in his first two years is paid a salary along with commissions, the firm providing some time for him to train, develop some expertise, and build a client base. After that, it's pure commissions. The split varies somewhat at different firms and changes after certain thresholds are met, but generally it breaks down to the broker keeping 40 percent of the commissions generated, and the firm taking the remaining 60 percent. This is a vital revenue stream for the firms, and they make a nice profit on their retail business.

Although most brokers have a range of clients, many end up focused on a certain level of the economic ladder. Some brokers concentrate almost solely on high-end clients — very wealthy individuals or families for whom they provide a variety of services. This is a very lucrative business, and many firms not associated with retail brokerage (such as Goldman Sachs) have established units to deal with the brokerage needs of the ultrarich. (Goldman calls its unit "private client services.") Morgan Stanley and other firms more closely associated with investment banking have similar units.

Because the commission business fluctuates widely, many firms are focused on making their brokers pure asset gatherers in hopes of creating a very predictable stream of revenue. In this scenario, the broker's role is not to buy and sell stocks for the clients but to help direct them to various asset managers employed by the firm. Fee-based services have the potential to keep you and the broker on the same side of the transaction, since he's less inclined to make a trade simply to generate a commission. But because these brokers are searching solely for money, rather than active clients, they tend to focus on people who have a lot of it. And keep in mind that under this arrangement you are still turning over some decision-making power to the broker. If he is recommending a professional money manager, then you are relying not on the broker's stock-picking ability but on his judgment in recommending the money manager who makes the decisions. In such a case, get the money manager's audited results — and make sure you get them over a long period; everyone looked like a genius from 1995 to 1999. Also make sure you understand the money manager's portfolio. If you want someone who is picking among the Dow components, pass if the manager's forte is trading mortgage and treasury derivatives. More on that in the next chapter. (Naturally, it also works in reverse.) If you already have a big-cap mutual fund, you might want a money manager who invests primarily in mid caps, not a guy who prides himself on his judgment of Merck versus Pfizer or Citigroup versus J.P. Morgan Chase. If your broker is recommending the wrong kind of money manager, then maybe you have the wrong broker.

Asset-management fees are negotiable, so don't automatically agree to the stated fee. Fees range from an annual charge of 1–3 percent of assets under management. The larger the account, the lower the percentage you ought to pay, and the greater negotiating leverage you have. Just as with asking a pit boss for comps in Las Vegas, you never know until you ask, and the worst thing that can happen is you'll find out you aren't as high a roller as you thought.

In fact, most aspects of the broker-customer relationship are negotiable. If you've stuck with a broker for a long time and he's not doing much more than processing trades, ask him for a break on the commissions. He's generally allowed by his firm to cut a discount, and if he thinks you will bolt for an online broker, he might cut his own share of the commission to keep the account. Believe it or not, brokers are usually unhappy when their customers lose money. If you are taking a beating, ask the broker for a break on commissions or money-management fees or any other fees you are paying. If you are not offended by a rejection and aren't unreasonable, you have nothing to lose.

Within many investment banks you'll also find brokers who focus largely on an institutional audience. These brokers are not to be confused with institutional salesmen, the guys who call the big mutual funds and hedge funds each morning to relay the research call from their respective firms. These guys are true brokers, but they typically perform their own detailed research and very often focus on recommending short sales to hedge fund managers. These guys can be huge producers at their firms, given the size of the orders they can generate from a strong investment idea. They can also very often be at odds with the firm's own research department, since many of their short ideas grow out of work they do on some of the very stocks that their firm is recommending.

The brokerage firms, in addition to trading common stocks and other publicly available issues, offer a range of services. In fact, the gigantic consolidation of the financial-services industry occurred so that the companies involved could vertically expand their product offerings. For example, Citigroup now encompasses Smith Barney's retail operations, Salomon's trading and bond expertise, Travelers' insurance products, and Citibank's banking and credit business. Meanwhile, each division's customers increase the number of people to whom products from the other divisions can be sold.

A lot of this cross-selling is beneficial to consumers. It's simple economy of scale: a company that's already spent a lot to get you as a customer of its brokerage doesn't have to spend quite as much to tell you about its life-insurance products or to re-enter your data on a mortgage application. Hopefully, some of those savings are passed along to you.

But what about products you don't really need? There have been numerous well-documented instances of conflicts of interest, overreaching, and just plain fraud by firms unloading their institutional clients' garbage on retail clients or larding transactions with so many fees and costs that only the brokerage firm makes money. Lawsuits and bad publicity have improved things, but you can count on these firms to be ingenious in pushing the envelope. I can tell you ways to protect yourself from such investments, but the best protection is understanding that this is one of the ways brokerage firms make their money.

How to Pick a Broker

You wouldn't hire a doctor or lawyer without scrutinizing credentials and demanding recommendations. So don't entrust your investment portfolio to someone you barely know.

One of the strange things about the brokerage business is the way in which brokers market themselves. When they're just starting out, brokers troll for customers by holding seminars at community gatherings — "Learn About the New Tax Changes" at a town breakfast, or "Will You Have Enough to Retire?" at the local college. These can be helpful, but the reality is that any broker hosting such an affair is either very green or not so good at his job. And unless you are the sort of person who would accept a marriage proposal from a stranger over the phone, don't listen to the nonsense peddled by some cold-calling broker.

So how do you find a broker who's both honest and smart?

INTEGRITY

Securities brokers are required to belong to the National Association of Securities Dealers, which keeps tabs in its Central Registration Depository (CRD). Before you send a check to some sweet-talking smoothie, ask him for both his own and his firm's CRD numbers. Any broker worth your time will know both and will be forthcoming with them. Then contact the NASD — easy, via their toll-free number (800–289-9999) or web site (www.nasdr. com) — and get the "rap sheet," which shows where the broker has worked and for how long. More important, the CRD contains any "disclosable information," such as disciplinary action taken by self-regulating agencies (e.g., the NYSE and NASD), the results and circumstances of any judgments (including arbitrations), and criminal convictions or indictments against the broker and/or his firm.

Brokers are often hit by spurious lawsuits or charges, so if you do see an infraction, you shouldn't necessarily be dissuaded. Ask the broker about it; his being honest and forthcoming with information can be a sign that he'll be honest and forthcoming in conducting your business. If, however, you see a rap sheet littered with infractions, run for the hills.

One story shows how thorny a broker's past can be. Chelsea Street Securities, Inc., was an Irving, Texas, brokerage started in 1990 by former Arizona State track star and world-class discus thrower Gary S. Williky, whose athletic career came to a conclusion after he tested positive for anabolic steroids in 1985. Chelsea's bread and butter were thinly traded penny stocks. In the fall of 1994 the SEC sued Williky for violating securities laws, including lying to investors about the prospects of the stocks Chelsea peddled and manipulating their prices. Williky cut a deal with the NASD to leave the securities business for two years and pay part of a $25,000 fine. Among the flashier elements of the firm's dissolution were a Chelsea officer punching a stockbroker who worked for him and a lawsuit by Milton Berle, who alleged that one of Chelsea's penny-stock companies owed him $100,000.

After Chelsea shut its doors for good in 1993, Williky was hired by Reynolds Kendrick Stratton (RKS) in Beverly Hills, which soon ran into troubles of its own when the firm aggressively promoted the stock of a company in which many of Reynolds Kendrick Stratton's board members were investors. In 1994 RKS changed its name, its strategy, and its board of directors. Redubbed JB Oxford, the discount brokerage cleaned up its act and joined the ranks of good corporate citizens (and CNBC advertisers!) shortly thereafter.

A clean CRD is a good sign but doesn't always prove that the broker is kosher. Careful investors should also check the broker's home-state securities office. Sometimes these agencies offer information that you don't find on the CRDs, such as personal bankruptcies or liens.

That figured prominently in one case I remember from 1996. A guy's "full-service" broker at a Long Island firm called Corporate Securities Group Inc. recommended a local company called Health Management Inc., which was trading at $14. He suggested placing a stop-loss order at $11, meaning that a sell would be automatically triggered if the stock slipped to $11, which would prevent a margin call that would happen at $8 or so. The guy bought 1,500 shares. He didn't hear from the broker for a couple of months, until a frantic call saying that the stock was at $3 and that he needed to send $7,700 immediately to satisfy the margin requirement.

As the devastated investor learned, it is not possible to place a stop-loss on a stock that trades on the Nasdaq. Not that the broker had told him that, of course. Many brokers offer to "keep an eye" on a stock and to call a client if it dips below the target. Proving that the broker offered such a thing is no easy task, though. Although brokerages claim to record their brokers' conversations with clients, my experience is that those tapes surface only when they confirm a broker's version of events.

There have been periodic movements to include more information on the CRDs, such as pending customer complaints, regulatory investigations, and employment termination under fishy circumstances. But for now the brokers have fought this stuff, so, again, don't take a lack of negatives as proof positive.

You can contact the NASD at 1735 K Street, NW, Washington, D.C., 20006-1506. Its toll-free number is (800) 289-9999, and its web site is at www.nasdr.com. To find out information about your state securities regulator, contact the North American Securities Administrators Association, 1 Massachusetts Avenue, NW, Suite 310, Washington, D.C., 20001. Its phone number is (202) 737-0900. It usually takes about five to ten days for the NASD to respond to telephone requests and only a day or so for Internet requests. Don't commit to a broker before you know anything about him, even if he says his hot tip won't keep.

The major firms have no monopoly on ethics and employ plenty of sleazebags, but smaller shops deserve even closer scrutiny. Their brokers can often be guys whom the big firms have either kicked out or wouldn't hire. It's tough enough getting comfortable with an individual broker without having to worry that the entire operation is geared toward separating you from your money.

Notorious penny-stock operators such as Blinder Robinson (known in the trade as "Blind 'em and rob 'em") and First Jersey Securities (run by notorious felon Robert E. Brennan) would rack up complaints, then simply shut down. The brokers, however, and even sometimes some of the principals would simply hang out a new shingle with a new name and begin the fresh hunt for suckers. Brennan showed up with Hibbard Brown in one of his many encores. The nasty firm of Stratton Oakmont was expelled from the NASD in December 1996, but it wasn't until June 1998 that thirteen of the principals were finally barred from the securities industry. You can bet that in the intervening eighteen months these swindlers were busy working at other lowlife brokerage firms. One of my favorite bucket shops was a firm called AS Goldmen, so named for founders Anthony and Salvatore Marchiano, who were going to be "gold men." Marchiano cut his teeth at one of the true models of thievery, D.H. Blair, before moving on to start Goldmen. His plan, however, was put on hold by multiple fraud allegations. Meanwhile, the firm's former CFO was convicted of plotting to murder the judge hearing one of the fraud cases.

BRAINS AND PERFORMANCE

A broker whose greatest attribute is that he's not trying to rob you blind doesn't quite deserve the job. Beyond honesty and customer service, you need someone who knows what he's talking about, and there is no sure-fire way to determine that. As with any professional, a good way to identify a good broker is recommendations from people you trust. But you must do more than ask — you must listen carefully to the basis of the recommendation. Too often people tell you about some great tip the broker supplied, something that has nothing to do with trustworthiness, honesty, or integrity. The ideal situation is not to hear stories about how the broker was way out in front on Yahoo! or EMC. Better to learn how the broker helped protect the client, keeping the investments stable and diverse, not exposing the portfolio to undue risk.

Failing to ask the right questions can really hurt. Consider this: in 1999 a forty-five-year-old software salesman at Microsoft put his entire investment and retirement portfolios — about $700,000 — into the hands of a couple of brokers at Morgan Stanley. By late 2001 he was down to $400 — and faced a $40,000 tax bill! The reason he picked those particular brokers? More than a dozen of his colleagues at Microsoft used the same guys (and most of them are broke or nearly so, too). Again, while asking people you trust for their advice on a broker is smart, don't stop there.

Focus on the broker's advice, not the client's returns. One broker I know of described a situation in which a client started investing in Cisco in 1995 and made a huge amount of money. He ran his account from $100,000 to $3 million with very little additional investment. In 1999, as the stock price hit $40, $50, $60, the broker said, "Why not take some profits, take a little money off the table?" The client ignored him; when Cisco started dropping, the client insisted on buying more, on margin. Today, the client's account is worth about $300,000. If you looked only at that client's financial returns, the broker's good advice is invisible.

Second, ask the broker about his own investing. I do not in any way recommend that you give a broker discretion to make investment decisions without your approval. But if this is a course you choose, then you should demand to see his personal trading records. A broker has them and if he won't part with those records, you should not give him discretion.

Even if you do not grant a broker any discretion, you must still have a detailed conversation in which he lays out his investing philosophy. What does he invest in? How has he done? What was the state of his portfolio when the Nasdaq tanked in the spring of 2000? Don't expect him to be a clairvoyant, but if he had his personal portfolio in Internet and tech stocks, he could hardly be expected to be the voice of reason when you stray from the path.

Third, take stories about hot stock tips with a grain of salt. Especially with the state of investing information today, brokers are in no better position than you to pick a good stock. One stock, one time, does not make a great adviser. I shall delve into the subject in more detail in chapter 6, but it's worth a word or two on brokers and rumors.

If your broker or a broker tries to get you to buy a stock based on a rumor, ask him how he came to be aware of this rumor. It's the simplest of questions but often goes unasked. In most cases, a retail broker is the end of the line for the rumor mill. Once it's been spun by an institution, played out by a trader, and worked its way across most of Wall Street, a broker may pick it up. And by then it is of little use to you. If your broker tells you he heard it from the trading desk or fails to tell you how it came to him, you probably should pass on the trade.

There are brokers who can put you on to profitable trading rumors. Usually they have a good sprinkling of senior management at various public companies among their clients. And when you ask them that key question, you get a different answer. If they tell you that one of their clients is buying options in the particular company and he was the college roommate of that company's CEO, that may be just the kind of rumor worth taking a shot on.

In addition to brokers who tend to focus on an institutional audience, so-called institutional brokers, there is also a class of brokers out there I call the "fast-money guys." Fast-money brokers deal in rumors. They try to have as many well-placed management types as possible among their client base for easy access to useful information. They know what all the brokers in their office are up to. They are very conversant with options. They make a lot of trades, and if they are good and stay out of jail, they can make you some money. You won't want to give a large percentage of your savings to a fast-money guy, but if you come across one, he can certainly keep things lively. Again, even with a fast-money broker, every trade should be cleared first.

INDEPENDENCE

A good broker can protect you from his firm. A bad broker can victimize you with an array of his company's schemes to sell you its products. How can you tell which is which?

An interesting phenomenon of the brokerage business revolves around who actually "owns" the customer: the broker or the firm. Whenever a broker leaves a firm, a whole series of contretemps is unleashed. The instant the firm hears of the impending departure, it tries to lock the guy out — literally. Other brokers from the firm divvy up the Rolodex and immediately begin calling the guy's clients. "This is Gary from Big Firm X. You may have heard that Joe Smith is no longer working for us — not quite sure why, but there's talk of a drinking problem and photos of farm animals in lingerie. So I'd like to offer you half-price commissions and free checking if you'll let me keep your account here at Big Firm X." No, that's not an exaggeration.

Meanwhile, the broker, who's landed at Big Firm Y, is certain to have duplicated his Rolodex. (It's not unheard-of for brokers to list fake numbers and contact names on their workplace Rolodexes, in preparation for a forthcoming exit.) From his new window office at Big Firm Y, he gets his clients on the phone. "Hey, big guy, your buddy Joe Smith here. I'm not at Big Firm X anymore — was hearing rumblings of SEC investigations and stuff. But all is rosy at Big Firm Y, and if you follow me here, I'll give you half-price commissions and free checking."

The fact is, the broker almost always wins this battle. Departing superstar brokers have been known to retain 90 percent of their clients, which proves that the relationship is much more important to investors than are the products or services a firm can offer. In effect, the account belongs to the broker, not the gigantic firm listed on his business card. So talk with the broker before you commit, and pay more attention to his style and trustworthiness than to his sales pitch about his firm's offerings. The broker's level of experience is relevant, too. Generally, the young brokers are more willing to believe the company line about how every single product it sells is great for the client or are desperate for the commissions and brownie points that come with selling in-house products.

One broker I know has been in the business for nearly twenty years, working with major firms such as E.F. Hutton, Shearson, Prudential, and Morgan Stanley Dean Witter. All the firms offered in-house limited partnerships and investment instruments, but he hasn't sold any since his days as a young Hutton broker. Why? "When I realized that the clients never seemed to make money, I stopped pushing them. Now I just ignore all the promotional materials the firm sends me."

Incidentally, getting a broker who has moved around is not automatically a bad thing. Investigate whether the broker was forced out for disciplinary reasons, of course, but his transience may actually indicate a broker who considers himself a free agent. That could be the kind of broker you want, one who takes his clients from firm to firm, more concerned with keeping them happy than sticking up for the firm to the clients' detriment.

You can simply ask about these things. If, for example, you ask about access to the company's research, you can get two kinds of answers:

A. "Opening an account with me will give you access to the best research on Wall Street."

B. "I'll send you whatever you want, but I have to tell you that most of these kids wouldn't know their ass from their elbow."

It should be obvious that I would recommend Broker B, though not for the reasons you would expect. I think Broker A has some problems understanding reality, but I wouldn't condemn him for that reason alone. The problem is that Broker A is obviously married to the firm or is giving you the hard sell. Broker B seems willing to risk muddying up a sales pitch by expressing some cynicism. That's exactly what you need in a broker. Ace Greenberg, chairman emeritus of Bear Stearns, was testifying at a trial in Delaware many years ago when the chancellor interrupted him and said, "You sound somewhat cynical, Mr. Greenberg." He replied, "I wasn't born that way." Take the cynical veteran when you can get him. But also keep in mind that simply because a broker is old doesn't mean he is smart.

You can also ask about the firm's in-house products. Or see how eager the broker is to bring them up and tout them. As with analysts, some may be good and some may be bad, but beware of the broker who is too enamored of the company line.

And speaking of being enamored: watch out for brokers who seem especially close to one company and its management. Retail brokers, along with many people on Wall Street, like to feel important. Nothing can get those feelings flowing faster than an opportunity to tell some other Wall Street guy, "I control seven percent of that company." And you would be surprised at just how often that is the case. Numerous brokers control accounts whose total assets climb well into the hundreds of millions. A broker who has the trust of his clients can often rally them to buy what amounts to a large position in a small- to midsize company. Although technically the ownership is controlled by each of those individuals, the broker who oversees their accounts is suddenly a big man with the company in question. Managements know this and on occasion seek out a broker who they believe could fall victim to their charms. Management treats the broker as it would a large institutional investor, complete with dinners, off-the-record phone calls, and golf games. Brokers don't often get treated to such attention and are often not experienced in dealing with upper management in a skeptical manner. They hang in there despite what might be bad signs.

A close friend suffered such a fate when her broker put her in shares of the HMO WellCare. The broker boasted of being close to management and said he was putting many of his clients in the shares. My friend invested $10,000, a large percentage of her net worth at the time, when the stock was in the low 20s. The stock moved into the high 30s a year later, and she asked the broker if it wasn't time to sell. He said no; "this is a fifty-dollar stock."

Not long after that, *Barron's* wrote a negative piece on Well-Care, questioning the company's accounting. The stock fell sharply. My friend called her broker and asked whether she should sell the stock. The broker, citing his ties to management, said he knew the company well and suggested she buy more stock, not sell. Luckily she didn't do that, but she didn't sell, either. WellCare eventually went bankrupt. She was wiped out.

How a Broker Can Hurt You

A broker can hurt you in two ways: by giving bad advice and by making bad investments. They're not the same thing. And if you let either occur, you have only yourself to blame, because you'll

WHERE CLASS ACTIONS COME FROM

I'm fascinated by the phenomenon of securities class-action suits. While part of me thinks they're antibusiness extortion by greedy lawyers and irresponsible investors, another part says they're a necessary check on the unbridled promises and self-dealing of corporate executives. Take Bill Lerach, for example. The king of class action is so despised by the tech community for his firm's tendency to sue just about everyone that *Wired* magazine ran a screed against him headlined BLOODSUCKING SCUMBAG. On the other hand, plenty of the 263 companies his firm, Milberg Weiss, is suing as of this writing have indeed turned out to be disasters or outright frauds: AremisSoft, Aurora Foods, eToys, and Sagent. (Sprint, Nike, and Coca-Cola also make the list.)

I asked one of my sources, a class-action lawyer, where the clients come from in securities cases. It turns out that it's all from relationships with stockbrokers. When the lawyer sniffs out a juicy case, he phones his broker contacts and asks if any of the guy's clients were holding XYZ between Date A and Date B. Since the Private Securities Law Reform Act of 1995, which requires that the plaintiff with the largest loss be "lead plaintiff," the lawyers have spent some time cozying up to institutional investors, but retail brokers are still key. The brokers don't cooperate out of the goodness of their little hearts. In exchange for the referrals, ball-game tickets, weekend trips, stays at fancy hotels, and other bribes are de rigueur. My source told me about one broker who was reluctant to cough up the name of a client in what was promising to be a lucrative class-action suit. The broker, who was from Detroit, indicated that he could be persuaded if my source could come up with a ticket to the Pistons-Bulls playoffs in Chicago, where he'd "never seen a game," the poor dear. My source frantically called all the scalpers in the sports-mad Windy City, finally landing a pair of decent seats for $2,000. The broker came down from Detroit, picked up the tickets, and then got pinched trying to scalp the seats outside the stadium and spent the game in a Cook County jail. The beauty of it was that he then needed the source to go to court for him to beat the scalping charge, which solidified the relationship and turned the reluctant broker into one of this lawyer's most reliable lead generators.

be able to see it coming. The scandalous practices of the big-time brokerage firms over the past twenty years are well known, and we are long past the time when a broker was considered a beneficent expert. Back in the sixties some firms referred to brokers as "investors' men." That's awfully close to "company men." A company man works for the company, not you.

Brokers are frequently in a bind. They provide a service, and benefit by keeping you satisfied. But their firm provides them support, prestige, a phone and desk, and — sometimes — incentive to do its bidding, to your detriment.

IN-HOUSE PRODUCTS

Every era has its scam, an investment idea that once made sense in a certain context but when applied on a mass scale to retail investors is merely a cash grab for the brokerage firm. In the eighties it was the in-house limited partnership. Most of the big firms sold them, but Prudential was the most notorious. It created more than seven hundred land and energy limited partnerships, raising $8 billion. At one time, 40 percent of Pru's retail customers owned at least one.

These investments were generally terrible. They were loaded with fees and commissions. The firm offered inducements and threats to make sure brokers pushed them on customers. The underlying assets of the partnerships were frequently acquired in non-arm's-length transactions in which Pru or one of its clients was a seller. So, after a big hunk of the investment went to pay commissions and overpay for the assets, many of the partnerships had as a general partner some Prudential-related entity or a client of the firm. This led to a continuing income stream — management fees, insurance costs, and other fees — for the general partner. Although Prudential generally denied wrongdoing, it paid hundreds of millions in settlements, fines, and legal fees to resolve the matter and was the subject of SEC and criminal investigations. Most of the owners of those limited-partnership interests ditched the firm, along with many brokers who were disgusted with the firm's sales practices. Some brokers even sued Prudential, claiming its strong-arm tactics in selling these lousy investments cost the brokers customers when the partnerships fell apart.

Prudential was far from alone. Many of the big brokerage houses peddled similar partnerships or created securities from underlying assets their institutional clients wouldn't touch. Back in the eighties Drexel packaged its most toxic junk bonds — the stuff Michael Milken couldn't get even his captive buyers to take — and marketed them as "high income trust securities" (HITS). The owners of these bonds found themselves standing in a very long line at bankruptcy court, divvying up what was left of the companies that issued them.

Limited partnerships may have gone the way of Drexel, but Wall Street's attempts to seize the flavor of the moment and force it on naive retail clients live on. The problem is that by the time the brokerage firms figure out what's hot and get around to creating a product to capitalize on that sentiment, they're usually too late. When the Street started floating the latest in dot-com- and telecom-related funds, the coming catastrophe for both sectors was dangerously close. (Retail clients would have benefited from funds that could short stocks of dot-com and telecom companies or funds that could buy the distressed-debt securities of selected telecom companies. Unfortunately, if the Street ever gets around to offering such vehicles, you can bet the telecom debacle will have ended.)

In late 1998 and 1999 some of the venture-capital firms that developed high profiles during the dot-com boom were starting to market venture-capital funds for retail investors. These efforts barely broke ground before the dot-com stocks fell apart, but had the boom gone on any longer, you definitely would have seen brokerage firms offering a chance to invest alongside the best brains in the sexy world of venture-capital investment. I don't think I'm speculating when I say that investors would have had to cough up big fees for this opportunity and been stuck with the leftovers that the general partner and/or adviser (the brokerage firm and a venture-capital outfit) didn't want to own themselves.

It may have been venture capital in the late 1990s, but at other times it's other things. Hollywood has always been hot. A number of years back Shearson Lehman Hutton, now scattered with the wind, and a few other firms marketed a series of limited partnerships from Disney called Silver Screen Partners. For $5,000, you could invest in financing a motion picture, just like the moguls. At one time more people owned Silver Screen limited partnerships than Disney common stock. The whole thing was designed so that Disney could finance its films on the cheap. If the films lost money, it charged enough in fees that you were left holding the bag. And if some of the films were hits, Disney still got all those management fees and also positioned itself first in line to get the box-office proceeds. Disney had enough money-makers that no one got burned too badly, but investors would have been much better off just buying Disney stock.

There are a number of things to keep in mind before taking a plunge into one of Wall Street's witches' brew. Many of these instruments are terribly illiquid (think roach motel). Don't buy in unless you're prepared to stay in for a very long time. Another important consideration: know who all the other parties are to the financial instrument. Know for a certainty how much the broker makes, and how much the firm makes, from selling you the investment. Stay away from anything with a legal or tax structure you don't understand or aren't willing to hire your own professionals to evaluate.

And, finally, don't buy without reading the prospectus. All these investments require you to sign a statement saying you have read and understand the prospectus. Beware of the broker who hands you the form at the same time as the prospectus and says, "Just sign this; it's a formality." The prospectuses for these investments are nightmares, but at least they are usually honest, since the seller uses the fact that he disclosed the crazy risks as a defense. These kinds of limited partnerships can exist only because *no one reads a prospectus!*

In the eighties a very hot Chicago real estate company, Van Kampen-Merritt-Stone (VMS), had brokerage firms selling limited partnerships in its realty properties. In essence, VMS was the principals' attempt to sell all these properties to retail investors and maintain lucrative management, lending, and insurance contracts. The prospectus was typical — filled with a lot of hard-to-follow mumbo jumbo. Still, they pretty much admitted that not only were they the sellers of the properties to the limited partnership but also, as general partners, they would be collecting management fees. Furthermore, just about every service the partnerships would need — insurance, property management, appraisal, financing — would be provided by some entity related to VMS or a participating brokerage firm.

A class-action lawyer I know initially refused to file a securities fraud case against VMS — a surprise considering that securities lawyers aren't exactly reluctant to sue, especially when major losses have occurred. "They disclosed every risk and dirty deal," he told me, "so no one could blame anyone but themselves." Happily for this lawyer, along with about fifty others, a case was eventually filed against VMS and all the related entities; they settled for hundreds of millions.

BAD ADVICE

Brokers are only human, so naturally they will make mistakes. Over the course of your investing life, so will you. That's why you are better off making your own decisions and picking your own investments. The responsibility should be yours. The broker's role should be to keep you on an even keel, letting you know when you are taking too many risks (or not enough risks) and helping you focus on your long-term goals. The reverse situation — when the broker makes the decisions, with you merely holding on for the ride — can be disastrous.

In 1992 a guy we'll call VG hired a broker at Merrill Lynch, who put a third of VG's portfolio into the Hyperion 1997 Term Trust, explaining that it'd pay dividends while preserving the principal. The pitch was remarkable: the low-cost units (typically, $10) had four key benefits — the best of mutual funds *and* individual stocks — each carefully spelled out by Merrill's army of brokers. Investors got:

1. Regular income of treasury bonds
2. Higher yield of mortgage-backed securities and other collateralized mortgage obligations
3. Managers who were expert at interest-rate predictions
4. The liquidity of stocks; because there was a set number of shares, investors could sell the units to other Merrill customers

At the end of the term — in VG's case, 1997 — the bonds would come due and the principal would be returned to investors.

Who better to raise money for these exciting new products than Lewis Ranieri? Brooklyn born and bred, Ranieri started in the securities business as a mailroom clerk at Salomon Brothers. Working his way up over the next twenty years, he helped make Solly's neglected mortgage-backed securities department a powerhouse, and he did it with a flair that helped make him the most interesting part of the bestseller *Liar's Poker.* After an unceremonious firing, Ranieri founded Hyperion, raising hundreds of millions from big investors. But small investors have money, too, and the four term trusts Hyperion offered raised $1.82 billion from individuals such as VG at Merrill.

Unfortunately, the return of the $10 turned out to be a goal, not a guarantee. A couple of wrong bets on the direction of interest rates sent all four Hyperion trusts into a tailspin. VG's broker at Merrill allegedly told him that the dividend would vary but that "we'll get our ten dollars back." Meantime, the price of the trust on the open market was falling fast, as lawsuits were filed

WHEN SOMETHING GOES WRONG:
Making Arbitration Less Arbitrary

The innocuous agreement every investor signs when opening a brokerage account contains one of those fine-print conditions that are regularly overlooked until it's too late: a promise to resolve any dispute with a securities industry professional through the arbitration process rather than the courts. For the most part, this is a good thing. The courts are clogged enough without every schmuck who lost $300 crying about cold-calling barracudas. But an understanding of how the process works and some savvy about how to navigate it are tools any investor can use.

So what do you do if a problem arises? Well, the first thing is to call the broker and explain exactly how and why you feel you've been wronged — and, without threatening, make it clear that you know about the arbitration process and how to begin the procedure. You might be surprised by the number of times a broker fixes a problem as soon as he realizes you're feeling wronged and intend to do something about it. If that fails to produce an acceptable result, call the brokerage's branch manager and follow up the call in writing, by registered mail or some other service that produces a delivery receipt. Detail the problem and include a log of when you contacted your broker and the results of those calls, so the manager knows you're establishing a paper trail.

If this, too, doesn't trigger a satisfactory offer, it's time to consider the arbitration process. Since you're looking at between $150 and $250 in filing fees, and you'll almost certainly recover less than 100 percent of your damages, don't bother unless you think you're out at least $500 or so. If your damages are considerable — say, more than $5,000 — consider hiring counsel. The brokerage firms have a staff of lawyers who take on these cases . . . better that you fight fire with fire. There are lawyers who specialize in helping wronged investors prepare filings and select a venue (the NASD may not be the best forum for certain types of cases). You might even consider a non-lawyer representative, from a firm such as Securities Arbitration Group in Marina Del Rey, California. Otherwise, the Public Investors Arbitration Bar Association (PIABA) is a reliable source of lawyer referrals, with members nationwide. Contact PIABA (888-621-7484 or www.piaba.org) for a list of securities attorneys near you. Regardless of who you choose, the Securities Arbitration Commentator (SAC) has a referral service (973-761-5880 or www.sacarbitration. com) and is sort of the all-round expert on matters related to going ten rounds with a broker. For $25 to $75, the SAC will send you a list of all the principals involved in arbitrations near you so you can gauge the efficacy of the representatives and call the represented for further references.

The odds aren't great. A recent analysis done by the SAC found that about one-fourth of arbitrations resulted in awards, and most of those weren't for the full amount requested. But if you decide to go the arbitration route, contact the National Association of Securities Dealers (800-289-9999 or www.nasdr.com). Ask which of the NASD's thirteen district offices would be best in which to file your complaint. On the long and scary form (you can download a copy, too), describe in detailed plain English your version of events. Don't get all Perry Mason on the form — clarity trumps legalese here. Include copies of letters you've sent to the broker and his manager, as well as copies of any receipts proving they received them. After submitting the form, you'll be notified whether your case warrants a hearing by an arbitrator. If it does, you'll present your case, the broker will present his, and a panel of industry pros will decide who wins, rewarding compensation and/or damages and/or legal fees to the prevailing party. It's quick, simple, and cheap, which is why arbitration replaced the courts in the first place. But it's not always equitable, so remember: you're responsible for your own dough, no matter what.

Consider this alternative: next time you open a brokerage account, simply cross out the fine print that commits you to settling disputes before an arbitrator. Your broker might tell you that you've got to sign the agreement as it's presented, but chances are good that he'll back down if you threaten to take your dollars elsewhere. Then you'll be free to use the arbitration system, should you deem it appropriate — and you probably will. But you won't be limiting your options should the magnitude of your problem warrant the legal assistance and fine-toothed comb of the "real" legal system.

against Hyperion and derivatives such as these acquired a bad reputation. When Hyperion's 1996 annual report raised doubt that the trust could pay the full $10, VG phoned his broker, who reassured him and said he'd get back to VG with the facts. After not hearing from the broker for several months — and being treated rudely when he called the branch office — VG moved his account to another Merrill branch. Merrill eventually settled with VG, who never believed that the $3,000 made up for what he perceived as deception by his broker, who suddenly stopped returning his calls.

How a Broker Can Help You

At every turn, your investments involve making judgments, sometimes without your even realizing it. Maybe something convinces you that Disney has been beaten down too long and you should load up on it. But if 20 percent of your portfolio is already in AOL Time Warner and Viacom, a good broker will caution you about overexposure to the entertainment industry. Likewise, if you already own Intel and Microsoft and start accumulating Dell, your broker may advise you to fund the purchase by selling some INTC and MSFT. Any good thing that happens with Dell should help Intel and Microsoft because their products are in every Dell computer.

This doesn't mean that the broker is always right or that you must always heed his advice. But the broker should always be prudent. That is where you get the benefit of the broker's experience. Pick a broker who strikes you as someone who can fulfill that role. It's great if your broker is the life of the party and becomes a close friend, but what you really want is a skeptical person who doesn't care about being well liked.

A broker's help in directing you toward a better portfolio can be formal or informal. Ask what services the broker provides on asset allocation and risk tolerance. Many brokers are trained to interview you about investment goals and generate a profile on the types of investments that are right for you. Others have financial models that evaluate the diversity of your portfolio and its exposure to particular risks. Get all these things. They are guidelines, not orders; use them to help define your investing goals and boundaries. And make sure the broker keeps these profiles around, so he can remind you when you are straying too far from your goals.

In addition to being the voice of reason, a good broker protects you from his firm's profiteering. Every broker you talk to will tell you that he wants to represent your interests, but pick the ones who don't drink their firm's Kool-Aid. Naturally, that means staying away from the guys who want to load you up on their firm's in-house products.

A good broker can help you separate the sense from the nonsense coming from his firm's research department. Those analyst reports contain valuable background information and occasionally some real insight but, as I have detailed ad nauseam, are frequently marketing documents for the investment bankers or quid pro quo for underwriting business. One Merrill broker sent me a hilarious (not for his clients) list of 330 companies that had lost between 51.75 percent and 100 percent of their value over the past year. Next to each of the companies that his firm covered, he marked exactly when Merrill's analyst went negative — invariably it was always far too late to do any of his clients any good. Given how many brokers feel burned by their firms' research departments, you should have an easier time finding independent-minded brokers these days than just a few years ago.

Remember, all these financial-services mergers are predicated on the idea that it is profitable for a firm to have a customer base to whom it can offer the full variety of services. Of course, these, uh, "synergies" only work within reason. An ex-con with two bankruptcies shouldn't expect that his $20,000 account at Salomon Smith Barney entitles him to a cut-rate, no-money-down mortgage from Citibank. Nevertheless, a good broker can be your friend, partner, and confidante as you stake out your financial future. And a bad one can ruin you. Choose carefully and you need not go it alone.

Lessons and reminders
What to look for if you're looking:

- An overseer of the risk and diversity in your portfolio
- A devil's advocate on your investment decisions
- Not a professional stock picker
- The source for locating a money manager
- Range of financial services on favorable terms and/or little hassle, such as insurance, mortgages, and credit cards
- Commission discounts on trades, if the broker isn't providing value-added services

When evaluating a full-service broker, consider the following qualities:

- Integrity
- The official NASD record of the broker (known as his CRD), including past employment and any judgments or suits against him or her
- Recommendations from people you know
- The broker's own investing track record and how well he or she has performed for clients
- Independence from the brokerage firm and its self-interest
- Cynicism (a/k/a honesty) about the sometimes-oppressive influence of the broker's own firm

Give virtually no weight to anecdotal accounts about brokers' past stock tips.

Beware of the following abuses brokers and brokerage firms can commit:

- Foisting in-house products on you that are illiquid, loaded with conflicts of interest, and commission-driven
- Stock tips, which could be based on unfounded rumors or in-house analysts who may be shilling for underwriting clients

If you and your broker are looking for a money manager, evaluate the following:

- Audited results over a long period
- Manager's area of expertise (e.g., big caps, municipal bonds, foreign funds)
- Negotiability of fees

5

FUN WITH FUNDS

I spend much of my workday talking on the telephone. And the people I speak most often with are men and women who run hedge funds. Like me, they spend much of their day hunting down information about companies. Unlike me, when finding information they believe can be useful from an investment perspective, they buy or sell a stock. When I find information that I believe can be useful from an investment perspective, I go on television and tell the world (or however many people happen to be watching at that given moment). So while our tasks are somewhat similar, our goals are not. Their goal is to make as much money as possible for themselves and hopefully for their investors, but my goal is to tell my viewers about things that are important to their investment decisions.

Still, although it might seem that we make odd bedfellows, the constant exchange of information is helpful to both of us. We both need action. I need to focus on events in which my ability to find things out can produce a story with investment implications; they, too, are looking for ideas, even if they're short-term, that can do the same. From hedge fund managers whom I trust, I get ideas and tips that I can then follow up on. They get feedback (though very limited when I confirm an important story) on those same tips, given that I am often able to speak to people who might not take their calls. When I broke the story in mid-September 2001 that the Bass family had been forced to sell $2 billion worth of Walt Disney stock in order to meet a margin call, the first word of the trade came from a hedge fund manager. (That manager, and the many others who called soon after, told me only that he knew a huge trade of Disney shares would soon hit the market and then speculated on whom the seller might be. I was able to determine without a doubt that the seller was the Bass family and that the reason was a margin call because someone who shall remain nameless had that information and chose to share it with me.)

Depending on your level of wealth, you may have the opportunity to invest in a hedge fund. But chances are that you will invest in some type of fund, most likely a mutual fund, during your lifetime. Therefore, it is important to understand how all funds work — whether they are mutual funds, hedge funds, or even private-equity funds. You may choose to avoid all types of funds and use the tools imparted in this book to make your own way in the stock market. I hope that's the case. But even if you never invest in a fund, by learning how they invest, you can pick up helpful ideas for your own investing. And in all instances, even if you are not parking your money with an institution or learning lessons from its moves, you should understand how funds move the market.

Hedge Funds Versus Mutual Funds

Hedge funds and mutual funds are similar. They consist of pools of money run by professional managers who collect fees and try to make money for the investors. Mutual funds are sold in shares, and the price of a share is called the net asset value (NAV). The NAV is priced each day (some funds have started pricing several

INSTITUTIONAL INVESTORS

In addition to mutual funds, private-equity funds, and hedge funds, there are other institutions that make the markets roll on: the massive pension funds, endowments, foundations, and insurance companies.

Insurance companies invest the premiums they receive in order to generate returns. Pension funds also invest their contributions in order to increase the size of the fund so that it can successfully meet the needs of retiring workers. Foundations and endowments invest their holdings for obvious reasons. Each of these institutions represents a major funding source for hedge funds, mutual funds, and private-equity funds.

All of these institutions also employ thousands of professionals in-house to manage their vast portfolios. Harvard University, for example, has an enormous endowment that is both managed by people employed by the university and allocated to various investment partnerships.

A man named John Myers is one of the heroes at General Electric. Myers has steered the company's pension fund to significant gains, which have even helped GE's bottom line (remember the balance-sheet section in chapter 2). But GE's pension fund also invests in hedge funds. It is the largest single contributor to Omega, for example, the giant hedge fund run by Lee Cooperman.

The largest pension funds are public, so if you are a teacher or firefighter, that's your money. CalPERS (California Public Employees' Retirement System) and TIAA-CREF (Teachers Insurance Annuity Association–College Retirement Equities Fund) are not household names, but each controls more money than Fidelity Magellan and the Janus Fund combined.

Although the credo of the institutional investor is generally "vote with your feet," some of these behemoths can't exit gracefully from a lousy company. If a pension fund holds 10 percent of, say, General Motors, simply selling isn't an option if the manager decides the CEO is a dolt. This has led some of the larger institutions — which also purport to carry a social conscience because they represent unionized public servants — to press for better corporate governance, threaten to side with insurgents in a proxy contest, or even lend their voices to a call for the CEO's ouster.

times a day) and reflects the dollar value of all the stocks in the portfolio divided by the number of shares. It's the number you see in the paper or online when you look up the price of a fund. The Securities and Exchange Commission (SEC) regulates mutual funds based on the Securities Act of 1933 and the Investment Company Act of 1940. The regulations consist primarily of very detailed disclosures to investors and regulators, on quarterly and annual bases, as well as the need for detailed disclosure before the fund raises money.

Proxy contest An attempt to unseat directors, change a corporate policy, or challenge a planned merger, through a shareholder vote. Shareholder voting materials are referred to as "proxies" because the shareholder is agreeing to allow a representative to cast his or her vote. Most shareholder votes are one-sided affairs, like old Soviet Union elections, in which management's slate runs unopposed or "recommends" how to vote. Proxy contests are among the most effective means for hostile bidders to remove directors or challenge an existing but not-yet-concluded merger. Shareholders can also use a proxy contest to try to defeat a merger plan, as was the case when Walter Hewlett battled the management of Hewlett-Packard over that company's plan to buy Compaq Computer.

Hedge funds operate under far fewer regulatory requirements and do not sell shares based on net asset value. Hedge funds are partnerships with less than one hundred or five hundred investors, depending on the regulations the fund is operating under. Those investors must be sufficiently "accredited." Accredited investors are supposed to be able to look out for themselves, but they are really just wealthy people. The definition of an accredited investor is generally someone who has earned at least $200,000 for the past two years or has a net worth of at least $1 million.

Because unregulated funds can accept money from relatively few investors, the minimum investment is much greater. It is not uncommon for hedge funds to require initial investments of at least $1 million, though many funds require less. And some funds make exceptions for investors with stakes below the stated minimum, either as a favor to friends and family or because the fund is hard up.

Lack of regulation has allowed hedge funds to be much more freewheeling in their investment strategy. Although they still prepare offering documents to prospective investors, they can be more vague than a mutual fund in stating their investment parameters. Hedge funds, unlike most mutual funds, can generally short stocks in addition to buying them. They can also invest in complex fixed-income securities, derivative instruments, distressed bank debt, and risk-arbitrage situations. Hedge funds also employ leverage (debt) when financing investments, not to mention having few restrictions on how much they must have invested at any one time. Although hedge funds are supposed to be able to better ride out down periods in the market because of their ability to short stocks or "hedge," all that freedom creates greater risk. The hedge funds are supposed to correct for that risk by outperforming the market averages and their peers in the mutual fund industry.

Of late, hedge funds have proliferated at an astonishing rate: there are now six thousand, running over $400 billion. At the start of the 1980s the hedge fund industry was made up of about seven guys (Michael Steinhardt, Julian Robertson, and George Soros were three of them) who managed $1 billion between them. I sometimes find myself shocked at the veritable rookies who today are able to raise hundreds of millions of dollars. Many of them are smart, but even with a modest fifteen years covering Wall Street, my experience puts theirs to shame. It does not make sense. What's more, many of these people were sell-side analysts! Then again, nobody said life was fair.

Mutual funds and hedge funds have vastly different fee structures.

Mutual funds' fees take two forms. The first is "loads," which some funds charge when an investor enters a fund (front-end load) or leaves it (back-end load). The load is the cover charge one pays to access the manager's supposed brilliance. Many funds do not have a load, but all mutual funds have fees that usually run about 1 percent of the fund's assets and pay for marketing expenses and overhead. One percent may not sound like much, but if you've got a $20 billion mutual fund, that's $200 million a year.

Hedge funds sport a fee structure, whose origin, while unknown, is adhered to by many in the business. The average hedge fund charges a 1 percent management fee, just as a mutual fund does, but also takes 20 percent of any profits it generates within the fund in a given year. A well-run hedge fund can thus make its limited partners richer (they're usually already rich) and its managing partners obscenely wealthy.

Some funds charge less and some charge more. A new fund with an unproven manager might be willing to accept 15 percent of the profits or might be willing to offer to cut fees for a very large investor or a high-profile investor whose presence would generate new investors.

George Soros invested some of the money entrusted to his care in other hedge funds, but when doing so, he would invariably ask for cut rates. The request was usually met: a fund manager with Soros money could use that as testimony to his own brilliance. Even if you're not a billionaire yourself, when business is slow, it can't hurt to ask for cut fees.

It also works the other way. Hedge fund managers with little to prove and little interest in raising new money display fee structures that would make Warren Buffet weep. Louis Bacon's Moore Capital charges a 3 percent management fee, as well as a whopping 25 percent of the profits. Stevie Cohen's SAC Capital does Bacon one better. Cohen charges investors 50 percent of the profits. Of course, most of the money in the fund is Cohen's anyway, so he's not really concerned with finding new money, though plenty is offered.

I have a good friend who recently started a small hedge fund after running his own money for many years. He wants it to stay small, so he instituted a creative fee structure. He will take 20 percent of the profits on the first 15 percent of return to investors and 50 percent of any profit beyond that.

One-Way Option

The halls of Tiger Management were empty and many desks unoccupied on the day I made my way to an interview with the legendary hedge fund manager Julian Robertson. The previous day I had broken the story that Tiger would be shutting down, and so was summoned along with my colleague Ron Insana to a rare sit-down with the courtly southern gentleman who at one time had overseen some $21 billion in assets.

It was sad to walk the halls at Tiger. The beautiful art had no one to look at it. The gorgeous view went unappreciated. Robertson was not in a mood to match the desolate state of his once great firm. He seemed rather pleased, actually, and was happy to offer as proof the eighty-five fold increase an investment in Tiger, net of fees, would have generated had it been made and held since inception.

Still, I found myself wondering, and asking, why he was going out on a down note. From its peak in August 1998 to March 2000, the Tiger funds went from $21 billion in assets to less than $7 billion. Tiger investors had withdrawn some $7.7 billion during that time; the market had taken the rest. Why would a man as proud as Robertson not try to fight back? Robertson said it was because he was a rational man investing in an irrational market and could no longer deal with that state of affairs (which would begin to change literally days after he closed down). I think it also had to do with something called a high-water mark.

Although hedge fund compensation is lavish, it is also honest in that it requires funds to make up for any investor losses before they can take their 20 percent of the profits. If a hedge fund begins business with $1 billion under management, it can earn its 20 percent only if the fund stays above $1 billion. If the first year out is a bad one and the fund drops 10 percent, to $900 million, the general partner cannot begin taking 20 percent of the profits until the fund is above $1 billion. In other words, a 10 percent drop to $900 million means that the manager has to be up 11 percent (back to $1 billion) before he can begin taking any cut of the profits. That's called a high-water mark, and it is something that can figure prominently in the decision of a hedge fund to fold its tent after a few bad years rather than fight its way back.

As a fund moves along in its life picking up new investors, each of them has his or her own — higher — high-water mark. And although early investors in Tiger had seen their high-water mark disappear in a blizzard of profits, late investors to the fund had no such luck. Robertson took in a great deal of money late in Tiger's life, and when you're down 30, 40, or 50 percent on that money, it is very hard to claw your way back to neutral. That may have been another reason that Robertson hit the showers.

Think about it. When times were good, Robertson was making an absolute fortune. When he was running Tiger at the $10 billion level and was up 30 percent, he pocketed not only a $100 million management fee but a stunning $600 million performance fee. He had a big organization through which he delivered part of that fee, but you get the idea. Now fast-forward a few years and consider that just to make any performance fee, Robertson would have to engineer his fund to an almost 100 percent gain. You can see why he may have chosen the exit.

George Soros's sudden decision to close down Soros Fund Management in the spring of 2000 may also have been due to an unyielding high-water mark. It is often too much effort for managers to fight back to break even . . . at least when they are already billionaires, as is the case with both Soros and Robertson. If the hedge fund does well, you score. If the hedge fund hits a bad patch, the manager may choose to close down rather than forge ahead.

Though that may look like a cowardly move, pay close attention to hedge fund managers who have bad years. Even if a fund is down by as little as 10 percent, it may be enough to force the manager to change his style of investing and take a riskier investment road than he otherwise would pursue. That can lead to a lot more trouble. As a rule, if you have invested in a hedge fund that's down 20 percent or more, get out. And even with a decline of 10 percent, pay very close attention thereafter.

Not So Diverse

If you've learned anything from this book (and I hope you have), it is that making your own investment decisions requires a good deal of work and a great deal of mental energy. You may not have the time or the inclination to expend both of those precious commodities on investment decisions. You may therefore choose to invest in a mutual fund. But even then, you need to do some work and should understand how mutual funds work in order to find one that may work for you.

One of the big selling points of mutual funds is that through the diversity of their portfolios, they can minimize the risk for an investor. That can be true to an extent. But although a mutual fund may hold the stocks of many companies, it can still be far from diverse. And that can cost you.

Most mutual funds must closely hew to a narrowly drawn prospectus that dictates the parameters of investment, which often include an inability to short stocks. I've spent considerable pages in this book discussing the virtues of short selling. So you might not be surprised that I think it's a real impediment to profits when you invest your hard-earned money in a fund that can benefit only when stocks go up. Stocks don't always go up, and sometimes because of events beyond our control, let alone our imagination, stocks are sent down. When you invest in most mutual funds, you're in for a one-way ticket.

Mutual fund managers are also expected to stay "fully invested," which means they can't run a mutual fund that has 20 percent of its money in cash even if they believe the market is overvalued and due for a fall. General guidelines about the manager's style of investing are also detailed. Even if the prospectus leaves a little leeway, the hall monitors at Morningstar and the personal finance mags will scold any manager guilty of "style drift," a fancy term for pursuing the best opportunities. In the end, the investment parameters require the fund manager to invest in stocks of companies that fit the prescribed style. A growth stock fund manager whose heart tells him that cash or bonds or value stocks are the best place to be can do very little to act on that belief. He's stuck.

That is why certain groups of funds do well in certain market environments. During the bull market of the mid to late 1990s, funds that focused on buying so-called growth stocks posted stellar returns. This is how the Janus family of funds came to prominence. Its investment style of finding companies with impressive earnings, cash-flow growth, and the potential for further growth fit well with a booming economy and market. Janus and its funds may also have been part of a virtuous cycle that helped propel many of its holdings: because as Janus's various funds posted impressive returns, investors flocked to the funds, and their money was used by Janus's portfolio managers to buy more shares of many of the same stocks they had already been buying. The buying by Janus helped those stocks go even higher, enhancing Janus's performance numbers and attracting still more money. Ah, the good old days.

An investment in most of Janus's funds would have paid off handsomely if it was made between 1995 and 1999. During that period, and especially in 1998 and 1999, the flagship Janus Fund posted huge gains and also outperformed the S&P 500 index by a significant amount. But the fund was far from risk-free. In fact,

Growth and momentum investing A definition of those investors who adhere to a strict model that calls for purchasing the stock of those companies whose earnings and revenue growth are increasing and selling the stock of companies that have slowing growth.

Momentum and growth stock investors don't always admit to having the same discipline, but it is virtually identical. Companies that have a consistent increase in growth garner the attention of such investors, only to suffer at their hands if the company should turn in one poor quarter.

Momentum investors may have seen their moment pass. During the bull market, such an approach yielded vast rewards and also resulted in huge one-day drops for certain stocks that failed to maintain the rates of growth demanded by momentum investors.

it proved to be downright risky because as the market changed, Janus could not. It could not abandon the investing discipline that it promised fundholders it would follow. It could not build up large cash positions even if its managers felt that growth for many companies was slowing. It could not short the stocks of companies that its research may have found would soon have problems. It could only sell and buy from what ended up being a relatively small universe of companies. And when EMC and AOL and Clear Channel Communications started going down, Janus went with them.

Despite astronomical returns of 23 percent in 1997, 39 percent in 1998, and 47 percent in 1999, the Janus Fund, in the fall of 2001, had a five-year annualized return of little more than 7 percent. If, as many retail investors chose to do, you had held the fund throughout that time, you didn't benefit much from those incredible years. And if you came in after 1998 or 1999, you were out of luck. As they say, past performance is not indicative of future returns. Failing to have diversified your ownership of mutual funds beyond those focused on growth stocks would have had bad results.

Of course, if you had diversified your ownership of funds

to include those that focus on buying value stocks, you would have been frustrated by the paltry returns of the mid to late nineties while growth funds were skyrocketing. But doing so would have ultimately helped protect your portfolio because although those funds never had a period of success equal to growth funds, they did hold up a great deal better in the market of the new millennium.

The Sector Snafu

Many mutual funds not only focus on a specific investing discipline but use that discipline within a certain industry sector. Whereas in a growth-style fund you'll at least get some diversity of industry, a sector fund eliminates such diversity and thereby increases the risk inherent in the fund. The guy managing a technology fund, for example, *must* buy companies he does not necessarily love. His job is to invest 100 percent of his capital in companies from a small list. His approach is not "is this a good investment?" but rather "is this a better investment than the other few companies on my list?"

As pointed out in chapter 4, many of the brokerage firms and fund families develop funds that reflect their immediate sense of what will sell. There's no point in starting a health-care-related fund when health-care stocks have been out of favor. And yet, that might well be the time to start such a fund or at least start investing in such a fund. Instead, you'll get dot-com and telecom funds proliferating after those sectors have peaked. In fact, when you see a plethora of funds being created in a certain industry sector, you might want to start thinking about going short in that very sector.

A few years back I knew some people who were day trading mutual funds. It seemed absurd at the time, but if you choose to invest in a sector fund, it may deserve day-to-day attention and should not be viewed as a long-term investment. Consider the pressures the fund manager is under. He can't range outside a certain group of companies and must be fully or near fully invested. If his sector is out of favor, all the fund manager can do is try to find stocks that will suffer the least. In general, that's not a recipe for long-term success. And given the attention and work that must go into making a bet on a sector, you might be better off buying one of the leading companies in that sector and leaving it at that.

Tax Time

In your own investments, you recognize gains and losses when you sell. You know when the hit is coming and you can even modify your selling strategy to fit your tax situation in a particular year. Because mutual funds are not taxed themselves, they pass their tax liabilities on to you through capital-gains distributions. Nothing is really "distributed" to you except your own money. One friend got introduced to this issue the hard way. His very first mutual fund investment, as with many investors, was in the fabled Fidelity Magellan Fund. He picked a bad year to jump in. The fund lost value. Planning to just buy it and forget it, he was surprised to find that despite not selling the fund and having the value of the fund go *down*, he had to pay substantial capital-gains taxes on the fund. It seems that the fund had a lot of embedded gains on stocks that weren't sold until a new manager took over and shifted the portfolio. This guy got hit for a pro rata share of taxes, even though he did not share in those gains.

In the long run, this phenomenon evens out. When this friend exits Magellan, he will cash out at a value that includes unrealized — and therefore untaxed — gains and leave the next group of investors holding the bag. But in the short term, you can do a few things to keep from getting hit unexpectedly by taxes. Look at the average turnover. For how long does the fund hold its positions? In general, you want to be in a fund with relatively low turnover because you will be hit with less frequent capital-gains distributions. You can also check — in the fund prospectus or on Morningstar.com or dozens of other financial web sites featuring mutual fund information — for the fund's unrealized gains as a percentage of assets.

Difficult tax situations are not exclusive to mutual funds. In the world of hedge funds, it's important to understand the investing style of the manager and whether the fund does a great deal of short-term trading. That's because many funds that trade a lot, if they do so successfully, can generate a huge capital-gains tax bill. You need to keep that in mind when considering a hedge fund and make certain to ask for the net return to investors after short-term capital-gains taxes. Some hedge funds that engage in frenzied trading post seemingly impressive returns, but those numbers come back to earth after taxes.

Some hedge funds, such as Steve Cohen's SAC Capital Management, have a two-year lockup on your money, meaning you can't ask for any of it back until two years have passed. If you invested with Steve Cohen, you probably don't have a problem with that, given his amazing returns. But during that time, Stevie was generating a big tax bill from all those short-term gains he was taking. You need to pay that tax bill every year but can't rely on cashing in some of your gains with Stevie to do it — another reason hedge funds demand a rich clientele.

Know Your Manager

If you're investing in a hedge fund, chances are that you have a good sense of its manager and his or her style. That is of primary importance — if you don't know whether your hedge fund manager is a growth or value investor, you haven't done your due diligence and may get burned as a result.

But that kind of familiarity with a manager should not be confined to hedge funds. When you invest in a mutual fund, it's also important to know who is making the investment decisions. After all, every conceivable fund has numerous competitors selling exactly the same product, and the only difference is the person generating the investment ideas. Is the fund manager sufficiently committed to the fund to have his or her own money invested with it? Has the manager been with the fund a long time? What was his or her training? Many of the fund families provide such information, and you should take advantage of that availability to investigate the background of the person you are entrusting with your money.

Equally important is to take note of a change in management. When Jeff Vinik was replaced by Robert Stansky as manager of the Magellan Fund, Stansky quickly went about remaking the portfolio. That is typical; a new manager has his or her own style and wants to put it to work. But if you invested in a particular mutual fund because you liked the track record of the manager, you may choose to get out once he or she leaves.

PERSONAL TRADING ACCOUNTS

In the world of funds a personal account (PA) often serves as your manager's ultimate distraction.

The danger of a personal account is simple: the guy who's supposed to be watching your money spends more time watching his own. While Jeff Vinik was running Fidelity's Magellan Fund, his personal trading habits were legendary (see chapter 3), largely because Vinik was privy to great information that he received as manager of the world's largest mutual fund but could not use to benefit that fund. Jeff's PA was probably the single best performing pool of funds at Fidelity, but no one except Jeff shared in the gains.

At the larger hedge funds, the danger is the same. Many of the large funds run by established managers hire younger guys to oversee a particular industry sector. They can usually be counted on to know their sector cold, but they're not afraid to range far and wide in their PAs. Why? In part because their compensation is not guaranteed and they feel a need to supplement it through other means. In part because though they may have money in the overall fund, they are not in charge of making the overall investment decisions for the fund and so want more control. In part, it's ego.

Again, the danger is that managers will focus too much on their own accounts and not enough on those they are managing. That is an especially big problem if the manager is not doing well in his PA. Imagine how that affects his psyche as an investor.

At a mutual fund, it's somewhat understandable, given the compensation structure, why managers engage in PA trading. It helps pay the bills. And for a sector fund manager, it's also an opportunity to invest in different parts of the market. Someone who manages a fund of telecom stocks or a small-cap value fund or even an index fund can't be expected to believe that the *only* worthwhile opportunities exist in those venues. Certain mutual funds encourage such trading, with the notion that it sharpens the investment skills of the manager. Other funds frown on it or prohibit such trading; still others prevent short selling in PAs. Perhaps the more sensible way to eliminate the disparity between personal and public trading would be to allow shorting in the mutual funds rather than banning it in PAs.

As an investor in a hedge fund or a mutual fund, you should inquire about the fund's policy on PAs. It may tip the balance in choosing one fund over another.

If you're a hedge fund investor, it's also important to look beyond the person who represents the fund. The hedge fund industry is populated by teams of people, one very good at selling, the other ostensibly good at investing. Try to meet them both because the so-called manager of the fund may be nothing more than a sweet-talking salesman who couldn't find a great investment if it hit him square in the face. That's okay, as long as he has assembled a team that knows what it's doing. You should also know who works for the fund beyond the front man so that you can be aware of when a departure from that team puts the fund in some jeopardy. And as a new investor, don't shy away from going in to meet the managers in charge of the fund's accounting and operations. It's important that you have confidence not only in the manager's investing acumen but in the competence and honesty of the fund's accounting and operations staff.

A number of the larger hedge funds have professionals who deal with the information needs of their investor base and market the fund to prospective investors. It's fine to deal with someone who represents the fund and is knowledgeable about its operations. But that doesn't mean you should not have access to the actual managers of the fund and those that craft its strategy. Deal with the firm's chosen personnel on matters relating to your account, but when it comes to checking on the mind-set of the managers, make sure you have at least a couple of sit-downs a year with the firm's decision makers.

Finally, make sure the manager of the fund has most of his net worth tied up in the same fund that you are investing in. A good rule is that as much as 75 percent of a manager's net worth should be invested in the fund. Senior employees of the fund should also be significant investors. Some funds have a much larger inside ownership than others, but the point is the same: ensuring that the managers to whom you are entrusting your money are investing right alongside you.

Make sure you understand the structure of the hedge fund. How many funds is the manager operating? Is there one fund in which the general partner is fully invested with you? Many managers have two funds — one in which the limited partners have their money, from which the manager gets 20 percent of the profits, and a separate fund in which the general partner and employees of the firm park much of their own dough. That creates numerous conflicts, one revealed at the tail end of the last bull market: some hedge fund managers were using the size of their funds (where you invested your money) to win them big allocations on initial public offerings. Many IPOs proved to be first-day rockets, so anyone getting in on the offering price was being handed a huge profit. A number of hedge funds took these IPO allocations into their second fund, the one controlled by the general partner and employees. That fund would then receive the benefit of an incredibly profitable trade, while the main fund saw none of it. If you find your manager doing anything like this, withdraw your money as quickly as possible.

Occasionally you may find that your hedge fund manager has split allegiances. It is hard to argue with the track record posted by Stanley Druckenmiller, the man who ran George Soros's Quantum Fund for more than a decade. But it's easier to argue with the fact that Druckenmiller was also managing an entirely separate hedge fund all those years he was running the Quantum Fund. Soros had agreed to let Druckenmiller keep his hedge fund, Duquesne Capital Management, when he hired him. It was a small hedge fund at the time, but it did very well through the years and didn't suffer the same setbacks that the Quantum Fund did. When Soros shut down the Quantum Fund, Druckenmiller took a brief leave from Wall Street, only to return to run the hedge fund he had never left, which had somehow grown to manage an enormous $4 billion in assets. It's unclear whether Druckenmiller's attention or allegiance was ever torn between his two funds (though it's not hard to imagine), and although this arrangement was somewhat unique, it is nonetheless worth keeping an eye out for.

Another thing to watch for is a fund's private-equity investments. I'll discuss private equity in some detail later in the chapter, but here I'm talking about investments by hedge funds in companies that are not yet public or investments in public companies that cannot be sold easily. Many hedge funds receive offers to participate in financings for not-yet-public companies or companies that want to offer stock or bonds in a private transaction. These deals can often be very lucrative, though very risky as well. And since these companies aren't trading yet, the funds can't sell their stakes right away. Therefore, these investments can't be made from a pool of capital that is subject to sudden shrinkage. So, many hedge funds establish separate funds with long lockup periods from which they make private investments. Again, this is very risky. Soros Fund Management had an entire division devoted to making such investments and is still suffering from deals done during the bull market.

A number of mutual funds also more closely resemble private-equity funds, given the size of their investment positions and lack of change in the fund's portfolio. Ronald Baron's $3.3 billion Baron Asset Fund has devoted more than a third of its assets to five core investments over the past few years, including Sotheby's Holdings, Polo Ralph Lauren, and Charles Schwab. The fund has often been the largest single institutional holder of Sotheby's and Polo Ralph Lauren, meaning that when you buy Baron Asset, you're buying into some big, illiquid positions.

Bigger Isn't Better

On many occasions, I've seen a successful fund manager start out small and in charge but drift away from his portfolio as it gets bigger and as he focuses on raising money rather than running the fund. And that leads me to one of the few controversial pieces of advice I may impart to you on funds.

I believe that small funds, whether mutual or hedge, are better than large funds. I am not talking about funds that invest in small companies. I am talking about funds that do not have more than $100 million to $150 million under management and that invest in whatever the manager might like. I have no idea whether there is any empirical data to support this contention. I am simply sharing an opinion based on my experience.

That experience has been that as funds get bigger, they lose their edge. I have seen it frequently. A fund manager who oversees a small portfolio is on top of every one of the fund's investments. But as a fund grows, it needs to make more investments in order to maintain enough diversity in its portfolio to mitigate undue risk. As the portfolio grows, it is harder for the manager to be on top of every investment. He needs to hire more people to help monitor investments. He gets farther away from the portfolio. He starts to manage people rather than money. He may not be very good at managing people. The fund suffers.

So although plenty of small funds have lousy returns and plenty of large funds perform very well, I believe that a money manager with a smaller amount of money would do better than a manager with the same level of investing acumen would do with a larger amount. Keep in mind that a successful small fund can grow very big very quickly. Tiger started with $8.8 million in 1980 and had $21 billion eighteen years later. Of course, given my advice about size, you may want to think about getting out as the fund goes about getting big.

Most managers, especially those who run hedge funds, want their funds to grow increasingly larger. That's how they make more money. They spend a great deal of time raising money based on the track record they have compiled while their portfolios were small. But there are many money managers who intentionally keep their funds small so they can spend their time evaluating companies rather than raising money, because they know that a smaller fund can better capitalize on a few good ideas.

One of my sources provided a textbook example of what I am talking about. We used to speak almost every day, in part because he was always on top of information. He ran a nice $30 million–$40 million fund. He posted big returns: up 90 percent one year, over 100 percent the next. And he became emboldened by that performance and attracted to the potential riches it might bring if he could use that track record to help him increase the size of his fund.

He went into money-raising mode. He spent much of his time meeting prospective investors. He raised $200 million and suddenly found that he needed to hire more people to handle client services and keep track of a widening array of investment positions. He moved farther and farther away from what he had done best. His returns declined markedly. We don't speak nearly as often as we used to.

Keep an eye out as well for hedge funds that grow so large that their managers begin looking beyond the stock market for opportunities. Tiger Management and Soros Fund Management, the two heavyweights of their day, both made significant moves into currency and fixed-income markets as they grew bigger. The funds were forced to make such "macro" bets, in part because their portfolio of stocks could not grow any larger, even as their funds did, without swamping internal research capabilities and making the fund start to look like a mirror image of the S&P 500 index. The moves were largely positive, as each made correct bets on the movements of currencies such as the British pound and Japanese yen. But the danger of size remains. Just as the manager of a small hedge fund gets removed from its portfolio as it grows bigger, so too the manager of a big fund that grows even bigger gets removed from the investing discipline that made him a success. Julian Robertson, Tiger's founder, forged his reputation as a value fund manager, not a guy who knew the ins and out of yen-dollar forward swaps.

Equity mutual funds can't engage in such activity, but as they grow larger, such funds need to take enormous positions in order for them to be able to make a difference to the performance of the portfolio. Consequently, these funds can't buy stocks that don't have a lot of shares outstanding and hence a lot of shares trading. They need stocks that trade a lot, another way of saying they need stocks that are "liquid."

Often the largest of the general mutual funds, such as Magellan, start to look an awful lot like a fund that tracks the performance of the S&P 500 index. How can it not, given a need to own the largest and most liquid stocks? You may be better off simply buying an index fund rather than paying the rich fees of a large mutual fund.

Market Movers

When Robert Stansky buys, people listen. That's because as the manager of the world's largest mutual fund, Fidelity's Magellan, Stansky can single-handedly move the price of a company's stock up significantly if he chooses to make that stock a big part of his $77 billion portfolio. Each of Magellan's top ten positions might constitute as much as 4 percent of the fund, meaning that Stansky would need to buy as much as $3 billion worth of a particular company's stock. That's an awful lot of stock. And rather than buying it in one fell swoop, traders at Fidelity rustle up that stock from brokers all across Wall Street, all the while trying not to let anyone know just how much they want to buy.

Let's use a real-life example. At the end of August 2001, AOL Time Warner was one of Magellan's top ten holdings and Wal-Mart was not. Both were hovering in the mid-40s. When September came to a close, that was no longer the case. AOL found itself replaced by Wal-Mart as a top ten holding. During the month of September, while AOL was being sold by Magellan, its stock price fell to the low 30s. Wal-Mart had a big move up to the low 50s during a brutal slide for the rest of the market. Next time you see a big change in one of Magellan's positions, take a look back at how the stock performed during the previous quarter. If the position was reduced or eliminated, chances are that the stock in question was down for the quarter, and if Magellan was building a position, chances are that the stock moved higher.

The ability of mutual funds to move the stock prices of even the largest companies is magnified when these funds are facing redemptions. During much of the market's move south, investors constantly invoked the fear-inducing cry that mutual fund redemptions would bring further slaughter to the equity markets. It didn't really happen, though the damage done was bad enough. It pays to understand which stocks the largest mutual funds hold. The Janus funds, for example, were often thought to be selling some of their bigger positions in order to prepare for redemptions. Rare was the day that went by in which I would not hear about rumors that Janus was creating the selling pressure behind a certain stock's fall. Sometimes it was true and sometimes it wasn't. You can imagine, however, that when a $15 billion mutual fund such as the Janus Twenty is down 40 percent for the year, some of its holders may decide to get out. It is certainly possible that Janus's selling will drive down the price of whatever it's unloading, whether it's Clear Channel Communications, Viacom, or Nokia (all big Janus holdings at various times). Also, a fund family such as Janus that focuses on one key buying strategy tends to own the same stocks in many of its funds. So when redemptions come in across many funds, it can still be the same stocks that suffer.

Professional investors keep a close eye on the portfolios of large mutual funds or hedge funds that have encountered difficult times. I know plenty of money managers who relished the opportunity to short some of Janus's top holdings, in anticipation of Janus's being forced to sell some of those stocks to raise money for redemptions. There wasn't nearly as much of that selling as they had anticipated, but their reasoning was basically sound.

Window Dressing

At the end of a quarter, mutual funds and hedge funds engage in a practice that has nothing to do with windows or dresses, but is called window dressing. Just before publicizing their mutual funds' holdings — required on a quarterly basis — many managers perform exotic gyrations, selling stinkers and buying stocks that have already racked up significant gains. This occasionally leads to heavy volume in the last days of a quarter, further extending the success or failure of a high-profile stock. Don't be fooled when you look at the portfolio. Compare the fund's year-to-date results with the year-to-date results of its biggest holdings. It's not unusual to see a fund down 10 percent, with all its biggest holdings up 20 percent. That's because the fund purchased the stocks *after* the run-up. Stay away from these funds — they are run by managers you can't trust.

Window dressing encompasses more than that childish practice, however. On the quarter's final day, mutual funds and hedge funds rush in as buyers of stocks they already own heavily. Even if they don't put a great deal of money to work, they can often move higher the shares of stocks that don't generally have a great deal of volume. A 5 percent move in many stocks being window-dressed is not uncommon. Do that to enough stocks and you can get your portfolio up 2 or even 3 percent as the quarter ends. Not bad for a day's work. Of course, those gains will disappear when the next quarter begins because they were not based on consistent buying of the stock in question, but you've got an entire quarter to worry about that; meanwhile, you just reported better numbers to your investors than you might have had otherwise.

Window dressing gets a bit more pernicious at the end of the year. I know a number of smaller hedge funds that buy smaller-capitalized companies. These are companies with stock prices that can be moved fairly easily on a little volume, and when year end comes, these hedge funds go to work bidding up their prices. That's more than window dressing — that's stealing, because those hedge fund managers are paid on their yearly performance and they have just juiced up that performance in an unsustainable manner. Keep an eye out for this practice by knowing what stocks your manager holds. If they are small-cap stocks, check out their performance on the last day of the year. If each of them was up 5 percent, you've got a cheat on your hands.

Know What They Do, Not What They Say

Leverage is the great elixir of the hedge fund world, allowing a portfolio of $1 billion, for example, to have the buying power of

$3 billion. Leverage is just a fancy word for debt; but it is still debt, and it can kill. Leverage introduces risk into an otherwise conservative strategy. Leverage places a deadline on the trade — loans accumulate interest and have to be repaid, derivative contracts have due dates, brokerage accounts have margin requirements. All this led to the well-known (but poorly understood) collapse of Long-Term Capital Management (LTCM) in 1998.

I followed the collapse of Long-Term Capital Management very closely and was the first to report that it was at death's door, hoping to be resuscitated by the banks that had loaned it much of the debt it used to supercharge its portfolio of barely profitable investments.

Not one of Long-Term's investors had any real idea of what the hell the firm was up to. They thought they didn't need to. After all, LTCM was the brainchild of John Meriwether, a talented bond trader formerly of Salomon Brothers. Meriwether started the fund in 1994 with some other Salomon alums and a couple of Nobel laureates in economics. Based on the founders' past success and pedigree, investors were only too happy to hand over their money without asking any questions. But after too many leveraged bets, LTCM was in danger of a forced liquidation due to a violation of margin requirements and account-maintenance rules at its clearing brokers. The Federal Reserve Bank of New York stepped in, kindly forcing commercial and investment banks to take over portions of the portfolio rather than forcing a liquidation, which could have touched off an additional economic crisis. The fund's investors, oblivious for so long to what the guys in Greenwich were actually up to, got back about nine cents for each dollar they had invested.

There is a danger in failing to understand what happened to Long-Term Capital Management. The problem was not institutional. They really had a great economic model. But the leverage introduced a degree of risk — an exposure to even a relatively short period of economic upheaval — that the fund never acknowledged or prepared for.

If you find yourself with an opportunity to get into a hedge fund, don't take its word on how much leverage it uses, or on how much hedging it does. Check it out for yourself. Ask to see a run on every stock held and every short position with the corresponding dollar amount, market price, gain or loss on the position, realized gain or loss, and leverage used. Every hedge fund has this run available every single day; indeed, the software that hedge funds use allows them to know their exact up-to-the-minute profit or loss. You shouldn't feel shy about asking to take a look before making a commitment.

A typical run on an $800 million hedge fund might comprise more than 150 short and long positions and end a good day with a tally that looks like this:

Total exposure: $1,153,945,528	Total profit and loss: $10,920,158
Long exposure: $769,887,758	Long profit and loss: $17,795,415
Short exposure: –$384,057,770	Short profit and loss: –$6,875,257

Ask the manager how much hedging is actually done. Ask about what kind of risk management is used and make sure you know how each day's final numbers were achieved. Be particularly wary of hedge funds that say they are short only. It's been my experience that such funds lie in order to garner money from investors who see such a strategy as a hedge to their other investments. In a strong market, these funds often have a hard time and frequently end up buying stock in order to generate some performance. This might be wise, but you don't want to deal with a fund that started out by misleading you about its investment approach.

You should similarly be wary of money managers with a particular expertise who face a market that can't reward those skills. Consider risk arbitrage: in a market without deals, a fund that focuses on risk arbitrage can't put a great deal of money to work. That's okay. What isn't okay is if the manager decides that's a situation he can't abide and makes investments outside his area of expertise. I know one brilliant risk arb who decided he was also a savvy investor in small toy companies. He wasn't. Many risk-arbitrage funds have also developed an expertise in distressed investing (investing in the securities of bankrupt or about-to-be-bankrupt companies). That's fine as well, as long as you know when you invest that this could become an area of concentration and that the fund is equipped to deal with it.

Many hedge funds get some of their best ideas from their own investors, who can typically be very well placed executives and really rich people with good connections. A number of hedge funds intentionally try to have CEOs among their investors to get access to inside information. Such access is not legal, but if the

GET MORE INFO

Hedge funds are partnerships, intentionally structured for maximum secrecy, so information comparing performance and holdings is not easy to find. Here are your best bets on the web.

- www.hedgeworld.com
  Self-described definitive hedge fund community, and deservedly so, but you have to pay to see the premium content.

- www.hedgefund247.com/funds2.html
  This front for TurtleTrader offers a massive list of all hedge funds, including performance data on lots of funds, although with important omissions. Pushes its Original Turtle Trading System course for $999

- www.vanhedge.com
  Maintains extensive data bank of information on approximately four thousand hedge funds.

- www.e-hedge.com

- www.hedgefund.net

CEO and the hedge fund manager are close, you might be surprised at what that manager is able to divine. One of the larger technology funds, which shall remain nameless, hired a number of former senior executives from Intel and always seemed to have a keen sense for what Intel's numbers would be. That can be a powerful edge.

Private-Equity Funds

In the old days, they used to be known as LBO funds, and they used to make a lot of money. Now they're called private-equity funds, and they barely make any money at all. There you have a two-sentence history of funds that seemed an anachronism through much of the 1990s as they waited for their turn in the sun to come again.

Private equity is much as it sounds: private investments are made from huge funds. Those investments can include purchasing all of a company, or making a large, illiquid investment in a company, such as buying a big tranche of convertible preferred stock.

As in hedge funds, the general partners of a private-equity fund insist on a lot of freedom on how they invest the money, and 20 percent of the profits for the effort. Limited partners can expect limited access to the manager and their money. Unlike in hedge funds, most of the investors in private-equity funds are not wealthy individuals but are large pension funds, insurance companies, and endowments. Private-equity funds usually require a commitment to invest rather than an immediate investment, and so in raising a $5 billion fund what they really have are firm commitments by their investors to fund $5 billion in equity investments.

Even though these investments involve public companies, they are usually illiquid. Most private-equity funds tell investors (informally, so they are not held to this prediction) that they invest with a four- to seven-year time horizon from entry to exit. When Tom Lee's fund bought Snapple in 1992, its investors (the largest of which, as in nearly all of Lee's funds, was GE's pension fund) had no idea how much money they would get back, or when. Lee took the company public again six months later, selling 13 percent to the public at a value representing more than eight times what the fund paid. By the end of 1994, Snapple agreed to be purchased by Quaker Oats for $1.7 billion. This included the cost of assuming Snapple's debt and buying out other shareholders, and Lee's $28 million investment ended up returning $900 million. That is a textbook example of how private equity is supposed to work. Often, even for Tom, the results are far from that favorable.

Since the late 1990s, private-equity results have been downright lousy. The junk bond market on which many of these funds rely for their financing has been very unpredictable. The proliferation of funds also led to bidding wars for properties that were far from first-rate. Through the bull market, valuations were simply too high for many of these firms to consider buying all of a company. Banks have also made things more difficult. In the 1980s an LBO fund could buy a company for $1 billion, spruce it up, and sell it two years later for $1.1 billion. That's a return of less than 5 percent per year, not enough to get you cover profile in *Fortune*. But if you found someone to loan you $900 million, and put up only $100 million of your own money, the same investment is a bonanza: you doubled your money! Those days are over, as banks have cut back on how much debt they are willing to lend for a given amount of equity.

Finally, these funds seemed to suffer from a complete lack of creativity. Whatever one might have thought about the corporate raiders of the 1980s and the LBO funds that Michael Milken put into business, they at least showed a combination of guts and ingenuity that has been sadly lacking in their firms ever since.

Private equity might still stage a stirring recovery. The brutal retreat in the equity markets has taken market values down for many companies and uncovered some that are trading at levels which might make a good old leveraged buyout possible. If the private-equity guys can get the financing, they may be heard from. But in any case, there's no reason to feel bad for these firms. Even in tough times, they are taking in a management fee that runs at about 1.5 percent of assets under management. And whenever there is a deal to be done, the general partners usually take banking fees. Kohlberg Kravis Roberts was famous in the late eighties for grabbing big investment banking fees up front for advice it gave its own fund, not to mention still more fees for arranging financing. Many investment banking firms have private-equity funds, which not only provide an opportunity for profit but guarantee a profit to the firm's bankers when they do a deal, good or bad.

Lessons and reminders
- Know your fund's expertise and make certain the fund does not stray far from it.
- Favor small funds over large funds.
- Don't be afraid to go with a type of investing regimen that is working (value or growth) and abandon it when it's not.
- Consider mutual funds that can go short.
- Stay away from sector funds when they are first created.

- Understand the tax ramifications of various funds.
- Check unrealized gains as a percentage of assets for mutual funds.
- Check the average turnover of the portfolio.
- With hedge funds, understand whether they are short-term traders who generate short-term capital gains (and if so, prepare for a big tax bill).

- Know your manager:

  Does your mutual fund manager have his own money in the fund?

  What is his work history?

Know when a change in manager is made and prepare to leave the fund if necessary.

Check on the fund's policy toward personal trading.

- Ensure that the hedge fund manager has much of his net worth invested in the fund and that it is the same fund you invest in.
- Check on whether the fund allows trading in personal accounts.
- Ask about other funds the manager may run, including those that make private investments.

- Know who other investors in the hedge fund are.
- Understand how much leverage is used in the portfolio.
- Understand the risk management used by the fund.
- Meet people other than the fund's manager.
- Understand the fund's lockup provisions.
- Ask for cut fees if the fund is starting out and you are an initial investor, or if you are committing a large percentage of your total capital.
- If your hedge fund is down 20 percent or more in a year, get out.

6

HOW TO PLAY M&A

I broke three of the biggest deal stories of my career because people couldn't keep their mouths shut. It is human nature to boast. And when you put that together with youthful exuberance, you find the ingredients for many of the finer scoops I've had the pleasure to uncover.

The tip that led me to break news of United Technologies' plan to buy Honeywell in October 2000 came from a young lawyer at Skadden, Arps. I don't know him (if I did, I could never tell this story), and he probably has no idea that he's the reason I found out about the deal. That's because he really didn't say much. He just casually told a friend who worked at a hedge fund that he was working on an "old economy," $40 billion deal that was close to being announced. The friend told his boss, who then told me. I nailed down the story in one day.

I have a junior banker at Lazard Frères to thank for the tip that led me to break the news of British Telecom's pending acquisition of MCI in late 1996. The banker unwittingly bragged to one of my sources at a private-equity firm that he was working on a telecom deal that would net Lazard a hefty $30 million fee. He mentioned no names — just an industry and a fee amount. It took me three full weeks to nail down the size, composition, and names behind that deal.

During the last week of December 1998, one of my hedge fund sources called me from poolside in Florida to tell me a deal was coming in telecom. He didn't know names and didn't know size, other than that it was "big." It took me about three days to ascertain that "big" meant more than $40 billion dollars, which probably meant that Bell Atlantic was going to take control of the wireless company AirTouch. I never asked my source how he knew of the pending deal. I don't want to know. But something tells me there's a good chance it was a young banker or lawyer doing a little bit of harmless bragging.

You'll notice a couple of things in the aforementioned stories. First, as the years went by, it took me much less time to confirm a story once I received a rock-solid tip. That's because of relationships with bankers, lawyers, and industry executives that have broadened and deepened with time. It's also testimony to the overall power of CNBC in helping me get my calls returned more quickly.

Chances are that you won't get the tips I do (I told you, people like to brag). And even if you do, you can't rely on my network of sources to determine whether what you are being told is true. Nevertheless, your investing acumen can be markedly improved by thinking as I do when you receive a tip of a takeover. And that brings me to the second point to be drawn from this brief list of takeover scoops: although each of the companies mentioned was acquired, none of the companies that acquired them was the potential buyer listed above. In each case, another company came in and paid more. In two of the cases, that was due in part to my reporting the pending deal before it was signed, but the point remains the same. Not only is there money to be made in accurately understanding the nature of takeover tips and their veracity, but there is also money to be made and saved by understanding when takeovers are likely, when other bidders may emerge, and when deals will go bad.

The Truth About Rumors

Rumors are essential to the health of any capital market. If we passed a law tomorrow making it illegal to discuss or trade on rumors, volume would contract significantly. Each day hundreds of stocks rise or fall based on information bruited about that may or may not be true. And at the very center of that maelstrom, occupying the most significant amount of real estate, is the takeover rumor. Takeover rumors, with their promise of quick riches, are the most alluring and dangerous ones in the mill.

I will report on rumors of all kinds when they are directly responsible for the change in value of a particular security. Naturally, I would always prefer to report only on facts or to debunk rumors I know to be false. But I believe investors are better off knowing why a particular security is moving, even if the news is not confirmed to be true. Sometimes the distinctions between fact and rumor seem to be lost on my viewers anyway.

Moments after I reported that United Tech was in talks to buy Honeywell, Jack Welch happened to be on the floor of the New York Stock Exchange. My colleague Bob Pisani told him, "Our own David Faber reports that United Tech and Honeywell are in talks. . . ." Jack's reaction was, "Well, that's quite a rumor." I later sent Welch a lighthearted e-mail teasing him for degrading a huge scoop broken on his own company's network. Jack is not alone. I often face instances when sophisticated investors take a rumor for the truth, and the truth for a rumor.

But what is a rumor? One of my favorite ridiculous terms is the *unconfirmed rumor*. What the hell does that mean? Can something be both rumor and fact? What about true rumors versus false facts? Do rumors refer to truthfulness, or to the degree to which the information is public?

To settle it, the authority — *Merriam-Webster's Collegiate Dictionary*, tenth edition:

rumor: 1. Talk or opinion widely disseminated with no discernible source. 2. A statement or report current without known authority for its truth.

fact: A piece of information presented as having objective reality.

But does this really clear up the controversy? Suppose I know that a story about Company A acquiring Company B is true. The CEO of A told me it's true and even faxed me a deal memorandum, but refused to allow me to identify him by name or share the terms of the deal. If I go on the air and report that "A is in talks to buy B, which I've confirmed with a high-level source close to the company," I feel that's a fact, not a rumor. But to the viewer, who may own shares of the companies in question, which were already moving before my report and continued to do so afterward, is it a fact or a rumor or both? It's a fact because I've presented the piece of information as having objective reality. Yet it's also talk that's widely disseminated, and my source, while known to me, is not known to my viewers. So who knows?

In any case, I never state that something is a rumor when I know it's a fact. If I can confirm that Amgen is in talks to buy Immunex (as I did), I don't report, "There are rumors that Amgen may buy Immunex" — I report the *fact* that the two companies are in talks. I distinguish these sources with phrases that are a journalist's best friend: the old "people close to the company" or "people familiar with the situation." To a sophisticated viewer, those two phrases should set off alarms that what I am reporting is fact and that the sources who have given me the information will not allow me to go beyond such an attribution.

The word *rumor* is occasionally invoked by companies that I have covered to invalidate what I have reported. I may report as a fact something that a company is not yet prepared to corroborate. When contacted by other news organizations following up on my story, it will issue the standard, useless, but legally safe comment: "We don't comment on rumors and speculation." If I know it's true but the company won't confirm it and no other reporter can confirm it, either, is what I've reported a fact or a rumor? Have I driven you up a wall with this yet? Perhaps it's time to move on, because though it is important to understand what a rumor is, it's more important for investors to understand what they can do upon hearing one.

As an investor, you may pick up rumors from a variety of sources: your broker, a friend or business associate, the Internet, a relative, or someone else who works on Wall Street. Very often it is the identity of the person who shares the rumor with you that speaks most clearly to its chances of being true. The neighbor who works at the big drug company in town and tells you he's hearing a rumor about a pharmaceutical company is a better bet than some smooth-talking broker. But since this book is about Wall Street, I'll start with who starts rumors there.

Rumors are often started by traders. To create liquidity for a big order (and get the price rising), the trader floats a rumor. Say Fidelity wants to sell 2 million shares of Yahoo! It tells Morgan Stanley to move 100,000 shares, with maybe more behind that. Fidelity won't lay the whole amount on Morgan Stanley at once. It doesn't even want Morgan to know how much it has to sell, but traders normally are able to tell if there's a lot more stock for sale. So Fidelity keeps an eye on how Morgan Stanley "works the order"; if Morgan appears to do a good job, Fidelity may lay another 100,000 shares on them.

The trader wants that business. Fidelity is a prized customer and generates hundreds of millions in commissions on Wall Street. So our particular trader working this Yahoo! sell order finds a buddy, such as a naive reporter or a portfolio manager, and says, "Remember the old Disney-Yahoo! rumors, and that analyst at Goldman who said Yahoo! needs a partner? Well, I'm hearing Disney might be taking a look. I don't know if this is true, but . . ." This particular rumor has some logical credibility. Disney and Yahoo! have done business together. AOL and Time

Warner already got together. Disney's stock has been weak, but Yahoo!'s is off by 90 percent.

Obviously, this rumor benefits Fidelity. Instead of Yahoo! sinking as Fido's 100,000 shares add to the supply, Yahoo!'s price is likely to be stable or move up if the notion that Disney is mulling a bid spreads through the market. And if the trader has some decent channels for quiet dissemination, chances are that it will. The rumor also benefits the Morgan Stanley trader who started it — in two ways. First, he has done a service for his client: Fidelity is selling its shares into a more liquid market but did not get its hands dirty in the process; in fact, it probably had no idea about the genesis of the rumor. Second, the rising price and volume might encourage Fidelity to let the trader sell more, earning more commissions.

Rumors can also be started by investment bankers to introduce an idea into the marketplace and get a sense from investors of its merits. Let's use our Disney/Yahoo! rumor (this is purely a hypothetical exercise). A banker might visit Disney's management team to pitch it on the idea of buying Yahoo! "It is a natural fit. You will diversify your streams of cash flow and create great synergy with your other media properties. Blah, blah, blah." Bob Iger, Disney's president, might answer the banker by saying, "It will kill our earnings because even now Yahoo! trades at a much higher multiple to earnings than we do, and our stock will get crushed. Please leave my office."

If our banker is a tenacious sort, he might choose to try to prove Iger wrong. If the rumor is floated into the market and gets Yahoo! shares moving up, while Disney shares do not move down, perhaps Iger will take notice. Maybe he'll even call back that banker and take another meeting on the idea. It's also possible that some large Disney shareholders, upon hearing the rumor, will encourage Iger to consider a Yahoo! purchase. It's a long shot, but bankers take that shot all the time.

This type of rumormongering is very different from the role that bankers play in spreading word of a potential deal. On occasion, after trying to nail down a particular takeover story, a banker will confirm the story for me and include every detail, such as the prospective ratio of shares to be exchanged. Let's assume that Disney decided to buy Yahoo! and I was picking up strong hints of the deal. I might call the banker I believed was advising Yahoo! and in this case he might confirm that a deal was near in which Disney was about to exchange a half share for each share of Yahoo! Why would a banker tell me that? Because even though the deal might be near signing, it might still require Yahoo!'s board of directors to agree that a price of half a Disney share was adequate for Yahoo! shareholders. By confirming details of a takeover story, bankers can check the market as to how the respective share prices would trade if the deal were announced. The market's reaction to my story gives the board of Yahoo! a good sense of how Disney's share price will perform once the deal is official. And if Disney shares slump markedly based on my report, Yahoo!'s board might request some price protection on the deal, or scrap it entirely.

Bankers also spread rumors of a deal as a smokescreen in order to shield from scrutiny a transaction they are working on. One of my worst moments in journalism occurred when rumors began to swirl that Deutsche Bank was in talks to buy J.P. Morgan. Morgan had been the fodder of takeover rumors for some time, and these rumors had intensified after CS First Boston announced its acquisition of Donaldson, Lufkin & Jenrette. But the rumors didn't make sense. J.P. Morgan's management was not likely to sell out to Deutsche Bank, and Deutsche Bank had already suffered mixed results from its acquisition of Bankers Trust just a couple of years earlier.

Still, I pursued the rumors until I was able to prove to my satisfaction that they were not valid. I reported my findings toward the end of the trading day. My timing could not have been worse. Ten minutes after telling viewers that J.P. Morgan was not in talks to be acquired by Deutsche Bank, we got word that it would be acquired by Chase. I had gone for the feint and missed the real story. It was a big mistake.

Rumors don't always originate in the capital markets. Many

times a rumor begins on Main Street and works its way onto Wall Street. I am talking about the tendency of people to share information when they should not. The wife or husband of a CEO tells a tennis partner or a college roommate that now would be a smart time to buy shares in the company. That person calls his or her broker and in addition to buying some stock buys some options. The broker, who likely knows very little of the reason behind this buying, nonetheless may be able to surmise that something is afoot. The rumor is now in the marketplace. And that leads me to the first of many checks an investor can undertake to determine whether a takeover rumor might be true.

Have Options Been Trading in a Strange Way?

A stock option is the right to buy or sell 100 shares of a stock at a predetermined price within a specific period. A "call" option represents the right to buy, and a "put" represents the right to sell. Buying a Dell "Oct. 50" call gives you the right — but not the obligation — to purchase 100 shares of Dell at $50 on or before the third Friday of October.

So how much is that right worth? It depends. If Dell is trading at $30 a week before the option expires, the right to pay $50 per share isn't worth much. But if Dell is at $49 three months before the option expires, the right to pay $50 for it could be worth quite a bit. That's because there's a good chance the stock will be above your "strike price" ($50) within the time you have to exercise the option. If Dell is trading at $65 by the time you exercise your option, then your right to buy 100 shares at $50 is worth $1,500 (you'd pay $5,000 for $6,500 worth of stock). And the same goes for puts: the right to sell at 40 is valuable if the stock is at 45 (and more so if it's at 35), but questionable if the stock's at 60.

In many of the stories I've broken, volume on the call options of the company about to be acquired was unusually high. Taken alone, this piece of information is not of great value. For weeks

UNDERSTANDING OPTIONS

Options are derivatives — they have no intrinsic value but "derive" their value based on the price of some other financial instrument. So the value of an option to buy or sell Dell stock is based on Dell's current stock price. In this case, Dell is called the "underlying security." The underlying can be a stock (like Dell) or even an entire stock index, such as the S&P 500.

Options aren't free. Buyers pay a premium, which is determined by the market's perception of the likelihood that the option will be worth something when it expires. The first variable is the price of the underlying stock. If a stock's at $80, a call at 90 will cost more than a call at 100. Time is the second critical variable. The more time before an option expires, the more chance the stock has to rise above the strike price. So if Dell is trading at 30 in February, the "June 40" call is more expensive than the "March 40" call because Dell has a longer period of time in which to reach the $40 level. The other major factor influencing an option's price is the volatility of the underlying stock. More volatile stocks have more expensive option premiums, since there's a greater chance the stock will move in one's favor.

Options volume is one of the things to check out when gauging the credibility of a particular rumor. Because of the leverage available through options — each call or put controls 100 shares — they are the vehicle of choice for those looking to make a quick killing without using vast amounts of capital. Of course, the risk is also much greater with options.

before the story broke that it was to be acquired by Daimler-Benz (a scoop by my dear friend Steven Lipin, formerly of the *Wall Street Journal*), Chrysler's call options were unusually active. I was alerted to that activity but was clearly not getting the information that Steve was turning up and therefore found nothing else to imply that the historic deal was near.

Even when you've got a lot more to go on, options volume is still not enough to prove there's a deal at hand. I was incredulous when I first started to hear that Exxon was working on a deal to acquire Mobil. The sheer size of the deal, not to mention potential regulatory constraints (more on that later), seemed to make such a deal unlikely. But I kept getting hints indicating that something was indeed going on, although I was unable to confirm as much with anyone actually involved. Here, I was let down by my lack of good sources in the oil and gas industry and a failure to reach the small group of bankers and lawyers who were actually working on the gargantuan deal. But I kept plugging away, in part because of the persistently high volume in the call options of Mobil. I never did nail down the story. The best I could muster was a report on the rumors and a list of reasons why those rumors might and might not be true. Pretty lame.

As an investor, you are not beholden to anyone but yourself. Nothing might have stopped you from buying some Mobil shares based on the information that I had. No need for you to be sure. But when it comes to options volume, a word of caution: though it can be a helpful tool in uncovering a deal, option activity can also be used to create the impression of a deal by those who are spreading fallacious rumors of the same deal. Think about it. The trader does a little volume way out of the money, such as buying 40 calls (options to buy shares at $40) when the stock is trading at $20. Then he starts a rumor and, as evidence that something is up, points to the increase in options activity — which he himself created! The trader plays on basic greed and mistrust: "He must know something, because why else would someone buy options so far out of the money?"

- For basic options info, the Chicago Board Options Exchange (www.cboe.com) provides free price and volume information for options on all exchanges, with a twenty-minute delay.
- At www.cboe.com, you can look at the 100 options that have

most exceeded their average monthly volume during the month, and you can download a spreadsheet that lists those figures for all options. Both sets are about two months out of date, unfortunately.

The most important checks on potential deals go to the heart of a simple question: Does the deal make sense?

IS THE ACQUIRER LARGER AND MORE "SIGNIFICANT"?

When I was working on confirming whether Exxon was actually talking to Mobil about buying it, the size of the transaction made a deal hard to imagine. But in fact it was possible for Exxon to pursue the deal. It was bigger than Mobil in every important category: revenues, earnings, and market value. In that important regard, the rumor held up to scrutiny.

Starting with size is as good a place as any to judge the merits of a particular story you may be hearing. A portfolio manager who makes frequent appearances on CNBC e-mailed me one fine day to let me know she was hearing that WorldCom might soon be acquired by Japan's NTT. This was back in the days when WorldCom's market value was still enormous. I knew the rumor was likely false, given that Japanese companies are historically cautious (not to mention that there would be some serious political ramifications of such a deal). And it was equally unlikely that WorldCom would buy NTT, given the barriers in the Japanese market to foreign ownership. But once I checked the size, I didn't need to check anything else: WorldCom was at the time a much more valuable company than NTT.

There are deals in which a smaller company is the acquirer, but very rarely when an exchange of stock is taking place. If Nokia was going to take control of Lucent, as was once briefly rumored, its shareholders would have had to wind up with the majority of the shares in the combined company, something that could happen only if Nokia was more highly valued than Lucent.

Even then, it wouldn't be a sure thing. Although Nokia was larger when the rumors (untrue) first emerged, that state of affairs had not been in existence for very long. The story might have made sense from a salvaging-value-while-in-decline perspective, but you have to be skeptical about whether a sudden reversal of fortune is enough to turn a formerly acquisitive giant into a target. It is rare for a company to rush to the altar after a rapid decline in its stock. It takes a while for the management of a company such as Lucent, which spent a year trading at $50–$80, to grow accustomed to the idea that its stock may not see that level again and that offers from smaller, less prestigious companies should be entertained should they materialize. By the time Lucent and Alcatel were talking in May 2001, Lucent's problems were so great that any grand expectations ceased to be a concern; the two companies were contemplating a deal that valued Lucent in the $8–$9 per share range.

Conversely, if the acquirer's stock has recently shot up, it is relatively unlikely that an acquirer will want to give the inflated currency full value. This is why there were relatively few mergers between Internet companies and more established companies during the dot-com boom. For all the rumors, the only large completed transaction was AOL and Time Warner, and that was because Gerry Levin was a true believer in the Internet and considered AOL's valuation to be real, and Steve Case was the rare Internet CEO who recognized the value of real assets and old-economy cash flow.

So consider size from the perspective not only of market cap but also of sales, earnings, cash flow, workforce, and history.

HOW DO THE BUSINESSES FIT?

Make this one of your first questions, since it should be the first question asked by the CEOs of both companies considering the deal.

Look at the annual reports to get a good description of the

business units. Are they in similar businesses, which if combined could produce economies of scale without major antitrust concern? (More on that in a minute.) Are they in similar businesses, which if combined would diversify their product lines sufficiently to produce more growth? Remember, deals among businesses in the same industries can be horizontal (extending your product line, such as owning a chain of gas stations and buying another) or vertical (extending your reach in the production chain by buying an oil-exploration operation when you already own a chain of gas stations).

Companies do illogical things and merge for the wrong reasons. So you may — despite knowing that the merger could be proposed only by a couple of morons — turn on the TV and see the two CEOs grinning like jack-o'-lanterns as they discuss the supposed merits of the transaction.

IS THE TRANSACTION ACCRETIVE?

In the Disney buying Yahoo! example, I fictitiously quote Bob Iger as being concerned about the earnings dilution Disney would suffer if it ever pursued such a deal. Concern about a deal's potential dilution is very real for any company considering a transaction. The concept here is fairly straightforward. Companies earn more or less per share after a transaction. When an acquiring company's earnings per share are less than they would have been without the acquisition, the transaction is said to be "dilutive" to the acquirer during the period of time that state of affairs persists. When the acquiring company's earnings are higher per share than they would have been, the transaction is or becomes "accretive" or "additive."

Companies with very high p/e ratios can more easily do accretive deals. If a company trading at 100 times earnings buys a company trading at ten times earnings, the acquirer is getting an awful lot of earnings for its money (and usually, that "money" is stock). For example, let's imagine two companies with 100 million shares outstanding. They each earned $100 million (EPS of $1/share), but Company A trades at fifty times earnings (giving it a p/e of 50) while Company B trades at ten (p/e of 10). Company B's market cap is $1 billion, so if A buys it for 20 million shares of its own stock ($1 billion), A's shareholders now have $200 million in earnings (double the EPS) while sacrificing only 20 percent of their shares. That's accretive.

P/E ratio The most widely accepted tool for determining the value of a company's stock price. It is the stock price divided by the per share earnings of the company. Or if you prefer, you can take the company's market value and divide it by the yearly net income of the company. Either way, you'll get the same number. If a stock has a price of $100 and earnings per share of $10, its p/e ratio is 10.

Taken another way, when you buy this company's stock, you are paying a price that is equal to ten years' worth of its earnings if those earnings remain unchanged. Think about that for a moment. If you were to buy the entire company at ten times earnings, you would get your money back in full after ten years if those earnings remain unchanged. That's a return of 10 percent on your money. If the earnings increase by 10 percent every year, you will get your money back in a little over seven years, increasing your rate of return to closer to 14 percent a year. With yields on the most risk-free asset (treasury bonds) at 3–4 percent, a 10 percent return or better doesn't look too bad. But that, of course, assumes earnings stay the same or improve. As we know, during a ten-year period there may be some years that don't go very well — which is why investors are happy to pay higher p/e ratios or multiples for companies such as GE, which deliver consistent earnings growth every year.

This is one of the reasons that companies such as WorldCom did deal after deal while their stocks traded at very high multiples to earnings. Each time a deal was completed for a company with a lower p/e, the earnings of the combination rose, in turn helping the stock price rise so it could be used for future deals.

(WorldCom may also have used each deal as an opportunity to bury operating expenses as one-time charges, thereby increasing its operating margins. WorldCom denies it; but either way, WorldCom's strong operating margins were one reason that investors were willing to award it a higher multiple to earnings than its peers, which helped keep its stock high. And around we go. But that's a story for another day.)

In getting back to our rumor example of Nokia and Lucent, Nokia had a much higher p/e than Lucent, and back then Lucent was still earning a decent amount of money, so a deal between them would have been accretive to Nokia. On this basis, the rumor might have made sense. But when we move on to another check of the cultural issues, it's a lot less compelling.

HOW DO THE CULTURAL ISSUES STACK UP?

There have been plenty of foreign acquirers of U.S. companies over the past decade, but many of the deals have not gone particularly well. That in part is because we do things differently here than they do over there. And though every foreign acquirer takes pains to say that it won't change a thing and is looking to learn from the U.S. counterpart, invariably it does try to bend the acquired company to seeing things its way.

Given the problems that such high-profile deals as Daimler's acquisition of Chrysler have encountered, not to mention the huge cultural impediments faced by Matsushita and Sony when they bought their way into the movie business by acquiring MCA and Sony in the early 1990s, it takes a very confident CEO to pull the trigger on a large cross-border deal. That's why while we can't dismiss the idea of Nokia's acquiring Lucent, it does seem to have its share of cultural hurdles. Of course, less than a year after the Nokia rumors emerged, Lucent did try to get bought by a French company (Alcatel). But, alas, that deal fell apart prior to signing because the two sides were unable to breach all the cultural gaps that separated them.

IS IT A SOCIAL FIT?

Lucent's CEO Henry Schacht is as fine a man as you're likely to find in the executive suite. But as tireless as he is, Henry was only too happy to find a graceful exit to his second tour of duty as Lucent's CEO. That's one of the reasons he was willing to consider the Alcatel transaction. There was no doubt about who would run the combined company. Henry was happy to take over the role of chairman and let his younger French counterpart, Serge Tchuruk, have the day-to-day operational responsibilities of Alcatel Lucent as its CEO. But that dynamic is not always the case.

A company is less likely to willingly sell out if its CEO believes he has a lot of leadership years left or has a strong senior management team that is eager to compete for the top job. When you hear a takeover rumor, check the ages and the management styles of the CEOs. If the talked-about deal features two young, ambitious CEOs who haven't shown previous interest in being acquired or acquiring, be skeptical. When I was chasing down the leads that led to my break of the Amgen-Immunex merger, I was first able to confirm that Amgen was going to buy a big biotech company, but unable to determine which one. My initial instinct was that Biogen might be Amgen's prize, because the deal would have added strongly to Amgen's earnings. But upon learning that Biogen's CEO was only forty-two years old and had been in the position for a short time, I quickly discounted Biogen. Other times the CEO's m.o. is precisely what makes the deal believable. In our Nokia-for-Lucent example, it was very possible that Henry Schacht was looking for a successor, and a deal would have given him an answer to that search.

TO TRUST OR ANTITRUST:
WILL THE REGULATORS PUT UP A FUSS?

The goal of U.S. antitrust law is to protect consumers. The best way to do so, consistent with the amount of involvement the gov-

ernment generally wants in business affairs, is to promote competition. The two types of conduct prohibited by U.S. antitrust
laws that are most often tested in merger situations are collusion
among competitors and abuse of monopoly power. The traditional focus of merger policy has been horizontal activity — either
dominating a market individually or colluding with competitors
to control it. Vertical activity — having an interest in several levels of an activity — can also be illegal but requires more proof of
abuse and harm.

When I was hearing rumors of WorldCom's plans to buy Sprint
(another story I failed to break), it always seemed to me and many
industry experts that the deal would have a hard time passing the
antitrust authorities. The companies were the number two and
number three players in the market for long-distance services, and
the government has rarely allowed the number two and number
three players in any market to get together when taken together
the top three control 90 percent of the market. That possibility did
not stop WorldCom and Sprint, who blithely pursued their deal
until it was given the boot by the Department of Justice.

The key to whether a deal will be challenged often centers on
what the government chooses to define as a market. When Staples
said it would buy Office Depot, few investors believed the government would object, because there didn't really seem to be a market
that could be defined as "the office superstore market." After all,
there are still thousands of small stationery stores competing with
Office Depot and Staples, so why shouldn't they be considered part
of the same market? The government didn't see things that way.
The deal was challenged in court, and the government won.

Conversely, when I was picking up rumors that Exxon was
close to buying Mobil, I discounted them in part because the two
companies were numbers one and two in their respective markets. What I failed to take into account was the number of competitors that would remain even if Exxon and Mobil did get
together. (The government did force the divestiture of thousands of their gas stations, but the overall deal was approved.)

In this day of heightened covert activity and national security, it's also important to remember that the federal government will be paying close attention to any national security issue arising out of cross-border deals. Given the tragedy of September 11, it is impossible to imagine the U.S. government letting Bell Labs (owned by Lucent) pass into the control of a French company (Alcatel) if the two companies had pursued their plans to merge.

Antitrust law is a moving target, changing with whatever administration is in power and with the geopolitical realities of the day. But the antitrust card, not only here in the United States but in Europe as well, must be well considered when one hears news of an impending deal.

DOES THE ALLEGED BUYER TYPICALLY ACQUIRE COMPANIES?

There are companies that live and often die by the deal. These serial acquirers convince shareholders that they know better how to manage companies, and use their high multiple stock price to acquire lesser multiple companies time after time after time. In the end many of these companies have gotten tripped up, either by doing a deal (think HSF-CUC) or by not being able to do a deal (think WorldCom-Sprint). In some ways these serial acquirers were a phenomenon of the long-lost bull market, but every market and every decade have their share of such companies.

Tyco had been the foremost serial acquirer left standing after the bear market of 2000–01. This diversified industrial company did deal after deal, but when its multiple to earnings crashed in early 2002, the company took a 180-degree turn and decided to break itself up, only to reverse that strategy when the market didn't like it. Still, in the next bull market, there's bound to be a company in a similar deal frenzy, so when you hear a rumor involving that company, it may have some validity given the acquirer's predilection for doing deals. This does not mean that you should rule out deals by companies that typically eschew them. Even Bell-South may someday decide that it needs to pursue a deal. Sometimes a company that has not used deals as a mechanism for growth decides to go on a buying spree. Amgen had eschewed any large deals throughout its history before embarking on biotech's largest acquisition of all time with the Immunex deal.

IS THERE TURMOIL AT THE POTENTIAL TARGET?

Turbulence at a target may make the company more willing to consider offers, but it also makes it more dangerous to acquire. In the case of Lucent, the company was suffering even more than competitors (who were suffering plenty) from a lack of demand for its products. An even bigger impediment to deals than temporary cyclical business issues are things like suspected misdeeds or revenue-recognition issues, such as the type Lucent announced right before the Nokia rumor was making the rounds. Such issues are deal killers. Even if the company's stock price declines dramatically because of such an announcement (as Lucent's did), few companies are willing to take on the risk of a deal when issues of accounting dog the potential prey. It's simply not worth the risk.

DO THE COMPANIES ALREADY WORK TOGETHER?

Companies having ongoing joint projects suggests that rumor has merit. Disney and Capital Cities–owned ABC jointly developed and owned the TV show *Home Improvement* before the merger and also had been working together to create an ESPN-themed attraction as part of Disney World. Chevron and Texaco had been partners in a joint petroleum venture in Asia for some sixty-five years before their merger. British Telecom already owned 20 percent of MCI before it made its bid for the rest.

DO THE COMPANIES SHARE BOARD MEMBERS?

Relationships between board members at the target and acquirer make it easy to imagine how discussions could have started. You can get a list of directors from many sources, but go right to the proxy statement. Many companies post the proxy statement on their web sites, but you can get them all from the Securities and Exchange Commission's (SEC) archive, EDGAR. Reading the directors' backgrounds could give you clues to affiliations among directors. Perhaps they have no common directors, but some of each company's directors may serve together on another board. This is not a key check, since there are many ways for companies to open the lines of communication. But it can be a helpful sign. Nokia and Lucent, for example, shared no board members or likely affiliations between members.

There's no one question on this list that reliably produces a definitive signal that a rumored deal will or will not happen. It's just that a positive answer leans toward likeliness while a negative exerts some debunking force. So, a whole bunch of positive answers indicates a rumor definitely worth considering or even acting upon, and a preponderance of negative means you can pretty safely bet that the rumor is false.

After the Announcement

After a deal has been announced for a company that you own shares in, what should you do? Before discussing what to do if you decide to hold on to those shares, I must tell you that selling those shares is as good a course as any. If you got into a stock because you liked the company's management and its strategy, a takeover offer that puts a few bucks in your pocket and will likely change what you liked about the company is a natural opportunity to consider saying good-bye.

The company in which you invested has substantially changed. If you own the target, and you invested because you thought the company had a certain amount of value, the acquirer's actions show that you have achieved your objective. If it is a stock deal, the company whose shares you will own will be much different from the one you originally chose. For all those reasons, it may make sense to sell when the deal is announced.

STOCK STORY:
Global Crossing, Frontier, and US West

Global Crossing's plan to buy US West was one of the more bizarre deals to come out of the bull market in telecom stocks. How I broke that story illustrates many of the skills to be used in navigating the tangled web of rumor traffic.

Before 1997 Global Crossing didn't even exist. Two years later it was becoming a major telecommunications player with an even more major market value. Two years after that it would collapse. In early 1999 I heard that it was working on a deal to acquire US West. When I first heard the rumor, I didn't believe it. The idea that one of the Baby Bells would accept the paper of an upstart company such as Global Crossing seemed absurd. Aside from what I thought would be US West's reluctance to accept a high-flying currency, I also wondered about regulatory risks, since a connection between local and long-distance providers appeared to break some laws. I was also curious how these two would fit both socially (two relatively young CEOs) and culturally (upstart versus bureaucratic behemoth).

The rumor came to me from a trusted source. When I asked him where he had heard it, he would say only that it was coming from a guy in Denver, where US West was based. The same source had passed along another rumor from the Denver guy a few months earlier that had turned out to be true but that I had ignored. Given this Denver guy's track record, I decided it was worth making a few calls.

On March 18, 1999, Global had reached an agreement to buy Frontier Communications for $11 billion in stock. Frontier was larger than Global in almost every way save market value. Given that deal, I was also quite curious as to why or how Global Crossing could pull off another deal without Frontier's permission.

I started making my calls to bankers and lawyers, but I also decided to speak with Michael Kaminsky, a portfolio manager at Neuberger Berman and a large shareholder of Global Crossing who didn't buy into the rumor. Portfolio managers are not usually privy to deal making, so I hadn't called Michael because I thought he would know if something was going on. Instead, I called him to get a sense of how Global Crossing shareholders would view the deal. Kaminsky also knew a number of people in management, people whom I would come to know well in later years but didn't have relationships with at that point. And I did think that upon hearing this rumor, he might be able to get a check from management on its veracity. (As it turned out, he called and was lied to.)

I also spoke with Paul Zoidis, an investment banker I thought might be working for US West. His firm, Lehman Brothers, had taken the lead in separating US West from its cable company, MediaOne, a few years earlier. Zoidis clearly had no idea of any deal — if he had, he would have gotten rid of me quickly. Instead, he dwelled leisurely on Section 271 of the Telecommunications Act of 1996, which requires Baby Bells to file a very detailed application for permission to provide long-distance services; Frontier and Global Crossing both provided long-distance service, but US West did not. Zoidis also questioned whether Global Crossing would want to be a facilities-based carrier — i.e., a company that owns and operates the switching machinery that actually makes the calls — since the infrastructure and its maintenance cost a fortune. He concluded by telling me, "It's not something I'd recommend. If they want to do a thirty-billion-dollar deal, they could buy better facilities. There are also social issues about who would run this company."

Then I called an attorney with whom I have a good relationship. He's someone who would never lie and will on occasion offer some guidance. I asked him what he knew. "I think your bunny has a good nose," he replied, then silence, *click,* dial tone. (The quote comes from the insider-trading scandals of the 1980s and was popularized in the movie *Wall Street.*) Suddenly and with one phone call, I went from thinking that I was chasing a useless rumor to knowing that something was going on.

My next calls were to Frontier's bankers at Morgan Stanley. "I think Global Crossing is going to merge with US West. What does that do to your deal?" I figured these guys had to be aware that their merger partner was already focusing on the next deal. So when one of the bankers told me that Global Crossing couldn't do a deal without Frontier's blessing, I realized that these guys didn't know what was going on. Finally, he admitted to hearing that Global Crossing's Gary Winnick "was out there trying to do something." But the banker assured me that Gary had to get Frontier's approval if he planned to issue more than $2.5 billion in stock (which would clearly be the case). "He has not requested permission, and I'd know if he did."

I talked with another senior telecom banker who had worked at Credit Suisse First Boston and went off on his own. "What's in it for Global Crossing?" "They get traffic," he told me, and traffic is worth a lot. Local phone customers of US West could become users of Global's network — the synergy argument. He also pointed out that this could be a classic case of using an inflated stock price to buy some real assets and cash flow. "Boy, they must be desperate at US West," he concluded, "if they are willing to take stock from Global Crossing."

Then I had a conversation with someone close to our friend Jack Grubman, Salomon Smith Barney's celebrity telecom banker-analyst, who I knew had strong ties to Global Crossing. Grubman was supposed to be in Spain, but I discovered that he was actually in Denver for the weekend. Well, what do you know? That's where US West has its headquarters.

Time was now of the essence. In speaking to bankers and lawyers and one portfolio manager, I'd put this rumor in the public domain where other reporters could get wind of it and start making some of the same calls I had. I also didn't want the rumor to move too far too fast and send US West's stock price up, bringing further media scrutiny.

A few days passed while I sat on the story and stewed. I still couldn't get someone to confirm it outright or give me some details. The week was drawing to a close, and if there was a deal near, it was likely to be announced on Monday morning and leaked to the *Wall Street Journal* over the weekend. I called someone who typically does investor relations for companies about to do deals. To my shock he confirmed the story flat out: Global was about to acquire US West. He gave me the confirmation because the story was starting to get

222 | THE FABER REPORT

out and rather than have it slowly leak into the market without details and the aid of some spin, he decided it was better to give me both.

The Section 271 issues, he told me, were being addressed, and no one worried about the outcome. Frontier did not know about the deal, and he claimed that it did not have a right to veto the agreement, anyway. One rationale for the deal, he explained, was that US West was way ahead of everyone else in hooking up DSL service for its customers, representing a huge potential revenue stream. "There are some interesting wrinkles. We're not tying Global Crossing to a dinosaur."

My next call was my favorite. I phoned Frontier's banker at Morgan Stanley and told him I knew that Global Crossing was buying US West. He didn't really say anything in response, so I hung up; I knew he was immediately dialing Frontier's CEO.

As I was preparing my story, I got a call from the investor-relations contact saying the deal had hit a big roadblock: Frontier was (surprise, surprise) furious that Global had left it out of the loop, not to mention that *I* somehow had gotten in the loop, and was threatening to block the deal.

As you know, Global Crossing did sign a deal to acquire US West. And, as I reported would be the case, Qwest came in to break up this marriage by bidding for both Frontier and US West. Qwest got US West, and in doing so may have ensured its survival, while Global Crossing completed the purchase of Frontier but filed bankruptcy three years later.

Investors can't necessarily replicate this kind of investigation. And even if an investor does find himself with, say, an M&A lawyer telling him that a deal is afoot, it's illegal to trade on that info. Nevertheless, it's vital to understand how the skills of a reporter can be used to be a good investor.

That said, you may choose for a variety of reasons not to sell. Perhaps the takeover premium was not to your liking. Perhaps there was no premium at all. Perhaps you believe that the combination resulting from the deal will be superior to the company you invested in or that a better offer will emerge. Those are all valid reasons for staying in after the announcement of a takeover or merger. But if you choose to do so, you had better read on.

Risk Arbitrage

The name sounds kind of sexy, but the profession is not. Those who are good at it are very smart, incredibly attentive to nuance and detail, and well versed in the law. Even then, they can get their heads handed to them — and often do.

Historically, arbitrage involved exploiting inefficiencies among different markets. If, for example, gold traded for more in Zurich than in London, an arbitrageur would buy in London and simultaneously sell in Zurich. As markets became more efficient, spreads on such things became smaller, but it also became possible to bet on more situations.

Collar In a stock-for-stock merger, the parties may agree to put in a protection for the target in an attempt to ensure that the value of the deal is maintained if the acquirer's stock price goes down. This protection, referred to as a collar, can alter the exchange ratio, depending on where the acquirer's stock price trades.

If the acquirer's stock price trades within the collar, but toward its higher end, the ratio of shares correspondingly adjusts lower: the value of the deal stays the same, but because the shares are valued at a higher level, fewer total shares need to be exchanged. Conversely, if the stock trades toward the bottom of the collar, the acquirer is forced to issue more shares in order to conserve the value. When the stock trades either above or below the collar, the ratio is fixed at whatever level was specified for the top or bottom of the collar. In some deals, the target has the opportunity to call off the deal if the acquirer's stock price trades below the collar for a certain number of days prior to the deal's closing. Many deals do not feature collars, a fact often seized upon by management of both companies to justify how confident they are that the deal is a good one and should be rewarded in the marketplace.

> **Exchange ratio** The ratio of stock traded between companies in a stock-for-stock merger. Typically, one company is designated the surviving entity, and its stock is distributed to the other company with its own shareholders keeping their stock. For example, when AOL and Time Warner announced their merger in January 2000, AOL was the acquiring entity. Its shareholders kept their shares while Time Warner shareholders received 1.5 shares of AOL for each Time Warner share they owned. The ratio, in comparison to the share prices of the two companies, represents the companies' view of the relative value of the two companies and what premium, if any, is due one of the companies.

In the eighties risk arbitrage was a more glamorous, mysterious business. It was also tinged with malfeasance, most notably reflected in the outright cheating undertaken by the best-known risk arbitrageur of his time, Ivan Boesky. Boesky and others made much of their money before a deal was announced by buying shares of companies they believed would soon be the subject of takeover offers. This was a day when Wall Street still didn't let a great deal of sunlight in. The arbitrageurs, the investment bankers, and the corporate raiders were all part of the same fraternity, where inside information was readily obtainable and the security laws had yet to catch up to the reality of the marketplace. Boesky was a slimeball who paid for information on deals, but other arbs, though less venal, also used connections to try to determine where the next deal would hit. While plenty of investors still try to find out what deal is next (hence the preceding section), risk arbitrage today is played on a much more level field.

Today's risk arbitrageurs are focused almost entirely on whether a deal, once announced, will go through as originally planned. It may not seem as daring as the way their forefathers practiced things in the 1980s, but it is not without its dramatic moments, both good and bad.

What are the key things that risk arbs and those who dabble in takeover investing focus on?

HOW RISK ARBITRAGE WORKS

The risk arbitrageur is there to buy shares from stockholders who sell once a deal is announced. The reward — and the risk — comes in the form of a spread between what the acquirer is willing to pay per share and what the stock of the company to be acquired is currently trading at. In other words, if an acquirer is planning to pay $55 in cash for every share of its target, whose stock price is currently trading at $50, the spread is $5, or 10 percent. Of course, if the deal collapses, the arbs can be in a lot of trouble.

In cash deals, the decision for risk arbs is simple: either buy the stock of the company to be acquired and wait until payday, or stay away from the deal. In stock deals, the arbs have a more complex set of circumstances with which to deal. If our $55/$50 example were a stock deal, the arb would short one share of the acquirer at $55 while at the same time buying an equal number of shares of the target at $50. When the deal closes, the arb receives one share of the acquiring company's stock for each share of the acquired company and uses those shares to cover the short position. Say the acquirer's shares rise to $60. The short position loses $5 a share, but it's made up for by the increased value of trading the $50 stock for one now worth $60. If the buyer's shares sink to $45, however, the $5 made on the short position is offset by the loss on the long position when the acquired company's shares sink.

The spread in a deal changes as the perception of the deal's certitude changes. As regulators sign off, shareholders vote in favor, and fundamentals remain as expected, the spread shrinks. If problems with regulators arise, fundamentals weaken, and the two sides start sniping at each other, chances are that the spread will widen, given the declining likelihood of the deal going through as originally planned (if at all). Throughout the deal, arbs are betting on that spread based on their perception of the risk of collapse. They can also attack that spread through the use of complex hedging strategies involving options and can use ratios that magnify their ability to profit if the deal goes through or hedge in case it doesn't.

RISK OF AN ADVERSE CHANGE IN BUSINESS

Even though merger agreements are crafted to protect the company being acquired from a sudden change of heart on the part of its acquirer, there can be adverse material changes in the business of the prey that allow the buyer to call things off. Those changes are typically defined in the material adverse change clause (MAC clause) of the merger agreement. This clause is always well reviewed by risk arbs since it defines what constitutes an "adverse change" and hence the ability of the acquiring company to walk away from a deal.

The sanctity of the material adverse change clause was reaffirmed by the Delaware Supreme Court in 2001. The court forced Tyson Foods to follow through on a purchase of food processor IBP, after Tyson had pulled out of the deal, citing a material adverse change. The judge ruled there had been no material change, only a change of heart by Tyson. Tyson completed the deal, much to the delight of risk arbitrageurs.

In a $10 billion lawsuit against Dynegy for pulling out of their merger agreement, Enron alleges that it never violated the merger agreement's material adverse change clause. Given the mischief going on at Enron, that could be tough to prove. But if a judge agrees, that MAC clause could represent the best hope any Enron creditors have of seeing some of what they are owed paid off.

In the wake of the horrific events of September 11, risk arbs were forced to examine closely the MAC clauses of any deals in the travel industry. Would Cendant, for example, be able to walk away from buying Galileo International now that its business in booking travel reservations was severely affected? If the lawyers have done a good job, material adverse changes that are suffered by all the players in an industry are excluded from reasons that a buyer can back out. Such was the case with Cendant and Galileo.

When there are changes sufficient to warrant invoking the MAC clause, it doesn't always mean that the deal will be called off. Many times the company to be acquired accepts a lower price from its suitor rather than run the risk of remaining independent. Such a move can still spell disaster for risk arbs or for any investors who have likewise chosen to wait until the deal closes before selling their shares.

Perhaps the ugliest price cut ever to hit the arbitrage community came in a deal that I was intimately familiar with. When I broke the news on November 1, 1996, of British Telecom's $22 billion acquisition of MCI, the arbs moved in fast. British Telecom (BT) was what they call a "good buyer" because it was large and steadfast. The deal was also to arbs' liking because its size allowed them to take large positions.

Cut to June 1997. MCI announces that it's going to lose $800 million on its local phone initiatives for the year — much worse than expected. Weeks pass with no word from BT, and the British financial press lays into the company's management for being snookered into overpaying for a crafty American company. The spread on the deal opens widely as investors fear a price cut or total abandonment by BT. Various analysts make pronouncements saying that their sources tell them BT will not cut the price. Lehman Brothers telecom analyst Blake Bath forever makes an enemy of the risk arbitrage community by assuring it that MCI management knows that the deal will hold. And then the ax falls: BT cuts its deal price by 20 percent, and MCI accepts.

BT investors love the new price, pushing British Telecom 5.7 percent higher on the day it's announced. Meanwhile, MCI plunges 18.7 percent in the two days following the announcement. The arbs get it on both sides since their short is going against them at the same time the long position is losing value. In the risk arbitrage world, that is the definition of pain.

I occasionally run into the former head of Salomon Brothers' risk arbitrage department who lost the firm a billion dollars in the MCI debacle. Sandy Weill eliminated the department after that hit. The trade, even all these years later, seems to haunt this gentleman, whose name I won't share out of respect. He still seems to be struggling to understand how BT could have cut the price with MCI's permission, and he shares that fact with me every time I see him, although many years have passed.

TIME VALUE OF MONEY

MCI did not go away as a public company until almost two years after I broke news of BT's bid. Deals take time to be consummated, and the acquirer's promise to pay you $55 in, say, six months is worth less than $55 today, just as a $100 savings bond that matures in seven years can be purchased for $50 today.

The spread in a deal widens and shrinks not only because of the perception of risk it won't make it to the finish line but also because the finish line may move farther and farther away, thus depressing the current value of the deal. It may be worth your while to hang around and capture a 10 percent spread, but if a deal is going to take eight months to close, keep in mind that the clock keeps ticking until you actually get paid. The main reason for delay? Antitrust.

REGULATORY REVIEW

Every merger or acquisition is subject to antitrust review by either the Department of Justice (DOJ) or the Federal Trade Commission. If the companies do any business in Europe or hope to (virtually every big company these days), the parties must also get the nod from the European Union's (EU) competition commission. I've already discussed the concerns raised in a regulatory review here in the United States. The EU tends to focus on concerns of competitors, as opposed to those of consumers. Given its importance in approving deals, the EU review adds another layer of complexity to determining whether a deal faces a tough and lengthy regulatory review.

It's not always easy to know which deals will be approved quickly and which ones will encounter serious opposition — as was certainly the case for the deal that was supposed to be Jack

Welch's career capper. GE's acquisition of Honeywell faced minimal opposition here in the United States, only to be waylaid by Mario Monti and his EU Competition Commission. The key issue was GE's ownership of both an aviation equipment manufacturer — which would be even larger and more powerful with the addition of Honeywell's line of aviation products — and a unit that finances the purchase of aviation equipment. Monti claimed that GE would be able to pressure airlines into buying only its products. His proposed solutions included GE's selling 19.9 percent of its Capital Aviation financing unit, presumably to a competitor such as Pratt & Whitney or Rolls-Royce. And despite many a risk arb's belief that Jack would somehow figure out a way to make the deal happen and offer Monti a face-saving opportunity to back down, it never happened.

The EU's public profile in this country, obviously, rose substantially with its rejection of the GE-Honeywell merger, but the EU has been a factor in big U.S. mergers as far back as 1997, when Monti's predecessor threatened to reject the Boeing–McDonnell Douglas merger. (Boeing agreed to some changes and, with pressure from the United States, the EU backed off.) After that, the EU generally worked in concert with the Justice Department, which had a similar antitrust agenda. Although the DOJ rejected the WorldCom-Sprint merger the day before the EU did, the EU made its dissatisfaction clear well before its rejection, on the murky grounds that the combined company would have too much control over the Internet's infrastructure.

Why are "they" allowed to interfere with "our" mergers? Well, U.S. companies have to obey the laws of the countries in which they do business. The same is true of non-U.S. companies doing business here; DaimlerChrysler can't ignore the National Highway Traffic Safety Administration's safety standards or EPA emissions standards by saying, "We made this Mercedes in Germany, so we have to obey only German law." Articles 81 and 82 of the Treaty of Amsterdam set out antitrust standards generally similar to U.S. standards, and the regulations give the Competition

Commission jurisdiction over any transaction in which the combined company has worldwide revenues of 5 billion Euros ($4.5 billion) and euro zone revenues of 250 million Euros ($225 million).

THE MARKET SAYS NO THANKS

The stock market can also react to news of the merger in such a negative way that it scares off the deal makers. The USA Networks–Lycos merger fell victim to this sort of market dislocation. Between the deal's announcement in February 1999 and when USA abandoned it in May, Lycos stock lost one-third of its value, and USA Networks's stock also declined. This was the first new media–old media merger, and it fell apart because one key Lycos shareholder couldn't get his mind around the idea that values in the Internet sector might be transient. David Wetherell, CMGI's founder and a board member of Lycos, had stood up and applauded when Lycos's board voted its approval of the deal, only to start booing a few days later when the market reacted negatively. As the prices continued to fall, others got nervous and the deal collapsed.

THE OVERBID

If there is one reason to hang around when your company receives a takeover bid, it is the belief that another company will come along and pay more. That's what Pfizer did for Warner-Lambert, what Norfolk Southern did for Conrail, what AT&T did for MediaOne, what WorldCom did for MCI, and what GE did for Honeywell — to name just a few.

It is not an easy thing to know when a company will be subject to another bid. But there are a few things to keep in mind.

Scarcity value. Is the company the last of its type that might be acquired or does it have some operations that are unique? AT&T, in buying TCI, had clearly decided to become the largest provider of broadband service. When MediaOne signed a deal to be acquired by Comcast, AT&T knew it couldn't let such an asset pass into the hands of a competitor; without MediaOne, AT&T's grand ambitions would not be realized. It had to make its move.

When the rails were consolidating at a rapid pace in the mid-nineties, the boys at Norfolk Southern couldn't let Conrail, one of the few remaining independents, get sold to CSX without a fight. Conrail and CSX tried to sell their deal as a merger of equals in order to hide behind the Delaware law protecting such "strategic partnerships." But it was not a merger of equals, and ultimately Norfolk Southern prevailed in buying much of the company.

I remember the shareholder vote on that deal well. I had to stand outside in mind-numbing cold (–3°) in front of the meeting place in Philadelphia to report on the progress of the vote. Inside, a long line of Conrail employees went up to the microphone to speak their piece. Each would list his or her modest holdings and go on to discuss how proud he or she was to have worked for the company and seen it through very tough times in the 1970s. Each had a story of his or her days working with the company's CEO, David LeVan. Each employee ended by supporting management's deal with CSX.

Then came a lone Wall Street guy. Eric Longmire of the risk arbitrage firm Wyser-Pratte & Company. Eric is a slight man (even in his big down jacket), and as he made his way to the microphone, I feared that he might be jumped. He listed the hundreds of thousands of shares his firm owned and was greeted with whistles from the crowd. He then explained why he would be voting his shares in support of the Norfolk Southern offer and was quickly greeted with a chorus of boos. Eric's speech was simple. There was no discussion of loyalty or sympathy or his days working on the rails. His firm favored Norfolk Southern because it was willing to pay more money for each share. Sometimes Wall Street can seem a cold place.

Scarcity value also played a role in Pfizer's decision not to stand idly by while Warner-Lambert took its rich portfolio of drugs to American Home Products. Pfizer had previously approached Warner-Lambert about a deal. Often such discussions must be detailed in the merger prospectus, which can be a good place to look to find out whether a company spurned any offers before deciding on its deal.

Is the industry consolidating? Global Crossing and Qwest fought over US West both because there were only so many regional Bells out there and because the new providers of telecommunications services were lining up with the traditional companies that had the customers. When everybody in the industry is buying or being bought, every deal draws scrutiny, and potential interest, from everybody else in that industry.

Is the deal price too cheap? If the premium in the announced deal is small, or the price is below multiples in other deals, or below where the stock traded in the past, a formerly reluctant suitor may come in because the bidding started low. First Union's agreement to acquire Wachovia in April 2001 included a price well below the book multiples of the bank deals of the previous five years. SunTrust mostly sat out that frenzy, having tried without success to negotiate a deal with Wachovia four months earlier. But with Wachovia agreeing to be acquired at little more than the market price, SunTrust stood a relatively small risk of overpaying by jumping in with its own bid.

FOR-SALE ANNOUNCEMENTS

One sure sign that a company might not be in much demand is an announcement that it's for sale, even though it hasn't received a bid. Sometimes a company announces that it is "evaluating strategic alternatives" and implies that it has received interest which prompted that action. Be leery if the subsequent auction goes on awhile. If there are viable buyers for a company at a premium, it simply should not take more than three or four months for a deal to arise. Within an industry, competitors that might consider a deal are already quite familiar with the company, and if they want to buy it, they can decide rather quickly if they are interested.

On occasion a company that produces strong cash flow attracts the interest of financial buyers — meaning those interested more in the financials of the target than in its core business. When those buyers are involved, a deal can take longer. But these acquiring firms are usually borrowing money in order to consummate a deal, and they can go only so high before banks or the bond market will cut them off or they simply cannot meet their own return expectations.

Sam Heyman put pressure on the chemical company Hercules to sell itself, which it then tried to do. The announced auction lasted more than six months, and that's on top of efforts to sell the company that were made prior to the announcement. (In fact, those preannouncement efforts are so common that the run-up following the announced auction can sometimes be a good shorting opportunity on the stock.) Don't be fooled by reports that many companies are visiting the so-called data rooms of companies that are for sale. Their competitors would be stupid not to take a free opportunity to look at the details of a rival's operation.

The danger of long auctions is embodied in the sad story of General Motors' Hughes Electronics (GMH). GM's focus on obtaining a tax-free agreement and its simple inability to get any deal done in a timely manner proved its ruin. When the sale process began, GMH's stock price was in the 40s. As the sale process neared an end, the stock had fallen to 12. During that time GMH's DirecTV business suffered slowing growth, the economy and market went into a tailspin, and the country was forced into war by a heinous terrorist attack. The point is well made: if there's an auction, make it fast.

After the Deal

MOST MERGERS DON'T WORK

For all the trillions of dollars in value changing hands in mergers and acquisitions — and the billions spent on legal, financial, and accounting experts — most deals don't work. This has been studied numerous times over the past several years, using every conceivable yardstick — return on invested capital, financial measures such as income and cash flow, opinions of senior executives, long-term stock price — and the studies uniformly conclude that most companies would have been better off without the deal.

- Mercer Management Consulting studied 150 deals valued at $500 million or more between 1990 and 1995 and concluded, comparing stock performance relative to S&P industry indexes, that only 17 percent created substantial value, 30 percent created marginal returns, 20 percent eroded returns, and 33 percent substantially eroded returns. Mercer also compared acquirers versus nonacquirers and found that nonacquirers outperformed industry indexes more often.

- Coopers & Lybrand looked at 125 companies in the post-merger period and found that over 60 percent were financially unsuccessful.

- McKinsey & Co. studied 116 acquisitions in 1987, concluding that 61 percent failed to earn back equity capital invested within three years.

- Mark Sirower of New York University evaluated 168 mergers between 1979 and 1990 and found that average returns were –20 percent by the fourth year post-merger. He, along with two members of the Finance Department at the University of Iowa, found that stock mergers — the main currency these days — perform worse than cash deals.

- KPMG studied 107 large cross-border mergers completed between 1996 and 1998. Only 17 percent of the mergers added value, 30 percent produced no discernable difference, and 53 percent actually destroyed value. KPMG looked at the companies' stock performance, relative to their industries, one year after the deal. A follow-up study conducted in 2001, reviewing 118 deals completed between 1997 and 1999, found that only 30 percent of the mergers created value, 39 percent did nothing, and 31 percent destroyed value. Better, but still nowhere near a passing grade.

▪ Management consultants A. T. Kearney looked at the fifty largest mergers and acquisitions from 1990 to 1999 and found that 69 percent of the surviving companies trailed their industry averages in total shareholder return in the two years after the deals were completed. Among the deals with the longest track record, 70 percent of the surviving companies underperformed their peers five years after the deals closed.

The anecdotal evidence from recent deals looks much the same. When you look at the biggest deal stories of the past few years, you can see why so many deals don't work out. Smaller acquisitions by large companies are difficult to judge since it's simply too hard to ascertain success. The big deals are easier to grade; they often fail because of unrealistic expectations, overpayment, or, most important, the inability of management to execute the integration.

Handicapping the Odds of Post-Merger Success

UNREALISTIC EXPECTATIONS

The people who make deals still have a long way to go before their expectations match reality. In KPMG's 1999 study, 82 percent of the respondents thought the deals had achieved their objectives; in fact, only 17 percent of the deals had actually created shareholder value. In 2001 KPMG updated the survey and concluded that things were getting better: 75 percent of the directors thought the mergers were working, and 30 percent of the deals had created value. But promises are easy to make, and given that a deal's survival can depend on the performance of the acquiring company's stock price, it is not surprising that many of those promises remain unfulfilled.

Wall Street wants to see results from a deal quickly, but on many occasions CEOs would be better off dampening expectations rather than raising them. There is little doubt that had C. Michael Armstrong not taken AT&T's business in a decidedly different direction than long distance, the stock would be a small shoe size. But Armstrong failed to recognize how long it would take before AT&T's move into broadband would show progress on the bottom line. He was too quick to offer rosy scenarios for growth; he should have simply explained that he was saving the company, but the new strategy would take time to play out.

During the presentation of its bid for MediaOne, AT&T made estimates of the cash flow it would produce from a broadband business that included MediaOne, which now seem naive. Armstrong may well have known then that the numbers were a

---

Bear hug Bear hugs are a poor man's hostile offer. Instead of making the offer through an outright tender for the sought-after company's shares, a bear hug takes the form of a publicly made offer to buy the company. The public appeal is designed to generate shareholder pressure on that company to negotiate.

Bear hugs are common because many companies' takeover defenses preclude a successful tender offer. They are also a cheap way for one company to get a sense of whether the market likes its proposal. And they are the only way one company can try to force another company to sell a part of itself (think Comcast and AT&T Broadband).

Bear hugs often fail if not followed by more aggressive action on the part of the suitor.

stretch, but he chose to put them forward in order to bolster the bid for MediaOne. A few years later those same inane projections would be used against Armstrong by Comcast to prove how badly managed the business had been.

Honeywell's merger with AlliedSignal was also the victim of unrealistic expectations. To sell investors on this merger of far-flung conglomerates, Honeywell CEO Michael Bonisignore made unrealistic promises about the growth of some mature businesses. The merged company's mediocre results blindsided Wall Street, which knocked down the stock and made the company takeover bait for United Technologies and then General Electric.

Disney's acquisition of Capital Cities/ABC in 1996 was based on the idea that the synergy — a frequent rationalization when it doesn't appear that a deal will contribute to earnings in the near term — between Disney's content and Cap Cities' distribution would improve both companies. If you have a hit program and also own the network, true, you may make more money. But what if you don't have any hit programs in the pipeline? Then not only do you lose money in the production division but the network is suddenly stuck with lousy product as well. And if the content divisions have too close a relationship with the distributors — Disney later merged Touchstone with ABC — it can be more difficult to sell to other distributors, who don't want to buy from a perceived competitor.

Sometimes the guys who promise the least deliver the most. If the CEO is conservative about cost savings and the market is lukewarm about the deal, you may have some upside once that skepticism gets priced into the stock. When Norwest merged with Wells Fargo, in contrast to most of the big bank mergers, CEO Dick Kovacevich did not promise big layoffs or cost savings. This kept morale high, and investors have been pleasantly surprised.

POOR POST-MERGER MANAGEMENT

Even when you put together two good companies and don't over-pay, the deal can — and often does — still fail because manage-ment can't really bring the two companies together. It is a very difficult job, and not surprisingly, the best companies at doing it are the ones with the most experience: GE, Tyco, and Cisco have been through the drill between fifty and five hundred times. Ex-perienced acquirers can still fail, by paying too much or buying someone else's problems, but inexperienced acquirers are likely to get tripped up by the difficult task of merging two large com-panies. The problem is compounded if the acquisition is out of the acquirer's wheelhouse or there are geographic or cultural differences.

If companies are not providing investors anything specific, it is probably because they don't really have it figured out. If they haven't tackled the hard issues, there could be problems. Daim-ler bought Chrysler because it wanted some of Chrysler's risk-taking culture. But while Daimler's Juergen Schrempp liked Chrysler's entrepreneurial spirit, he never figured out how to capture it. After the deal, which was misrepresented as a merger of equals, the executives responsible for that entrepreneurial culture departed or were forced out, which left the combined company with the same problems Chrysler had always had and without the executives who gave it its strength. And it isn't just ex-ecutives at the company being acquired that deserve watching. In many instances long-time management at the acquirer promptly takes the money and runs, leaving the integration process floundering.

AT&T lost billions on its purchase of NCR in 1991 in part be-cause the acquisition process was long and hostile, which cost AT&T some of NCR's top management. The computer business was outside AT&T's field of expertise; in fact, part of the reason it bought NCR was in the hope that NCR could fix AT&T's own money-losing computer division. When results were not immediately up to AT&T's expectations, it reversed an earlier promise to keep NCR intact, replacing a bunch of executives, ordering layoffs, and even changing the company's name. It incurred more than $3 billion in losses during its four-year ownership and spun it off to shareholders, at a market value of half of what it paid.

The 1996 merger of Union Pacific and Southern Pacific was so poorly executed that it literally created a national crisis. Union Pacific was just not ready to integrate the companies, from computer systems down the line. Management just didn't understand how much work it was going to take to put together the operations of these two railroads. The merger put the malfunctioning combined company on so many tracks that it single-handedly created traffic gridlock in rail transportation across the United States and led to massive freight delays. It was such a mess that the Surface Transportation Board called a moratorium on further consolidation in the industry.

Look at the quality of the management and read what they say about their post-merger plans, taking pains to look beyond the spin. Do they already know who is going to be in the key positions? Are they specific about where the cost savings will come from? Are they doing something — other than just slapping one another's backs — to arrange for the integration of the two operations? Look for situations in which there's a clear organizational chart and it's known up front who's in what job and how many people are going to be laid off. That shows evidence of planning and an understanding of the issues the company will face. When either those things are unknown or the companies won't say, look for trouble. It's a sign of arrogance and it unsettles investors. And without a clear sense of direction and a forceful leader, very little work gets done as people wait to learn their fates.

The management team from the old Chemical Bank could write a book on how to approach integrations. Their first deal was a merger of equals and out of necessity with Manufacturers

Hanover Trust. It went quite well as executive SWAT teams low-
ered the boom quickly and with precision on various units within
the bank. The next deal was called a merger of equals but was
really a takeover of Chase Manhattan in which Chemical proved
all too happy to give up its name for the honor. That deal also
went well as the Chemical guys followed the same game plan,
choosing quickly among various managers. Chase's purchase of
J.P. Morgan was not a merger of equals, but again the old Chemical management team proved more than happy to subjugate
their new name to the best one yet, that of J.P. Morgan. Once
again, management worked together to nail down the first thousand management positions for the post-merger company.

Integration is not required for a deal to work. The merger of
Morgan Stanley and Dean Witter has worked precisely because
they have chosen not to integrate. Bankers from Morgan Stanley
didn't even mention Dean Witter, so much so that they finally got

Poison pill This takeover defense was devised by attorney Marty Lip-
ton to help companies defend against hostile offers by making them
prohibitively expensive. A poison pill typically calls for the issuance of
special stock rights in the event someone acquires a certain percentage
of the company's stock — usually 15 percent — without the consent of
the board of directors. These rights allow existing shareholders to purchase special additional shares of stock that (a) dilute the ownership of
the hostile acquirer and (b) have to be redeemed at a premium if there is
a change in control. The goal of the poison pill is to force accumulators
of a company's stock to negotiate with the company rather than at-
tempting to take control by acquiring stock in the open market. A company making a hostile offer for another company can try to remove that
company's board of directors and replace them with directors friendly to
its offer, for which they will then vote to lift the poison pill. An even more
venomous form of the poison pill has cropped up in some corporations.
Known as the "dead hand pill," this poison pill can be removed only by
the old board of directors, even if they have been replaced. The "dead
hand pill" has been ruled illegal for companies incorporated in Delaware.

rid of the name. Morgan maintains its position at the top of the investment banking chain but at the same time gets the benefits of having a network of brokers to sell products, along with a credit-card business that throws off a lot of cash.

> **Staggered board** In order to make it harder for an interloper to replace a board through a proxy fight, companies have begun staggering the terms of their directors so that they are not all up for reelection at the same time. During Weyerhaeuser's eighteen-month struggle to buy Willamette, Weyerhaeuser waged and won a proxy fight to replace three of the company's directors but still did not control the board.

OVERPAYING

Back when Kohlberg Kravis Roberts (KKR) did the biggest LBO ever, the $25 billion purchase of RJR Nabisco in 1989, it had to outbid management and most of the LBO funds and investment banks on Wall Street. The price was so high that by the time KKR finished dismantling the company several years later, it barely broke even. In competitive situations, the danger of a buyer overpaying becomes more pronounced. And when the buyer is using stock as the currency (as is most often the case), it doesn't worry as much about the result. So you get bad deals, such as World-Com's purchase of MCI, or even worse deals, such as BancOne's purchase of First USA in early 1997 for more than five times book value, a 43 percent premium to its predeal stock price.

POWER SHARING

For a while the notion that two CEOs could share power was in vogue. It thankfully didn't last long, but companies aching to get together still settle on this strange leadership coupling rather than breaking off their talks. Take a jaundiced view of such arrangements. Most of the high-profile power sharing of the past several years has been the result of one CEO mollifying the other by pretending to share power, with the other CEO being oblivious to the designs of his counterpart. Look at what happened at Citigroup. A lot of people doubted that the companies' cultures could mesh or that Sandy Weill and John Reed could get along as co-CEOs. It actually worked out great; Weill simply pushed Reed aside.

How clear is the power structure once the deal becomes known? If the CEOs are vague about it in the spin sessions, then they probably recognize that it is a problem and don't want to mess up the negotiation with a fight. (That might have gotten Alcatel and Lucent to the altar, but if there is going to be a fight over who runs the company, better they should have it before making the deal.)

CULTURE CLASH

As an investor, you can look for many things to decide whether cultural issues will wreck a deal. How smoothly running are any joint projects the companies already have? Do they have a history of working well with others? How do they perform in international markets? For all these things, look at annual reports and company profiles. A KPMG study in 1999 of large cross-border mergers concluded that companies that confronted and resolved issues about who would get what management positions and how to deal with cultural differences before the merger were significantly more likely to improve stock performance in the three years after the deal.

Lessons and reminders
Where do takeover rumors come from?

- Traders, trying to create liquidity for big orders
- Investment bankers, trying to drum up business
- Investment bankers, testing the market during price negotiations on a deal

- Investment bankers, to create a smokescreen hiding their real activities
- Company insiders who tell friends to buy the stock

Use the existence or absence of as many factors as possible to determine whether takeover rumors are true. Rumors are more likely to be true if you find the following:

- An acquirer large enough to pull off the rumored deal
- A logical fit between the businesses of the acquirer and target
- The transaction being accretive to the acquirer's earnings
- A cultural fit that suggests a lack of resistance to new or combined leadership
- Lack of regulatory issues that would have deterred consideration of the deal
- A rumored acquirer with an aggressive reputation
- Turmoil at the potential target
- A prior relationship between the companies
- Common board members or officer affiliations

The announcement of a deal may significantly move the stock of the companies involved. The likelihood of the deal's completion becomes an investment consideration. The following factors can undo a deal:

- An adverse change in either company's business
- Regulatory review
- Stock market's rejection of the deal
- Another bidder

A bidding war can drive up the price of the target's stock (or, if the acquirer's shareholders aren't thrilled with the deal, can affect the price of the potential acquirer's stock). The following factors can point to additional bidders emerging:

- Scarcity value
- Rapidly consolidating industry
- Suggestion that the acquirer is getting the target on the cheap

After the deal, you have to determine whether the combination will create or destroy value. Most mergers, unfortunately, do the latter. These are the factors to look at that wreck most combinations:

- Unrealistic expectations
- Poor post-merger management, including exodus of key managers and unworkable power-sharing arrangements
- Overpayment
- Clash of cultures

7

CEOS ARE PEOPLE, TOO

I'm fairly certain I conducted the last television interview granted by Tyco's CEO, Dennis Kozlowski. It was mid-April of 2002, about six weeks before he would be forced to resign when the Manhattan D.A. charged him with tax evasion. That, of course, was to be the least of his alleged infractions. But on this evening, I was not yet aware that Kozlowski had stolen from the government or his own shareholders. I didn't know that this CEO, once tabbed by *Barron's* as the next Jack Welch, was actually swindling his shareholders of hundreds of millions of dollars.

I only knew that Dennis Kozlowski had some problems at the company he ran — problems of his own making that he was now desperately trying to dig his way out of. And I knew that Tyco, a company that had grown to enormous size during the 1990s by pursuing a strategy of acquisitions, had shockingly decided to change direction early in 2002 and split itself apart.

Kozlowski had agreed to appear with me after the company had reversed course again. In the face of a withering assault from investors and the critics who had always believed the company was not honest with its financial results, Tyco had dropped the idea to split into four parts only three months after it committed itself to that course.

Kozlowski is far from an attractive man. And when he's sweating, as one often does under the hot studio lights, the pallor of his already ruddy complexion becomes crimson. And so it came to pass that the final television interview of Dennis Kozlowski's career as Tyco's CEO practically ended with paramedics being called. I've wondered since whether it wasn't the studio lights but the weight of the lies Kozlowski was spewing that may have been giving him the sweats.

It's hard for me to know now whether Dennis Kozlowski ever told anyone the truth about Tyco. He definitely lost his connection to the truth somewhere along the road. I distinctly remember a morning on *Squawk Box* when Kozlowski joined us for an interview to try to arrest the slide in Tyco's stock price that ensued after the company's decision to split itself into four parts. Jack Welch was our guest host on the show, and during a commercial break, after Kozlowski had seemed uncomfortable answering questions, Welch glared at him and beseeched him to "just tell the truth." It was an amazing moment, but while Kozlowski seemed to want to please Jack, he also seemed truly confused by the idea.

It's still a point of debate whether there was significant fraud at Tyco, but one thing that seems certain is that the enrichment of upper management was the sole purpose of the entire enterprise.

My favorite allegation (none of the trials have yet begun) concerns the multimillion-dollar bonuses that Kozlowski and his number two, Mark Swartz, would pay themselves for conducting ordinary business. When Tyco successfully spun off part of its telecom business, the company took a $76.5 million charge associated with the transaction. The charge was solely to pay bonuses to Kozlowski and Swartz. I loved that one, especially because Tyco would soon choose to buy back the portion of Tycom it had taken public. Kozlowski and Swartz didn't give back their bonuses.

On the day he announced his resignation, one of my sources, a longtime Tyco shareholder, spoke with Kozlowski. When asked about his plans, the Newark-raised Kozlowski said, "I'm going to go out on my boat and have a lot of sex."

Most CEOs are not Dennis Kozlowski. They are not even bad people. They're also not the stars that we in the media make them out to be.

In my sixteen years covering business, I've met and interviewed many of the leaders in corporate America. They are not, taken together, an overly impressive bunch. But there are exceptions. Some have great minds, others charisma, and others an ability to motivate large groups of people. None of those qualities may be indicative of whether the company they run will encounter success.

During the bull market of the 1990s, the media went out of its way to link the performance of a particular company to its leader. There is no doubt that the decisions made by a CEO during the course of their tenure have an impact on the success or failure of a company. But the belief that CEOs are omnipotent and solely responsible for success or failure is a fallacy. Especially when we consider success to be a share price that goes up.

Consider my former boss Jack Welch and my current boss, the chairman and CEO of General Electric, Jeffrey Immelt.

My interaction with Mr. Immelt, while not extensive, has been frequent enough for me to conclude that he is the equal of if not superior to Jack Welch. (How's that for kissing up?) That opinion and $2.50 will get you a cup of latte at Starbucks. And thus far during his tenure, judging by the stock market, Jeff Immelt has not been a success. GE has lost hundreds of billions in market value since he took over in September 2001.

It is not possible to understand all of the challenges faced by a corporate chief. It is not possible to know how the stock market will behave or what hand fate will deal. And so it is not possible to know whether GE's stock price will rise because of Jeff Immelt's great leadership, whether it will rise in spite of his leadership, whether it will fall in spite of great leadership, or fall because he fails.

There is no doubt that good management can turn a company around or propel it forward and that bad management can eventually sink even a great company. I can tip you off to some things to look for as predictors of particularly good or bad managers, but this is a subjective exercise. I can give you some clues, but we're talking about people. They can look great and perform badly. Or they can act like *schlubs* and become tremendously successful. And one thing I cannot do is predict what the stock market will do.

A CEO is just one guy or gal. A CEO does not in any way represent the sum total of management's acumen. But when it comes to judging that management, the CEO is your most visible source of information. And his or her decisions, over time, can mean the difference between success and failure.

Part of the modern CEO's job is to be bulletproof — never surprised, never insecure, never in doubt. A big-company CEO has gotten to the top of a ruthless food chain. Even a lousy CEO is either extremely intelligent or adept at faking it, a PR expert, a political in-fighter, and a great representative of the company. Even without the help of the corporate machinery, these guys (and yes, they're still almost all guys — more so than even the Senate) got where they are by understanding the media as well as the people reporting on them, and they have large operations devoted to preventing surprises, preparing answers, and generally frustrating any attempt to cross those inner bridges to find unguarded truth and insight.

Chances are that your exposure to a CEO is made up of television appearances, magazine and newspaper profiles, and the correspondence from the CEO that is often found once a year in your annual report's shareholder letter. That's not enough information on which to rely for a decision to buy or sell a stock. Even if you wanted to, these guys are just too smooth to judge by the sound of their voices or by their quotes in an article. Follow what they do more than what they say. And use the information you can glean about the CEO, if it's positive, to enforce other good reasons behind an investment. Or if the information is negative, use it to scrutinize more carefully a decision to invest in a company.

That lesson cannot be more forcefully made clear than by relating my own impressions of a CEO which turned out to be terribly wrong.

Rich McGinn had all the equipment necessary for success: long and varied experience at AT&T and Illinois Bell; an apprenticeship under Lucent's original CEO, Henry Schacht; a competitive yet friendly persona; and, most important, a phenomenal track record in helping to grow Lucent's business. But what most impressed me about McGinn was the way he handled Lucent's first failure to meet earnings expectations.

CEOs are so well coached these days, it's almost impossible to wrench an unfiltered word out of them. Like baseball players talking about "team effort" and "giving 110 percent," top executives work from a well-rehearsed and colorless script — especially when things go wrong. Seldom is responsibility taken or the problems specifically identified. Instead, blame is firmly affixed to broad slowdowns in business or a lack of visibility. Worse, plenty of executives simply hide at the first sign of trouble, speaking to the media (and thus their shareholders) only through spokespersons who are even better trained in the art of spin.

That's what made Rich McGinn such a refreshing exception. When things started heading south at Lucent in January 2000, McGinn dazzled my colleagues and me at CNBC. Lucent had just missed its quarterly earnings estimate, the first time it had done so since becoming a public company. The stock was going to open dramatically lower as investors sold on the belief that Lucent's heretofore compelling story of growth was in jeopardy. Most CEOs would have run the other way, but McGinn showed up that very morning in our studios to come on *Squawk Box.*

In a twenty-minute interview in which Mark Haines, Joe Kernen, and I peppered McGinn with questions, he never ducked. He took personal responsibility for Lucent's revenue shortfall, identified the division that had caused it, and promised to hold accountable managers whose targets hadn't been met. He gave every impression of a boss in charge, someone who recognized a problem and had made decisive moves to ensure that it would not be repeated. It was a very refreshing attitude.

After he left, Mark, Joe, and I kept remarking to one another about what a breath of fresh air McGinn was. A take-charge guy, a CEO who tells you he made mistakes, explains them, and explains why they won't be repeated. I have always believed CEOs who are willing to admit mistakes are the ones you want to get behind. Every company is going to encounter its share of problems. Only CEOs who admit that "giving 110 percent" might not be enough to solve those problems will implement meaningful solutions.

Rich McGinn shot that theory to hell.

Rich McGinn is an extremely engaging and personable fellow. I don't know him well — I've had a couple of meals with him and maybe ten face-to-face chats — but he's always been casual and warm, and seemed to know his business very well. He was always up front about challenges and shortcomings — and not just on that one occasion on *Squawk Box*. But McGinn faked me — and a couple of million investors — out. While he was talking about Lucent's staggering growth, we all missed the big picture. All those quarters of beating analyst estimates had come at an enormous price. McGinn and the rest of his management team, dangerously obsessed with impressing the Street, had flooded the product channel, cutting prices and piling orders on customers. To keep its growth machine going, Lucent had to give customers so much equipment that the market was oversupplied. Furthermore, that mind-set led to aggressive accounting and questionable sales. McGinn was able to keep the stock propped up for the first six months following its initial earnings miss, but then Lucent missed its numbers again and again, and by January 2001 Rich McGinn was gone and the company was thoroughly out of control.

Lucent had been the most widely held stock in the world (i.e., it had the most shareholders). But as the bad news piled on, the share price fell from $80 to $5 and the market value swooned from $250 billion to $20 billion. As I explain in detail in chapter 2, there was a great deal of information in Lucent's balance sheet that spelled out its eventual doom. But if you simply used its straight-talking CEO as a guide, chances are that you would have held on while more than $200 billion of market value simply disappeared.

The Hot Seat

I like Carl Icahn. I like him because when I'm interviewing him on CNBC he'll say things like: "You really have what I call an 'anti-Darwinian principle.' It's survival of the unfittest. You get a guy who's been at the company a long time or bought into a company, and he's not too bright but he's a good mixer. He's like a fraternity president. If you had a family company, you would never let him run it. But he's there, and the board likes him. He doesn't bother anybody, but he's not the guy who's really going to be entrepreneurial. . . . And he's never going to let a number two guy come in better than him. So by definition the number two guy is worse than that. Eventually you're going to have idiots running it. That's the problem with the whole deal."

Carl admits that there are plenty of exceptions, but the fact is that CEOs too rarely get taken to task for being bad at what they do. Still, boards reach more quickly for the ax than they once did. Rich McGinn was given a few quarters to prove he could work his way out of a jam, but that was it.

The fact is, customers and owners are more impatient these days. If a perennial contender misses the playoffs for a couple of seasons, the owner who is shelling out $90 million a year in salaries may want to try a different approach. Investors, from giant institutions to individuals, act much the same. And the big money creates bigger expectations. Just getting hired as a CEO is a life-transforming event: rare is the CEO who doesn't sign on for a seven-figure salary and a pension in that league — and that's before stock options. It is not unusual for a successful CEO of a big company to eventually earn a dynastic fortune, and even washouts routinely walk away with $10 million to $20 million in stock for a few years of unsatisfactory leadership. Given those wages, nobody wants excuses.

Yet, it is hard to be a good CEO, and rare indeed to find those corporate leaders who can master all the myriad tasks their job requires. The best CEOs combine skills that include the following:

- Visionary — the CEO has to be the architect of the company's long-term plan
- Motivator — that plan has to be communicated throughout the company, and everybody has to be convinced that the plan is a good one
- Financier — even with a good CFO, the CEO has to be visible to Wall Street and trusted
- Marketer — the CEO has to understand how the company's products or services are sold, be the public face for the company, and get involved in large deals or contracts
- Deal Maker — the CEO has to understand the strategic rationale behind decisions to buy or not to buy other companies, and manage any combinations that occur as a result
- Operator — the CEO has to know enough about the nuts and bolts of operations to make plans on the basis of more than just spreadsheets or summaries, and deal with operational problems that threaten plans
- PR Specialist — apart from being the most visible person in the company, the CEO has to be able to respond quickly and properly to crises, whether of the company's making or of a national nature
- Investor Relations Expert — he has the primary responsibility for communicating the company's direction to investors

The fact is that very few CEOs master all of those tasks. But what a good CEO must have is an ability to succeed on either a strategic or a tactical level. By that, I'm speaking of two distinct sets of skills. The strategic CEO is one who understands deal making and understands the ways in which his company must change in order to succeed. The tactical CEO is one who knows how to get the most out of a given set of assets. Some CEOs are strong tacticians; others are excellent strategic thinkers. Few combine both skills. That's why a man like Jack Welch is considered the model for the modern-day CEO.

I worked for Welch for eight years. I reported on him throughout that time and interviewed him more times than I can remember. I was also able to see Jack from time to time in a more casual setting and get a sense of his thinking. But I certainly wouldn't lay claim to being an expert on the man. Still, his legacy is so large, and the lessons so helpful, that it is worthwhile to boil Jack Welch down to a few characteristics that you can hopefully spot in other up-and-comers before everybody else discovers them.

- *Will to win.* I ran into Jack a few weeks after his retirement began. He, like all of us, was taking the World Trade Center disaster hard. But that didn't stop him from telling me that his new book, *Jack,* was the number one bestseller in the nation — "and without any publicity." It's that kind of fire to excel and win that has made Jack Welch the success he is.
- *Eye on the bottom line.* Welch was jeered as "Neutron Jack" in his early days as CEO, but not by stockholders. If GE was not employing its capital as efficiently as possible, Welch never hesitated to make changes. That meant selling or shutting down high-cost, low-return operations, as well as rooting out and cutting unnecessary expenses, including employees. Not only did GE become a leaner, more efficient company virtually every year Jack Welch was CEO, it also grew to employ far more people by the time Welch left than it would have had he never fired a soul.
- *People power.* Contrary to his early nickname, Welch was always adamant about doing the utmost to keep the best people

from leaving GE. He always stressed that the strength of GE was in its employees, and made sure that managers worked to create an environment in which the best could thrive.

▪ *Ability to develop a plan and get people to stick to it.* Who can say how much Jack Welch knows about airplane engines or MRI scanners? Regardless, he learned enough to oversee those and other far-flung businesses, not just setting financial targets but learning each company's risks and opportunities, then fitting them into his plans and making sure the hands-on managers followed those plans.

▪ *Consummate team player.* Jack's icon status came largely in recent years as his pending retirement became a media obsession. Though GE's superb financial returns have long made him the subject of glowing articles and books, he has never been a camera hog. He gave his managers room to operate and share the credit, both publicly and financially, when they did well. He never failed to be the front man when something went wrong. Many great managers left GE in the past several years to run other large companies, but virtually none left because he didn't like the interaction with Welch.

▪ *Eye for deals.* Welch showed great discipline with acquisitions, but took to them with vigor. He had final approval over all investments exceeding $15 million, but had a team of people whose analysis of potential deals kept GE ready to pounce if an opportunity presented itself.

▪ *Perpetual salesman.* At the biannual business council meetings, Jack would hunt down other CEOs and personally pitch them on the benefits of leasing a Boeing business jet. GE, of course, is Boeing's partner in that venture, but it was still always stunning to see the top man making the hard sell. Jack believed completely in the product, and proved a wonderful salesman.

▪ *Eye on succession.* Five years before he was set to retire, I started asking Jack Welch about his plan for that eventuality. And even back then, he calmly told me that it was becoming a focus for him and would become one of his highest priorities in the years ahead. He was good on his word. The process of choosing his successor was orderly. In one of my favorite moves, Jack promoted the three contenders and then promoted three other people to each of their former jobs, ready for the day that one would win and the other two would leave (which is exactly what occurred).

That is a great deal to look for, and you could probably expand the list. There are a number of situations to watch for that can signal the development of positive management at a company.

Money Talks

By the time someone becomes a CEO of a big company, he is already wealthy, and base wages ensure that he will get wealthier. If the CEO is willing to put a substantial amount of that compensation package at risk based on results, or if he puts up his own money to buy the stock, your interests become aligned. And here I am not talking about stock options. I think stock options can work as a motivational tool for employees throughout an organization, but too often they are delivered in vast quantities to upper management without requiring that they risk any capital.

I'm most encouraged when I see a new CEO buy stock or an old one exercise options and then keep the stock (meaning that capital had to be put up and taxes paid). But be careful, because companies also make forgivable loans to their top executives, allowing them to buy the stock and forgiving the loan after a few years have passed. That once again limits any risk on the CEO's part if things don't turn out well.

Just as one of the first questions asked a fund manager should be whether his own money resides in the fund, a CEO with something to lose is a CEO who works hard to protect and enhance the share price. Of course, not all stock positions are created equal. If the founder, a guy like Warren Buffett or Bill Gates, is running the company, he is not going to have to take out a second mortgage after a bad quarter. Still, it's comforting to know that much of the CEO's net worth is wrapped up in his company.

Sumner Redstone is the finest example of this phenomenon. I've interviewed Sumner numerous times. I've had dinner with him. And I can tell you that the man has no inner life. Sumner Redstone lives and breathes Viacom. It is all that occupies his thoughts. Every dollar of his vast fortune is tied up in that company, a share of which, he is always happy to point out, he has never sold. Sumner may not show much range on topics of conversation over dinner, but his appetite for Viacom shares forever aligns him with his shareholders.

Seeing the CEO buy the stock, if he doesn't already own a lot, is a positive sign. Bruce Nelson became CEO of Office Depot in July 2000 after the company's faltering performance drove the stock down from $24 to $6. As an officer of the company, he bought 100,000 shares in the open market during the slump, and told analysts so in his first conference call. He said, don't bet against Office Depot over the long term. He put his money where his mouth was, and a year later Office Depot's stock price doubled in a bad retail climate.

Jamie Dimon made this point even more dramatically. He left a forced retirement to run Bank One in March 2000. When he signed on, Jamie bought 2 million shares of Bank One stock with $57 million of his own money. His buy-in was $28 per share, though the stock took a quick run-up to $35 (which quickly reversed itself) on the announcement that Bank One had hired him. In his first fifteen months at Bank One — not a particularly good time for the banking business — the stock traded in the mid to high 30s. Too soon to "take to the bank," but certainly an early sign that Dimon (who also received a load of cash, restricted shares, and options) is doing the job you'd expect with his own money on the line.

This indicator, of course, isn't always surefire. Sometimes, a CEO can get too deep in for his or anyone's good. WorldCom's Bernie Ebbers continued buying WorldCom on margin as it started its slide. When the stock fell below $15 in October 2000, a margin call forced him to sell 3 million shares. In order to meet further margin calls without giving up a large part of his equity in the company, WorldCom loaned Ebbers $75 million. When WorldCom shares dove even deeper in early 2002, the company loaned Ebbers an astonishing $400 million to cover new margin calls. That sort of thing never helps a balance sheet.

OUT OF OPTIONS

During the recent bull market, companies that widely issued stock options to employees instead of paying them in cash were able to garner a dual benefit. They were able to attract talented employees and, because option compensation is not counted as salary, were able to save money on cash compensation, which must be run through the income statement. A number of companies, led by Coca-Cola and GE, have begun to account for stock options as an expense.

Still, options can cause problems when stocks go down. Companies are at risk of losing employees while at the same time being forced to increase costs as cash replaces stock as the key form of compensation. In the falling stock market, many large companies, including Microsoft, Sprint, and Amazon.com, raced to reissue or reprice stock options.

Sprint, in particular, showed the inequity of using stock options as remuneration. In October 1999 the company allowed all stock options held by its employees to vest once Sprint shareholders approved the company's acquisition by WorldCom. They did approve the deal, in April 2000. The problem? The deal never happened. Shareholders took a bath when antitrust regulators scotched the deal, but executives who were smart enough to quickly exercise their newly vested options made a personal fortune. Adding insult to injury, shareholders were screwed even worse because many top managers had left, thanks to those options.

Class-action lawyers and the AFL-CIO ripped into Sprint, claiming that the vesting provisions accelerated $600 million in options for the top five executives alone. CEO William Esrey received $69.3 million in total compensation and stock options in 2000, as well as $64.1 million from exercising stock options that had been granted in prior years. I had an opportunity to talk to Esrey about this situation one evening more than a year after the fact. Esrey, like so many CEOs, is an engaging guy. He's a lean, athletic man who normally shows an easygoing demeanor. But on this evening, the moment I mentioned the options, Esrey sprang quickly to the task of defending his company. The provision for vesting, he said, was something that had been on the books of the company for a very long time and was not of his doing. He went on to admit that it would have been better had it not happened but added that few employees actually left.

Esrey probably wishes he had never heard the word *option*. In early 2003 Sprint's board fired him after concluding that a shelter he used to avoid paying taxes on options put him in conflict with the company's auditor. Esrey lost his job and stands to lose most of his money if the shelter is ultimately ruled illegal by the IRS.

Time Warner's deal with AOL did Sprint one better. Time Warner had the audacity to let all outstanding options vest on the *announcement* of the deal. Lawyers who worked on the deal told me they had never seen anything like it before. It meant that if the deal fell apart the next day, or shareholders voted against it, or regulators prevented it, management would still have had the opportunity on that day to cash in their options, regardless of whether they had received them only a few weeks earlier. Given the huge jump in shares of Time Warner on the deal announcement, there was plenty of money to be made.

It's not just options that misalign the interests of shareholders and management. You're probably getting sick of MCI and British Telecom. But allow me one more reference.

When MCI ran into an awful earnings miss and BT came back offering 20 percent less, MCI president Tim Price claimed to be happy with the new offer. "We came down in price — or restructured the deal — so this would be a win-win arrangement for both companies," he said at the time.

Given the fact that WorldCom stepped in, eventually buying MCI for $40 billion — more than twice the reduced BT offer — one wonders what Price was smoking when he was so cheerful about the cut-rate price his company agreed to after the renegotiation. As it turns out, the contract between BT and MCI contained an unusual clause. Management was scheduled to participate in a $100 million retention pool if the deal closed — even if it closed on terms different from the original agreement! No wonder Price was so sanguine — his sacred retention pool was safe, even though MCI's renegotiation almost cost his shareholders a great deal of money. In fact, people involved in all the negotiations involving MCI tell me that management's main concern was the size of the retention pool and the bonuses to be paid out to executives who stayed with the company for at least a year after the deal closed.

The Visionary Brings in a Professional

Good companies, particularly in technology and entertainment, often develop in the image of the founder's or leader's visionary genius. Steve Case was a true believer about the power of linking individual computer users with one another, information, and, finally, the Internet. By 1996 he had turned AOL into a powerhouse, but an erratic one: there were frequent questions about the quality of service, accounting practices, increasing competition, the business model, and the depth of management. Bob Pittman joined AOL management, later became president and COO, and led AOL through the dot-com boom and bust, bloodied but bigger than ever and possessing enough value to use its stock as currency to merge with Time Warner and get AOL's shareholders a majority holding in the combined company. While investors bid AOL stock to stratospheric multiples, Pittman focused on creating new revenue streams and attaining profitability.

In the early eighties Roy Disney Jr. threw open the doors at Disney to whomever would take it over or run it better. Michael Eisner, a studio head at Paramount with a reputation as a creative dynamo, was chosen as the man with the vision to revitalize the moribund movie and theme-park company. In addition to Eisner, the junta ruling Disney (a combination of corporate raiders, white-knight investors, and Disney family members) lured Frank Wells, a former Warner executive with a superb grasp of financial details. The combination was perfect. While Eisner improved each aspect of Disney's operations — movies, animation, theme parks, and merchandising — and broadened the Disney brand, Wells focused on a series of financial maneuvers that wrung out maximum dollars.

A combination of leaders can always backfire, however, so don't automatically assume that your money is safe just because the visionary has brought in a manager. In 1983 Steve Jobs brought in John Sculley to provide managerial experience and play off Jobs's ability to sell his vision of the user-friendly computer to a mass audience. Sculley successfully strengthened Apple's management, and the company further entered the mainstream of the personal computer business, but Sculley could not sustain Apple's gains. He did, however, consolidate his power, pushing out Jobs. It's an understatement to say that Jobs can be a difficult guy to work with, but he should have played a role. Under Sculley, Apple lost its focus, failed to seize the opportunity to license its operating system before Microsoft created something at least as good, and floundered.

How to Play the Saviors

What do Al Dunlap (Sunbeam), Tom Rogers (Primedia), Gary Wendt (Conseco), and C. Michael Armstrong (AT&T) all have in common? Each took over a company in trouble and through nothing more than his appointment was able to generate huge gains in the stock price of the company he joined.

In each case, though with a sharp variance, the troubles of the company proved difficult to overcome in a short period of time. The rise in the stock that greeted his appointment was erased within eighteen months of his having taken over. What lesson is there to be learned from all this? That once a company goes bad, it is awfully hard to make it good again. Don't overlook the fact that companies that have been poorly run for a long time are not going to be cured overnight. Too often, investors treat a supposed savior's appointment as though the saving can happen that quickly. Just as a successful culture takes years to develop, a culture of failure also takes years to root out.

Of course, the appointment of a new but well-known face to run a troubled company can be used as a good opportunity to buy the stock, since it invariably seems to rise with anticipation. Just remember that years can pass before a company is truly turned around, and you're probably better off using a high-profile CEO appointment as an opportunity to trade rather than to invest.

Succession Failure

Succession brings on a risk that many investors may want to do without. It happened to Lucent. It happened to Coke. It happened to Procter & Gamble and Xerox and Honeywell, too. A longtime CEO is replaced, and the company somehow loses its way.

The risk can be much greater when the CEO does not establish a clear successor or appear to have any interest in being succeeded. Sandy Weill loves being the chief of Citigroup. He has some able people who work for him, including former U.S. Treasury Secretary Robert Rubin. But no one who knows Sandy believes that he will ever willingly relinquish his job, and he has yet to anoint a successor. For years it was assumed that Sandy's boy wonder Jamie Dimon was his heir apparent. But Sandy never seemed to get over the fact that Jamie once fired Weill's daughter, Jessica Biblowitz. Their relationship cooled markedly after that, and soon after Sandy sent Jamie packing. Sandy hasn't had an heir apparent since.

Sumner Redstone has also had his share of high-profile number twos. From Frank Biondi to Mel Karmazin, Sumner seems happy to bring in a strong second banana and then let him go a few years later. No one doubts that Karmazin could successfully lead Viacom if Sumner ever decides to retire. But few people I know expect Sumner to ever retire, including Karmazin.

Perhaps it's a way to cheat impending death, or perhaps it's their way of implying that no one can do better, but Sumner and Sandy are doing a disservice to their shareholders. Jack Welch spent years running a well-honed process to help him select GE's next CEO, and he did it with a great deal of help from his company's board of directors. Nothing guarantees that even the most thorough process will find the right guy, but it is certainly better than the alternative.

Sometimes companies run a process that then goes haywire. If the CEO, for example, starts firing the guys under him, especially after the board or his age or health suggest that finding a successor is appropriate, it's only a matter of time before the guy starts fondling ball bearings and complaining about who stole the strawberries.

The CEO Versus the Board

One of a board's most important roles is to protect investors from the excesses and shortcomings of the CEO. And that means both firing the CEO when it's clear a change in leadership is needed and pushing the CEO to delineate a plan of succession when it's clear he doesn't want to leave.

Too Many Deals

I've told you about numerous CEOs who have gotten into trouble as a result of doing one deal too many — or received acclaim they didn't deserve for doing ten deals too many — so I won't belabor the point. It bears mentioning, though, that until the other shoe drops on these CEOs, no one is going to step up to criticize them.

As Bernie Ebbers was building WorldCom through acquisitions, most of the PR focused on his colorful ascent from gym teacher to telecom giant rather than the prices he was paying or the profitability of the businesses he was acquiring. Henry Silverman, likewise, had an adoring crowd of investment bankers to trumpet his success, until Cendant came crashing down with the CUC deal.

Everyone is quick to proclaim the CEO a hero if he is shuffling a lot of assets. This is nothing new. During the sixties Ling-Temco-Vought (later LTV) became one of the highest-profile conglomerates of the period thanks to the deals of James Ling. Ling was featured on magazine covers, and his constant buying and selling, with its array of spin-offs, holding companies, partial stock sales, debt offering, warrants, and exchange offers not only employed an army of investment bankers but had so many analysts and investors confused that they bid up the stock on the assumption that Ling had to be a genius if he could do all these things. Ling eventually bought into a bad business, had regulatory problems with a big acquisition, and couldn't use all those assets to bail him out when the market suddenly turned skeptical of his deals.

Where There's Smoke

A bad CEO is like an iceberg; you only see about 10 percent. Companies are so good at hiding their flaws and spinning the news that if you get just an inkling that something is wrong, it is better to err on the side of caution.

When you see the CEO make a fool of himself over something routine, it's a sign that he and his staff are out of touch with reality. Remember that picture of Dukakis giving the thumbs-up from the tank? CEOs sometimes do the same thing, and it isn't pretty. Several years ago, when Joe Antonini was floundering with Kmart, he took a reporter on a tour of some new stores to show how the turnaround was going. The tour mainly featured employees enthusiastically grinning and nodding because the boss was coming through, punctuated by numerous embarrassing, uncomfortable moments. At a jewelry counter, Antonini asked how the gold collection was doing. The clerk said "real well," then revealed she had been working at Kmart for only three days and hadn't actually sold any items from the gold collection. Later a checkout clerk mentioned that she was having problems with the scanner, a sore subject because Wal-Mart was at that moment raiding Kmart's market share with its superior inventory technology. The performance should have convinced investors that things would only get worse, and they did.

PR Machine

Companies whose CEOs are incredibly aggressive at promoting themselves and their companies should be watched closely. It is important for a CEO to be known and seen, and it's likewise important for a company's accomplishments to become well recognized. But it's a tricky balance between being available and being promotional. Sometimes CEOs go a bit too far. I've written at length about the promotional aspect of those who commit fraud. Here, I'm talking more about honest but overdone public relations.

Anyone familiar with New York real estate and politics, for example, knew when Donald Trump rose to prominence in the eighties that his father's clout and money helped make it happen. To the mostly ignorant masses, Donald's claim that he pulled himself up by his own bootstraps won him their respect. (I became suspicious of Donald in the late 1980s when he would claim to be holding 4.9 percent positions — which could not be verified — in a series of companies that received takeover offers. It made him look like a genius, but I'm fairly certain that he didn't actually own as much of the stocks as he said.) Trump realized that building an image of vast wealth could help him sell buildings and, amazingly, allow him to borrow hundreds of millions of dollars to buy buildings without being subjected to the due diligence banks perform for much smaller loans. The loan officers were swayed in the same way many others were, by the image of "The Donald." And he does have that fabulous hair. But when it comes to Donald's public companies such as the Taj Mahal, great PR has not led to profits.

That was not the case for EMC, a company whose CEO, Michael Ruettgers, would do an interview anywhere anytime. I was always somewhat suspicious of EMC, given the aggressive nature of the company's PR. But I was dead wrong. EMC was one of the best-performing stocks in history, and its business did pretty damn well also. The company clearly knew what it was doing with its PR and was able to back up its words with deeds. Until of course the stock fell 90 percent in 2001. Good PR can only go so far when your customers stop buying your product.

Lessons and reminders
Look for

- CEOs with a financial stake in the success of the company, beyond the standard options and stock grants
- A good balance between visionary strategists and hands-on operators
- A deep bench: when the company has enough management talent in the ranks that other high-profile companies

consistently come looking for leadership, it's a sign that management grooming is successful.

- A board of directors with a lot of stock ownership and some strong personalities who won't be afraid to challenge the CEO

Certain things should be taken as warning signs:

- A CEO very reluctant to choose a successor
- A CEO's offspring taking over the company, unless the business is sufficiently simple that a new generation can grow into the role
- A focus on deals and financial maneuvers seeming to outweigh attention devoted to operations
- A CEO who consistently looks bad in public, despite the efforts of the PR machine
- A CEO who publicizes himself too aggressively

CONCLUSION

I asked Michael Eisner once why he didn't trust people. I had just read him a quote from the noted media banker Herbert A. Allen, who said of Eisner: "He's a gigantic talent with great creativity who doesn't trust people." Eisner was not taken aback by the quote or the question. Everyone is selling something, he explained, and those who make their living on Wall Street are no exception. Eisner said it wasn't surprising that a banker would say he doesn't trust people, because when it comes to Wall Street, he had often evinced a strong skepticism for the products from that industry. "If you are a buyer, the person who is selling to you is probably going to exaggerate the value of his product or company."

Herb Allen is a cultured, worldly, decent man, and Eisner meant him no offense. The two have worked together on deals and strategy through the years; Allen himself once admitted he could teach his dog to be an investment banker. That's why I appreciate this little anecdote. It encapsulates my own view of Wall Street. It's a place populated by smart, decent people who work in an industry that should not be blindly trusted — something the people who work there will gladly acknowledge, but those who invest there don't seem to want to know.

I get e-mails from viewers asking me why I'm so negative. I've never understood them. I've never understood how people who are investing their money could be upset to learn more about what they are investing in. When I report, I'm not trying to be negative or positive. I'm simply trying to be informative. I've always believed that information and understanding are an important component of making good decisions. And I firmly believe that a dose of skepticism is healthy for investors making their way on Wall Street.

I hope this book has helped in that effort. I hope it's helped you understand how Wall Street really works. I hope it will help guide your decision-making process in the future. And I hope you'll take away a dose of skepticism, but know that Wall Street can still be a profitable place to invest.

It's funny. I never get e-mails from people who work on Wall Street telling me I'm being too negative. They seem to accept my reporting in the spirit in which it's delivered. I appreciate that and I appreciate them. What Winston Churchill said of democracy is easily applied to my own feelings about Wall Street. No one should believe it is perfect or all wise. But to those who would say it is much worse than that, I would counter that it is better than anything else I've seen.

ACKNOWLEDGMENTS

Look at any acknowledgments page in the book of a first-time author and you're likely to read about how much harder it was to write the book than he could ever have imagined. I wish I could tell you different.

Writing this book was hard. Very hard. And it's only thanks to a lot of great people that it was possible at all.

This book is drawn from my experiences as a financial reporter over the past fifteen-plus years. During those years, it was always the people on the other end of the phone or the other side of a dinner table who were teaching me about Wall Street. I've made some wonderful friends as a result of all that reporting, and many of those same people have been instrumental in helping shape the content of this book. But it's a funny thing about a reporter's sources. They don't really like seeing their names in print. So to the countless men and women in whose debt I firmly remain, I offer my deepest appreciation. You know who you are.

There are a handful of people to whom I can offer public thanks for their time and wisdom. My thanks to Larry Robbins, Lee Degenstein, Gary Kaminsky, Bruce Prescott, Allison Rosen,

Hope Taitz, George Sard, Seth Tobias, Stuart Conrad, Bob Olstein, Carl Icahn, Rick Shottenfeld, and David Berman.

I would also like to express my gratitude to a number of very smart risk arbitrageurs who have taught me a great deal through the many years I've covered mergers and acquisitions: Morgan Rutman, David Simon, and Rick Schneider. I'm afraid that all the lawyers and bankers with whom I've shared confidences must remain in the shadows. But I owe a great deal to them as well.

I learned how to be a reporter in the trenches of the newsletter division of *Institutional Investor*. It was a place where old-fashioned reporting skills were stressed and being first with the news was everything. I owe a great deal to the man who still runs that division, Tom Lamont, who taught me to be fearless in pursuit of a story. The constant urgings of my first editor at *Institutional Investor*, Mark Voorhees, to make more phone calls and always be skeptical have stayed with me to this day.

I also want to thank all my colleagues at CNBC, whose professionalism day in and day out have helped to make our network the success it is. I've enjoyed every minute of my eight and a half years with them. I've had a particularly good time every morning, thanks to my partners on *Squawk Box,* Joe Kernen and Mark Haines, and thanks to the show's longtime producer, Matt Quayle. At CNBC, I also want to thank my assistant Sonya Uribe, who is simply the most pleasant person I've ever had the pleasure of working with, and Samantha Wright, who has been the most helpful person I've ever worked with.

Two of my closest friends are a part of Wall Street. For years, Steve Lipin was my fierce competitor from his post at the *Wall Street Journal* in addition to being a loyal friend. He's always been a great supporter, despite digging up many scoops that might otherwise have come my way. My dear friend Russell Sarachek is one of the best hedge fund managers I know. And I know plenty. He's also been a great help on this book.

My friend and former agent David Fishof encouraged me to write this book for years. When I finally responded, it took me over a year to write the proposal. That led me to the conclusion that unless I found some help, the book might take ten years to write. I found that help in the person of Ken Kurson, a student of Wall Street whose attitude matches my own. Ken's tireless enthusiasm for this book, not to mention his ability to put up with me, made our every moment fun and productive. I have no doubt that without his enormous contribution, this book would have suffered greatly.

Ken would like to acknowledge a number of people: his wife, Rebecca; Michael Craig for his invaluable research; Bob Safian, David Granger, and Flip Brophy.

I would also like to thank David Vigliano and Dean Williamson for their help in finding the right home for this book. Little, Brown is that home, and my editor Geoff Shandler's deft touch helped tighten and toughen this text. He also kept me from being too alliterative.

This is not the book my mom might have thought her English-major son would author. But it's only because of her love and support that I was in a position to author anything at all. Perhaps a work of drama or literature will follow one day, but I know that regardless, she'll still be in my corner. She always is.

My thanks to my father for giving me the strength to make good decisions and never criticizing me when I made bad ones.

The best decision I ever made is named Jenny Harris. My wife makes every day a joy. She has been my steadfast partner throughout the writing process and didn't complain during all those months when I could no longer be her playmate.

New York City

INDEX

The board of Merrill Lynch recently made its preference known when it came to selecting a successor to CEO David Komansky. Komansky wanted Jeff Peek, who ran Merrill's asset-management business, to take over. But the board was more impressed by Stanley O'Neal, Merrill's head of its U.S. Private Client Group and brokerage operations. The board convinced Komansky that his initial choice had to be changed.

Don't be fooled by what appear to be some respected names on a board. Having a powerful lawyer or former government official or banker or venture capitalist or professor on the board isn't going to help the company with its business. That's management's job, and if they need the help, they can always hire consultants. If you are looking at the board of directors at all, ask yourself whether you can imagine these people standing up to the CEO when things go bad.

Disney has had a famously weak board of directors. Its sixteen members include an L.A. schoolteacher, the actor Sidney Poitier, a theology professor, an architect, the publisher of an L.A. Spanish-language newspaper, and former senator George Mitchell. Chairman Michael Eisner defends the board, saying that an entertainment and real estate company should have board members such as actors, architects, and schoolteachers. Perhaps he's right. But you can also be sure that these are not the types of people to tell Eisner that he has to sell some assets that are bleeding the company dry or that he should have settled that Katzenberg lawsuit earlier.

But even if there are heavyweights (and Disney has its share of them as well, including Roy Disney and Tom Murphy, the legendary former CEO of Cap Cities), bear in mind what John Malone once told me about his board experience at AT&T: "I'm a team player . . . I'll go along with it even though I have my reservations." So although you can check a board of directors to see whether it has strong members, it's not a surefire recipe that the board will keep the CEO on a short leash.

If you look at GE's board, you'll notice that it has quite a few outsiders with experience running big companies: Silas Cathcart (former CEO, Illinois Tool Works), Paolo Fresco (chairman, Fiat SpA), Claudio González (CEO, Kimberly-Clark de México), Andrea Jung (CEO, Avon), Ken Langone (a founder of Home Depot), Rochelle Lazarus (CEO, Ogilvy & Mather Worldwide), Scott McNealy (Sun Microsystems), Andrew Sigler (former CEO, Champion International), Douglas Warner (chairman, J.P. Morgan Chase). In addition, six of these eight directors own more than $5 million in GE stock. But let's not kid ourselves. The best measure of a board's effectiveness is the company's performance, and for GE's board, it was mostly a matter of staying out of the way. Likewise, Disney had a ten-year winning streak with its board. But to protect against things going bad, you want to see some directors you can imagine duking it out with the chief, and you want them to own some stock.

Junior

Brian Roberts is a nerd who wants to take over the world. And all he had to do to give it a shot was take over his father's cable company. Brian is a very smart guy and a good manager as well. But when it comes to junior stepping in, it's not always that easy. It is not an accident that monarchies have long passed from world dominance. An able leader can come from anywhere, and bloodlines do not correspond with management skills. So investing in a company when it's clear that bloodlines will win out over brains is not always the smart thing to do.

That being said, family ownership can also prove immensely rewarding. The Dolans at Cablevision, the Roberts at Comcast, and the Redstones at Viacom (to name just a few) have posted amazing fifteen-year track records for the performance of their respective stock prices. Though both Cablevision and Comcast have seen day-to-day management turned over to the sons of the pioneers, Charles Dolan at Cablevision and Ralph Roberts at

Comcast (soon to be Comcast/AT&T) are still actively involved in their companies. That's a big help for their sons.

Sometimes subsequent generations can get into trouble, especially if the business is already in a difficult period in its development. Chris Galvin, the third family member to run Motorola, founded by his grandfather in 1928, is struggling under the weight of a high-tech company that was both successful and troubled when he took over in 1997. Galvin's first problem — a natural one in son-succeeding-father situations — was the difficulty in cutting ties to his father's mistakes. Robert Galvin was hailed as an excellent manager who built niches for Motorola in numerous high-tech businesses, but the company was disorganized as a result of too many acquisitions, consolidations, and technological developments. In addition, Motorola's investment in satellite-phone provider Iridium racked up enormous losses. Chris Galvin delayed shutting down Iridium and delayed fixing the organizational problems. In the meantime, rivals took away business in wireless phones, and the company has not developed any significant new technology, a requirement to survive in its many fast-changing businesses.

On the other hand, at Anheuser-Busch, family leadership has stayed strong. The Busch family has always been active in hands-on operations. August Busch III is the fourth generation of his family to run the company, and its stock has consistently marched higher over the past several years, regardless of bear markets or new-economy crazes. His son, August IV, is a group vice president who recently won a slew of awards for supervising the company's advertising campaigns.

So how about this for a rule of thumb: if they advertise and sell beer, the CEO's son can run the company, but if they have a lot of technology issues, keep it out of the family. You would have missed out on IBM, one of the most successful companies of all time, with that rule. Thomas Watson Sr. made IBM successful, but it was his son, Thomas Jr., who pushed the company into the computer business and created the corporate culture that made it the standard for corporate America in the sixties and seventies. But if you are looking for a guideline, this is not far off the point.

Consider the situation of two Chicago companies, Wrigley and Comdisco, which both faced succession crises over the past several years and chose the CEO's son to lead the company, with dramatically different results.

At Wrigley, the chewing-gum company, William Jr., then thirty-five, took over in March 1999 after his father's death. He looked too young to run the company. He was largely unknown to analysts and the media. To fill the void left by his father and other executives nearing retirement, he quickly brought in two Procter & Gamble veterans and the former controller of Gillette as his CFO. After two years he seems to have the sometimes-sleepy company poised for greater growth.

At Comdisco, the computer-leasing company, Kenneth Pontikes, before dying in 1994, made it clear to his board that he wanted his son (who then had been with the company only two years) to succeed him. By 1997 a caretaker CEO retired and Nicholas, only thirty-three, became CEO. Nick, with his prior apprenticeships at Drexel and Blackstone Group, hit the ground doing deals. Comdisco needed its business to evolve, but the younger Pontikes got caught up in the dot-com fad, allowing its more established businesses to languish while doing deals with forgettable companies such as Webvan, eToys, and Ask Jeeves. He also bought a DSL company, which went out of business after Comdisco spent more than $500 million buying and developing it.

In contrast to Nick Pontikes, there were numerous signs that Bill Wrigley could handle the job. First, chewing gum is probably an easier business to learn than computer leasing and disaster recovery. If anything, the rap on Wrigley was that it had been dull and stagnant. Those may not be long-term virtues, but that's an easier environment in which to land than one that's a mix of venture finance, high tech, and Internet hysteria, like the one Pontikes was thrown into.